EVANGELICAL THEOLOGY

A DEFENCE OF
EVANGELICAL THEOLOGY

BY

Wallace Nicholson
MA., Th.M., B.D.

FREE CHURCH MANSE
PLOCKTON, ROSS-SHIRE, SCOTLAND

Printed by
John G. Eccles, Longman Industrial Estate, Inverness, Scotland.

TABLE OF CONTENTS

I. GOD

II. MAN

III. THE PERSON AND WORK OF CHRIST

IV. THE WORKS OF GRACE

V. THE LAST THINGS

VI. THE CHURCH

VII. THE SACRAMENTS

PREFACE

These studies in Evangelical Theology are now presented to the Christian Church in the hope that they may be of some assistance to students, lay preachers, and intelligent Christians of which there are not a few in the Highlands and Islands of Scotland.

In this book an attempt has been made within a short compass to bring out the essence of the Evangelical Faith in line with the best and highest theological thought in the Christian Church. Hence the reader will find himself in company with the thoughts of the best and greatest theologians that the ages of the world have produced; while he engages with them in dealing with the lofty subjects which have been the topics of discussion by the noblest minds during the past fifteen centuries.

The field covered has already been subject to the closest investigation by the most eminent theologians of the ages; and the only originality claimed by the writer, on the themes connected with man's relation to God, is the gathering of ideas from various sources and expressing them as clearly as he can.

The presentation of old truths, looked at from various standpoints and simplified where possible, will familiarise the diligent reader with the doctrines of the sacred Scriptures and so lead his thoughts into further acquaintance with the Words and Works of our Lord and Saviour Jesus Christ.

I am advised that Chapters I and IV should be omitted by the ordinary lay reader as being rather difficult. Most of the rest of the work is easier reading, but one must remind the reader that it is a book of reference as well as a book to read.

It gives me pleasure to express my indebtedness to Rev. John MacSween, M.A., Point, Lewis; Rev. Murdo MacAulay, M.A., Back, Lewis; and Rev. Donald Gillies, M.A., Crossbost, Lewis, who advised me and made necessary corrections.

The Free Church Manse,
Plockton, Ross-shire,
Scotland.

March 1969.

CHAPTER I

THE EXISTENCE OF GOD

I. THEISTIC PROOFS
   1. The Ontological Argument, (1) Plato, (2) Anselm, (3) Descartes, (4) Clarke.
   2. The Historical Argument.
   3. The Moral Argument.
   4. The Teleological Argument.
   5. The Cosmological Argument.
   6. The Scriptural Argument.

II. ANTI-THEISTIC THEORIES
   1. Atheism.
   2. Pantheism.
   3. Polytheism.
   4. Deism.
   5. Materialism.
   6. Evolution.

The primary doctrine of religion is the existence of God. The Christian usually considers the subject to be above discussion and, hence, little attention is paid to it, but the truth itself is possessed of inestimable importance and sublimity; and a review of the evidence presented constitutes a useful exercise, not only to confirm the believer and enable him to give a reason for the hope that is in him, but also to provide him with materials to repel the assaults of sceptics. At the same time we must recognise that some of the proofs advanced in support of the evidence are so abstruse as to be of little value to the ordinary reader.

I. THE THEISTIC PROOFS

The question may be asked as to whether it is proper to engage in this exercise of proving the existence of God. If, however, we believe that God has revealed himself in creation and providence, it is not only proper but also our bounden duty to make a prudent investigation of the evidence presented. The word **proof** is used here in the sense that the evidence is sufficient to produce conviction of the being and character of God. While it has been said that the mind of man is depraved and that he will not accept the evidence presented, this could be said of any kind of evidence. In any case, if the evidence is sufficient, the unbeliever will be left without excuse. Besides, we must not rule out the possibility that the Holy Spirit will convict the unbeliever and ultimately convert him. And although the light of nature is not redemptive, there are important reasons why the natural man should be confronted with the self-revelation of God, which is to be discovered in man's being, and in the world around him.

1. The Ontological Argument

The word **ontological** means the science of real existence. This proof has been variously stated since the days of Plato. It should be noted here that any brief statement of some of these profound arguments can hardly be set forth without the sacrifice of preciseness and logical consistency; therefore, those who wish to make a special study of their structure and matter must read them in their original forms.

(1) **Plato.** This philosopher states that the only objects of certain knowledge are the ideas conceived in the human mind. These ideas, however, are merely apprehended by reason and must have their origin in the divine Mind, who is the cause and reason of them and whose existence is the foundation of all that exists or can be called into existence. This argument was admitted by Augustine and referred to by Anselm and Aquinas.[1]

(2) **Anselm.** The view of Anselm on this subject is: that man possesses an idea of an absolutely perfect Being, that existence is an attribute of perfection, and that, therefore, an absolutely perfect Being must exist. Anselm was not so naive as to think that a mere idea in the mind was proof that God exists, but he regarded this unique idea he possessed of a Being, "a greater than which cannot be

1. Wm. Fleming, D.D., **Moral Philosophy** (London 1874) p. 323.

conceived", as evidence that the Being he conceived of must exist.

(3) **Descartes.** Descartes says that the idea of an infinitely perfect Being which we possess could not have originated in a finite source and must, therefore, proceed from God himself. He also states that according to the clarity of an idea so is the objective reality; and since one of the clearest ideas in the human mind is the idea of God, we must therefore believe that he exists.

(4) **Clarke.** Dr Samuel Clarke makes the statement that since something exists now, something must have existed from eternity. This something must necessarily exist; and since the material world cannot be the first original being, we are unavoidably led to the necessarily existent being of God.

These arguments are extremely difficult to grasp and have been criticised by the friends and foes of religion; and, however valuable they may be, they should not be unduly relied upon. After all, we must distinguish between the evidence that confronts us of the being of God, and the structure and matter of the human arguments advanced on the basis of that evidence.

The ontological argument has been supported by the greatest theologians of the Christian Church; and even if a valid demonstration for the existence of God cannot be drawn from it, it can form the basis of a rational probability and so add to the cumulative effect of other arguments. Dr Dick thinks the specific argument put forward by Descartes is too abstruse and shadowy to produce a strong effect upon the human mind.[2] Dr Shedd believes that the ontological argument has the endorsement of Scripture. "And God said to Moses I AM THAT I AM." (Ex. 3:14). This passage of Scripture, says Dr Shedd, denotes the necessity of the divine existence and shows that the idea of a necessarily existent Being is one which the human mind readily accepts.[3]

2. Dr John Dick, **Lectures on Theology** (Edin. 1834) Vol. I, p. 284.

3. Dr W. T. Shedd, **Dogmatic Theology** (Edin. 1889) Vol. I, p. 239.

2. The Historical Argument

This scheme is based upon the truth that all nations acknowledge the existence of a Supreme Being who created and governs the world. This belief can be traced back to the remotest ages. It has been claimed that some tribes have been discovered who have no notions of a Supreme Being, but no sufficient data have been produced to establish this claim; and even if some tribes have been encountered whose powers of reason were subnormal, this would not impair the validity of the argument. And if this truth has been denied by certain thinkers, this should create no prejudice against the general agreement among men. Even where men have believed in a multiplicity of gods, the general principle was admitted by some that there is one supreme Being who governs the rest. The Athenians who were notorious idolaters erected an altar to the UNKNOWN GOD.

The sceptic will reply that the variety, order, and regularity of the manifold parts of the universe, and the benefits resulting therefrom, can be accounted for by the laws of nature, but since he cannot explain those laws his assertion cannot produce conviction. The evidence which abounds in the universe points to a sovereign Power and Intelligence superior to the laws of nature which directs the manifold operations taking place in the world. In the meantime the sceptic continues to cling to the resistless and remorseless laws of nature which know no pity and spare none, while the believer commits himself to a supreme Ruler and gracious Benefactor, who will continue to care for his temporal and eternal welfare amidst the changes and disappointments of this life.

3. The Moral Argument

This argument seeks to establish the existence of God from the phenomena of conscience. This, together with the universal feeling of dependence, it is said, constitutes the religious sentiments of humanity. Man is essentially a moral being, having inherent in his constitution the sense of absolute dependence and morality. Besides, the economy of human relations in the world can be explained only by the fact that an intelligent and moral Being, rules the world.

A simple way of stating this truth is that the conscience or moral faculty testifies to the fact of obedience or disobedience to a moral law. This implies a lawgiver. And, incidentally, the existence of such a moral faculty demonstrates the infinite and impassable gulf which separates man from the lower species. If it is admitted that man is a personal, intelligent, moral being, subject to moral obligations, the admission leads to the truth that a supreme and righteous Being superintends the moral destinies of the world. The above is the mode of argument employed by Calvin and Turretin. Kant thinks it is superior to all others as a proof of the existence of God.

4. The Teleological Argument.

The principle asserted here is that the general intellectual order of the universe implies a supreme Intellignce as the moving cause. The word **telos** is used to express **end,** or the science of final cause or design. This argument is based upon the principle that being and organic life and their development are due to conscious motive and purpose. And when we observe that the intellectual order of the universe implies intelligence as the moving cause, we are led to the existence of the first Cause. We are told that the evidence of design in the adaptation of the eye implies an intelligent designer : Aristotle remarks that if the end or final cause is not discovered, science is impossible.

5. The Cosmological Argument

The principle here is that the **cosmos,** or universe, must be the product of a first cause, since every effect supposes an adequate cause; and according to the Christian philosophic mind an acceptance of the premise leaves no alternative except God the Creator who is the first and only cause. The conviction that every effect must have an adequate cause is a necessary element in our thinking processes. This argument is supported by almost all scientific thinkers, whether or not they are agreed as to what this cause may be. The relation between cause and effect has been assailed by Hume and Mill, but A. A. Hodge remarks that they and all others use the same argument in their philosophic discussions. Clarke and Kant also dispute this argument. Kant thinks an acceptance of the premise would lead us to seeking a cause for the existence of God himself. This objection overlooks the fact that when we speak of a cause producing an effect, we exclude the eternal cause. Dr Dabney replies to Kant by saying that his objection may be removed by stating that "nothing can **begin** to exist without a cause outside itself."[4] If the world is temporal we must look for an adequate cause of its being and changes, but it would be illogical to seek a cause for that which is eternal and immutable; and since the cosmos is temporal and subject to change, we must look for an adequate cause, and this we find in the Supreme Being who is eternal and unchangeable, and so uncaused.

6. The Scriptural Argument

This mode of proving the existence of God is not usually included under the so-called rational proofs for the existence of God, as it is dealt with under other captions; yet it does appeal to some types of mind. In any case, the only possible way in which the existence of God can be known must issue from God's revelation of himself. This he had made known in creation and common providence. The Word of God indeed presupposes his being and character and serves to set forth more clearly his eternal power and Godhead. Here God is described as the Creator of all things, the Preserver of his creatures, and the Supreme Ruler and Judge of all. The internal evidence of Scripture as a proof of his being and character is intellectually invincible when presented in its full force and in its proper order to the unbiassed reasoning faculty; and this holds even when the corrupt heart of man rebels against the Truth. The writings of Scripture evidence the production of a supernatural Mind. The Old and New Testaments and the exposition and exegesis of all their parts set before us the same God : infinitely powerful, immutably righteous, full of goodness, and unchangeable in his purposes; and that same Word of God makes a full discovery of the only way of salvation consistent with his holiness and goodness; while the efficacy of

4. Dr Dabney, **Systematic Theology** (St. Louis, 1878) p. 11.

its teachings in solving the problems connected with the history and destiny of mankind is adequately manifested in the change of heart and life produced in a countless multitude of its readers. These Scriptures consisting of so many books written by different persons through successive centuries, free from error and therefore infallibly and eternally true, are sufficient evidence of the superintending providence of one intelligent presiding Mind.

II. ANTI-THEISTIC THEORIES

The being and nature of God as acknowledged by the Christian Church has been denied by various sceptics, such as: atheists, pantheists, polytheists, deists, materialists, and evolutionists.

1. Atheism

Atheism has been divided into various categories. Intellectual atheism may be **dogmatic** when it is maintained either, that God does not exist, or that we possess no proof that he does. **Sceptical** atheism is a profession of doubt as to God's existence or a refusal to accept the evidence presented. **Virtual** atheism maintains ideas inconsistent with the Christian conception of God, or denies to him attributes essential to his nature. **Practical** atheism professes to believe in God but refuses to acknowledge him in heart and life.

It is questionable if any reasonable being in a healthy state of mind holds settled convictions that there is no God. But if there are those who maintain this error and assert that they are sincere in their unbelief, they must be dealt with accordingly, and their attacks repelled. The atheist may not venture to prove that there is no God but will state that the evidence presented by the theist is inconclusive. If asked for an explanation he will sometimes be driven to acknowledge that no rational account can be given for the nature of things; neither can **he** give any reasonable account of what the laws of nature may be. Frequently he will repel the arguments advanced by the theist by objecting to the explanations given or by asking questions that are unanswerable. This to him is proof that he is right, and that his opponent is wrong or defective in his argumentation.

It is not always unprofitable, however, to reason with the sceptic, and it is possible to convert him to theism without converting him to Christianity. In ordinary cases it is worse than useless to throttle him with arguments or to threaten him with judgments. The atheist and every other religious objector is to be met with reason, not railing. There have been cases on record in which a courteous and reasoned argumentation by a devout believer, though it may not apparently have produced any impression at the time, has afterwards found lodgment in the reason and conscience. The courteous and stirring sermon by Paul on Mars' Hill should be studied in this connection.

2. Pantheism

This theory supposes that there is only one substance in existence and that all being in its various modifications is an attribute of God, so that all phenomena whether spiritual or material are attributes of this one universal substance. While atheism asserts that there is **no God,** pantheism maintains that **everything** is God. The god of pantheism is a universal, unconscious, and impersonal essence to which all attributes belong, and all changeable substances are parts of this universal substance which is not outside of them but contained in them. Pantheism has dominated the religion and customs of India for untold centuries. According to Spinoza, its modern exponent, God is one substance possessing thought and extension from which this intellectual and physical world eternally evolves. By implication, this degrading theory seeks to eliminate the distinction between mind and matter, good and evil, selfconscious purpose and unconscious self-development and reduces the Creator to a blind, unreasoning, chaotic substance destitute of personality, will, or morality.

3. Polytheism.

Polytheism, according to the derivation of the word, is a belief in many gods. This theory prevailed since the early history of man. The history of Greece and Rome affords abundant evidence of a refined polytheism, which was taken for granted by the most eminent philosophers of the time. Some of them, however, recognised one Supreme Being above all the others, such as THE UNKNOWN GOD of the Athenians. Theism, which is the belief in one personal God, was the primary religion of man, whereas this superstitious belief was simply a product of man's degeneration.

4. Deism

This system, while admitting the existence of one personal God, denies his controlling presence in the world, his immediate moral government, and all supernatural intervention and revelation. The effect of this theory is to deprive God of some of his essential attributes and to reduce him to almost human dimensions. Some of the philosophers whose names are associated with this system are Hobbes, Bolingbroke, Paine, and Voltaire. These philosophers denied that Scripture was a revelation from God and insisted that man could perform his duty to God just as well without any written revelation. A profound weakness of deism is that these men were urging such considerations in an age when the knowledge and influence of written revelation affected themselves and others. The truth is that the great thinkers of heathen antiquity such as Socrates and Plato were groping after such a light. These modern philosophers, however, professed to despise written revelation while they used its advantages to further their own theories.

5. Materialism

Materialists maintain that there is but one substance containing atoms and force. Intelligence is simply a function of material organisation which is dependent upon laws inherent in matter. Order and development are not products of intelligence but constituents of matter itself so that all changes in nature are the result of the operation of mechanical forces contained in matter. The materialism of the modern age is just a revival of the theories of Democritus and Epicurus. And it is gravely questionable whether the new materialist has improved upon the old. It should be conceded, however, that materialistic doctrines have contributed to the knowledge of the physical sciences and have brought forth views which are valuable for the prosecution of researches in that sphere. On the other hand, the materialist is forced to acknowledge that the nature of matter and the causes at work to produce organic forms is a mystery. If this is the case, why does the materialist waste time and energy in uttering declarations about the non-existence of the unknowable? Hodge has stated :

> If the phenomena of consciousness are resolved into modifications of matter and force, i.e. ultimately into some mode of motion, then all ultimate and necessary truth is impossible, duty has no absolute obligation, conscience is a lie, consciousness a delusion, and freedom of will absurd. All truth and duty, all honour and hope, all morality and religion would be dissolved.[5]

It is not likely that materialists would agree that this is true of their theory or practice, but this is the inevitable consequence of their reasoning.

6. Evolution

Evolution is the unfolding or development of matter through active forces resident in existing material. Some of the ancient philosophers asserted the eternity of matter while they admitted the power of God in its formation into its present existing forms. Darwin, the modern exponent of evolution, attempted by various arguments to prove that man is descended from the lower animals by a perfectly natural process controlled entirely by inherent forces. Darwin's **Origin of Species** was once thought to have solved the problem of the origin of humanity, but someone said there was a lie in the title of the book since Darwin gave no explanation of the **origin** of species. Some prominent evolutionists now regard the origin of species as a complete mystery. Indeed, evolution does not deal with origins or originals but with the development of materials already existing. Some of the evolutionists continue to believe in the eternity of matter, and they account for the origin of life by the process of spontaneous generation.

There is an evolution which does not deny creation or Scripture history, and will frankly admit such facts as the

5. A. A. Hodge, **Outlines of Theology** (London, 1891) p. 50.

development of the embryo and various other relevant processes in accordance with the truth that God created all things out of nothing and subsequently developed certain organisms through divine activity. Unhappily, certain professed Christian philosophers, while admitting the creation, will have it that evolution holds an important place in the history of humanity. Some will say that man descended from an inferior species; other speak of pre-Adamite man. The result of these theories is to destroy the integrity of the sacred records and to turn the first several chapters of Genesis into an allegory. Men who are wedded to their own theories will receive little impression from an exposition and exegesis of the relevant passages of Scripture, which contain a true account of man's origin.

Before the creation of Adam it is plainly stated that "there was not a man to till the ground". It is also stated in the clearest fashion that God formed man's body from earthly materials and breathed into his nostrils the breath of life. There is, however, a striking contrast between the creation of man and the lower animals. The latter were created after their kind; the waters brought forth and the earth brought forth after their kind. But in the creation of man the divine counsels were engaged and the pair created were made in God's image, and dominion was given to them over all the lower species. It is also significant that the lower animals were not addressed or consulted about their duty. But our first parents were addressed and commanded in accordance with their rationality. When they were created, they were blessed and commanded to be fruitful and multiply and replenish the earth and subdue it. The creation ordinances were necessary to the development of all that is useful in the history of the human race; and a trained scholar requires only very ordinary ability to study these first several chapters of Genesis and to understand that the working out of human history is a proof of the unique formation, character, and dignity of the primal pair in utter contradistinction to the origin and destiny of the lower animals.

Unhappily, the term **evolution** can be used in more senses than one, and the evolutionist will prove his evolution in the one sense and then argue for evolution in the anti-Scriptural sense. Our main objection to the evolution theory is that it has led men to juggle Scriptural history and facts, while at the same time its supporters very often profess to adhere to the doctrine of creation for the purpose of bringing unsuspecting individuals to their own point of view. The believer is bound to hold to the doctrine of creation in the strictest sense, and to God's providential and supernatural activity in the whole realm of nature and human history. Apart from the Scriptural arguments, which are self-evident in every ordinary devout reader of Scripture, almost every philosopher of eminence must be forced to agree that personality is not to be found in any of the lower species by any of the manifold tests conducted by scientists. The lower animals possess consciousness and determination, but personality, which involves self-consciousness, and self-determination, can be attributed only to man, who was made in the image of God.

"Consistent evolution is atheistic; it does not take God into account. It holds that living forms developed of themselves without divine plan or control. There is, however, a theory known as 'theistic evolution' which holds that evolution was God's method of creation of living things. This is really a contradiction in terms, for 'theistic' means 'connected with belief in God', while evolution means 'developing of itself without outside control'. This idea of 'theistic evolution is not consistent and it has been held chiefly by religious scholars who were embarrassed by the claims of unbelieving scientists. Really 'theistic evolution' is ruled out by the Genesis account just as truly as atheistic evolution. Those who talk about creation by evolution do not understand the real meaning of the terms 'creation and evolution'. Creation is by definition supernatural; evolution is by definition a natural process. To speak of creation by evolution is like speaking of an honest thief or a truthful liar." (Blue Banner, April 1954, Rev. J. Vos).

CHAPTER II

THE KNOWLEDGE OF GOD

I. FORMS OF KNOWLEDGE
II. SAVING KNOWLEDGE
III. THE CONTENT OF KNOWLEDGE

This subject has received special attention through the discussions of modern Christian philosophers, who assert that God is unknowable. The Scriptures expressly state that God reveals himself: and if man was made in the image of God, we must conclude that he is knowable. "The LORD is known by the judgment which he executeth." (Psalm 9 : 16). "God is known in her palaces for a refuge." (Psalm 48 : 3). "In Judah is God known." (Psalm 76 : 1). "Thou shalt know that I the LORD am thy Saviour and thy Redeemer, the mighty One of Jacob." (Isa. 60 : 16).

It has been said that we do not know God as he really and truly is but only as he wills us to think of him; that is, we can have no real and personal knowledge of God's being and attributes since he is a hidden God. His transcendence precludes any real knowledge of him. This is in line with the Kantian philosophy that we do not know things in themselves; we know only the phenomena or appearances of things. But the phenomenon is part of the thing; therefore, we must possess some knowledge of the thing itself. Even though persons cannot be completely known, we may possess a personal, true, and adequate knowledge of them; and even if we cannot possess an immediate or physical knowledge of God, we may know him personally. We may possess a true and spiritual apprehension though we cannot comprehend him. If this is not so, then we do not know him at all; and it would follow that we cannot have communion with God. This would invalidate many passages of Scripture. To know a person is to possess some personal knowledge of his physical, mental, and moral character; and to know God is to possess an intelligent cognition of his being and character as he has revealed himself in nature and in grace.

I. FORMS OF KNOWLEDGE

A distinction has been made between a **natural** and a **supernatural** knowledge. The former is implanted in man's constitution and communicated to him through the world of nature. The latter is given when God speaks to man by his Word or Spirit and is of such a character as could not be acquired by reason or the study of the world of nature. Others speak of a **general** and a **special** revelation. The former is communicated to men to meet their natural needs, and the latter is addressed to sinners to meet their spiritual needs. These distinctions are useful as general categories but must not be unduly relied upon or too sharply distinguished. The revelation of God to his creatures is of a manifold nature.

In the state of innocence the knowledge of God was implanted in man's being and communicated to him through God's handiworks. Besides, God held communion with man in the pre-lapsarian state, and after the fall he spoke to Adam (Gen. 3 : 9), to Hagar (Gen. 16 : 13), to Abimelech (Gen. 20 : 3). That he appeared to men at sundry times and in diverse manners is evident even from a cursory reading of the Old Testament.

It is significant also that God revealed himself to sinners who were outside the pale of written revelation. We may note the force of Rom. 1 : 32 and Rom. 2 : 14, 15 taken in their context as an exposition of this subject. We may gather from these passages that the natural man possesses some knowledge of God's being and attributes. This knowledge is not saving, yet it is adequate to leave men without excuse for their ungodliness and unrighteousness. There is a knowledge of his righteousness, his requirements (the work of the law written in their hearts), his wrath against sin, his goodness, and his eternal power and Godhead. We are taught here also that the heathen possessed settled convictions of moral virtues such as respect for sacred persons, obedience to parents, and a regard for truth, honesty, and chastity. An observance of these virtues produced approval in their consciences or disapproval as they violated these precepts (Rom. 2 : 15; Rom. 1 : 32). Man as man, therefore, knows himself to be a creature of God and subject to his righteous commands. The knowledge referred to is an internal cognition of the invisible God and his perfections in much the same way as the external eye conveys to the mind the world of nature. This natural knowledge is not a mere speculative belief, for it affects the conscience, leaving man without excuse. At the same time, it produces fear and hatred rather than reverence and love and is received only to be distorted and rejected by the carnal heart.

"They (referring to the heathen) perceive how wonderfully God works within them, and experience teaches them what a variety of blessings they receive from his liberality. They are constrained to know, whether willingly or not, that these are proofs of his divinity, yet they suppress this knowledge in their hearts."[6]

II. SAVING KNOWLEDGE

A saving knowledge of God is obtained through his Word and Spirit. Before Scripture was enshrined in writing "it pleased the Lord, at sundry times, and in divers manners, to reveal Himself, and to declare . . . his will unto the church"; afterwards it pleased him "to commit the same wholly unto writing; which maketh the holy scripture to be most necessary; those former ways of God's revealing his will to his people being now ceased."[7] The Word affirms what natural revelation does not reveal, the way of salvation for sinners. The Word, as Calvin says, is as spectacles given to old men by which they are able to see distinctly. Even Scripture, however, will not of itself produce a saving knowledge of God without the agency of the Holy Ghost. If this were so there would be no need for the Holy Spirit to enlighten our minds in the knowledge of Christ. But some would have it that God sometimes uses Scripture to enlighten our minds. This would seem to attribute the main part of our salvation to the Word rather than to the Spirit. On this Warfield says:

"Calvin's formula here is the Word and the Spirit. Only in the conjunction of the two can an effective revelation be made to the sin-darkened mind of man. The Word supplies

6. Calvin, **Institutes,** 1 : 5 : 4 John Allen (Grand Rapids, 1949).
7. Westminster **Confession of Faith.** 1 : 1.

the objective factor : the Spirit the subjective factor; and only in the union of the objective and the subjective factors is the result accomplished. The whole objective revelation of God lies, thus, in the Word of God. But the whole subjective capacitating for the reception of this revelation lies in the will of the Spirit. Either by itself is wholly ineffective to the result aimed at — the production of knowledge in the human mind.[3]

"In that doctrine the Spirit is not, with the Lutherans, conceived of as in the Word, conveyed and applied wherever the Word goes: nor is the Word, with the mystics, conceived of as in the Spirit always essentially present wherever He is present in His power as the Spirit of revelation and truth. The two are severally contemplated inseparable factors, in the one work of God in producing the knowledge of Himself, which is eternal life in the souls of His people : separable factors which must both, however, be present in this knowledge of God that is produced. For it is the function of the Word to set before the soul the object to be believed; and it is the function of the Spirit to quicken in the soul belief in this object; and neither performs the work of the other or its own work apart from the other."[9]

It is difficult to make a sharp distinction between the knowledge possessed by the natural and the spiritual man. Is the knowledge different in kind or degree or in both? in kind, we think; and is the knowledge in the one case merely intellectual, and in the other also emotional and volitional? (see John 17 : 3) : or may it not be proper to seek the difference in the moral state? In any case, the knowledge revealed, whether to the natural or the spiritual man, must be true and not false. We must remember, however, that a knowledge of God which is vague and distorted is called ignorance in Scripture. (Gal. 4 : 8; Eph. 2 : 12).

"It will always be evident to persons of correct judgment that the idea of a Deity impressed on the mind of man is indelible. That all have by nature an innate persuasion of

8. B. B. Warfield, **Calvin and Calvinism** (New York: 1931), pp. 82, 83.

9. **Ibid.** pp 83, 94.

the Divine existence, a persuasion inseparable from their very constitution, we have abundant evidence in the contumacy of the wicked, whose furious struggles to extricate themselves from the fear of God are unavailing."[10]

III. THE CONTENT OF KNOWLEDGE

It has been generally maintained that knowledge, and especially natural knowledge, is confined to the intellect, but Scripture speaks of knowledge as being more comprehensive than this. To **know** in Scripture is to understand, to ponder, to experience, to be persuaded, to approve, and to love. May we not suppose that spiritual knowledge may include all these aspects? Indeed, thought is emotional and volitional, and volition is emotional and intellectual. The Word of God in dealing with these moral subjects defies the speculations of epistemology. Spiritual knowledge is not merely an intellectual exercise, but it also involves the sentiments of reverence, delight, desire and complacency.

We have a striking conception of the working of knowledge very early in the history of the Church. "And when the woman **saw** that the tree was **good** for food, and that it was pleasant to the eyes, and a tree to be **desired** to make one wise, she took of the fruit thereof, and did eat, and gave to her husband with her; and he did eat." (Gen. 3 : 6). We have here far more than a bare speculative knowledge, for it involved the affections and will. "And the eyes of them both were opened, and they knew that they were naked." (Gen. 3 : 7). This knowledge involved the exercise of the moral faculty as well as the understanding. The knowledge referred to in Gen. 3 : 5 denotes experience. In Psalm 1 : 6 it is used in the sense of approval and delight, and in Amos 3 : 2 it carries the idea of choice. All these meanings or aspects of the word **know** are derived from the same Hebrew verb. The conclusion we arrive at is that the exercise of feeling and volition may be found in knowledge, though this does not mean that we may not possess a bare and speculative knowledge of persons or things in which we have no interest. There is in knowledge not only an

10. Calvin, **Institutes,** I : II; 3.

apprehension of the object but also of its qualities and the appropriate state of feeling which accompanies that cognition, whether pleasing or otherwise.

It must appear to us that a saving knowledge differs from a mere natural knowledge through the possession of the following sentiments, among others : a spiritual conception of the matchless glory of God as the alone Creator and Sustainer of all being, whether material or spiritual, and of the infinite excellence of his perfections; a delightful view of God's provision in grace to meet the needs of lost sinners, with a proper conception of the glory of Christ as God Himself, a Saviour clothed in our nature; a spiritual view of the infinite efficacy of his atoning blood to cleanse from all sin; enlarged views of the fullness, freeness, and availability of Gospel blessings in Christ for lost sinners; and a feeling of delight, desire, and complacency in the person of Christ as a Saviour all-sufficient to meet our every need. How such a knowledge could exist or survive in the human heart without the appropriate responses of godliness and righteousness in the life and conduct is inconceivable. That one may have a correct knowledge of God and his perfections and the way of salvation as set forth in the Gospel, possess real convictions of sin and enlarged views of Gospel mysteries, and still remain unconverted seems evident from Scripture and Church history. "A man may," says Bunyan, "know like an angel and yet be no Christian."

Spiritual, saving knowledge is not a mere change in outlook, habits, or exercises; it is inherent in a regenerated and sanctified heart. "Verily, verily, I say unto thee, except a man be born again, He cannot see the Kingdom of God."

CHAPTER III

THE ATTRIBUTES OF GOD

1. The Spirituality of God
2. The Infinity of God
3. The Eternity of God
4. The Immutability of God
5. The Wisdom of God

6. The Power of God
7. The Will of God
8. The Holiness of God
9. The Justice of God (1) God's Rectoral Justice, (2) God's Remunerative Justice, (3) God's Retributive Justice
10. The Goodness of God (1) The Love of God, (2) The Mercy of God
11. The Truth of God

Introduction

Some theologians have discussed the Being of God before taking up the subject of the divine attributes. Others prefer to consider the Being of God in connection with his other perfections. The doctrine of God was discussed by the Scholastics under three headings. **An sit Deus? Quid est Deus? Qualis sit Deus?** Is there a God? What is God? What is God like? The first question involves the truth of his existence. The second and third questions have been considered in relation to his attributes since he has revealed himself in these. Calvin asserts that it is useless to speculate upon the difference between his essence (what he is) and his attributes (what he is like) since our interest lies in possessing a knowledge of his perfections as they determine his being or nature.[12]

Various methods have been adopted to classify the perfections of God, but the subject is too sublime and mysterious to admit of any appropriate mode of classification. The two following are the most common: (1) the incommunicable and the communicable attributes. The former, such as infinity and eternity, can be predicated of God only; the latter, such as wisdom and power, are to be found in rational beings. This method must not be taken too literally since God's attributes are infinite and man's finite. (2) The natural and moral attributes. The former belong to the constitutional nature of God, such as eternity and infinity. The latter, such as holiness and love, belong to God's moral nature. God's power and will have also been called sovereign attributes. The definition adopted by the Westminster Shorter Catechism, which distinguishes

12. Calvin, **Institutes**, I : II: 2.

between the incommunicable and the communicable attributes, is the most natural and the simplest : "God is a Spirit, infinite, eternal, and unchangeable in his being, wisdom, power, holiness, justice, goodness, and truth."

1. The Spirituality of God

Spiritual substance is said to be that which is conscious, thinks, feels, and wills; while material substance is unconscious, thoughtless, helpless, and inert. We are profoundly ignorant of the essence of both spirit and matter, having no idea of either apart from their qualities. The denial of the existence of spirit logically involves the denial of the existence of matter since they are both unknown to us apart from their properties. We may say we cannot deny matter because it produces effects, but we deny spirit because we do not see it producing results. We should rather reason that matter never produces results; it is spirit that controls matter as evidenced in the power we possess over our own bodies and movements.

The Scripture declares that God is spirit, and theologians tell us that by his spirituality is meant that he is distinct from the world and is immaterial, invisible, simple and unextended, manifesting himself to us directly in our self-consciousness or inferentially by words and signs. The Westminster Confession describes God as being "a most pure spirit, invisible, without body, parts, or passions." When the **simplicity** of God is referred to, it is meant that his spirituality is not complex like that of man's; and that in contrast with finite spirits his essence and attributes are inseparable. The **impassibility** of God, according to the etymology of the word, denotes that he is incapable of suffering, being infinitely and immutably blessed. God is, however, spoken of as being complacent toward good and displacent toward evil; this is explained as being the activity of his holiness toward the two opposites of right and wrong. The ascription of bodily parts to God, such as eyes and hands, is an accommodation to our finite modes of thought to indicate his knowledge and power, for he possesses none of the properties of matter while all the properties of spirit are attributed to him in an infinite degree. Dr Shedd says that the two main predicates which are of fundamental importance in determining the spirituality of God are substantiality and personality.[13] Substantiality refers to the reality of the divine essence as opposed to some forms of pantheism and idealism which refer to God as an absolute idea. Pantheism denies that God is a spiritual substance and idealism maintains that God is an idea in the mind. Personality stresses the self-consciousness and self-determination of God.

2. The Infinity of God

By God's infinity is meant the perfection by which he is free from all limitations in relation to space. The word **infinite** should be understood intensively and means that God is not extended through the universe in a pantheistic sense. Since God's immensity is spiritual, possessing no extension of substance, it transcends all space, while more particularly his omnipresence characterizes his relation to his various creatures wherever they subsist. Bodies, says Turretin, exist in space **circumscriptively** as they are bounded by space; created spirits exist in space **definitely** though they occupy no space; but God is in space **repletively** because his essence fills and transcends all space.[13a] God is present in his **essence** and **knowledge** everywhere and always, but he manifests his presence to his creatures and exercises his power when and how he wills. He is present to his people as he is not to the world; and he is present in heaven by his boundless grace to his redeemed, and in hell in the manifestation of his wrath. "If I ascend up into heaven, thou art there; if I make my bed in hell, behold, thou art there." (Psa. 139 : 8).

The omnipresence of God should deter us from sin, as our motives and activities are always open to his inspection. "Can any hide himself in secret places that I shall not see him? saith the LORD. Do not I fill heaven and earth? saith the LORD" (Jer. 23 : 24). "Neither is there any creature that is not manifest in his sight: but all things are naked and opened unto the eyes of him with whom we have

13. Dr W. T. Shedd, **Dogmatic Theology** (Edinburgh, 1889) Vol. I, p. 178.

13a. Dr A. A. Hodge, **Outlines of Theology** p 141.

to do" (Heb. 4 : 13). His presence everywhere and always is a source of consolation and strength to his people, for it brings to them the assurance of his nearness and his ready and effective aid. "Nevertheless I am continually with thee: thou has holden me by my right hand. Thou shalt guide me with thy counsel, and afterward receive me to glory" (Psa. 73 : 23, 24).

3. The Eternity of God

The immensity and omnipresence of God refers to his relation to space; his eternity expresses his relation to time, or rather to eternal duration. Time is limited duration and in reference to our perceptions is divided into past, present, and future. Eternity is infinite duration without beginning, succession, or end; or rather it is no duration at all: it is not a plane but a circle without a centre and without a circumference, and that is almost inconceivable. Eternity is ascribed to that which transcends all temporal limitations. God is the eternal I AM and is infinitely elevated above all temporal conceptions. The eternity of God is timeless and super-temporal, and with him eternal duration is a present now. In the eternal essence or consciousness there is no evolution or development. He is the Ancient of days and his years shall not fail. To him alone belong the predicates of absolute, underived, and necessary eternity. He is the Lord Almighty which was, and is, and is to come.

This subject is far beyond our comprehension, for our modes of thought are unable to grasp the ideas suggested by infinite space and everlasting duration since the category they belong to is indefinable. Sir Isaac Newton says that God endures always and is present everywhere, and by existing always and everywhere constitutes time and space. We know that time and space exist, but we have no means of knowing how these stand related to God, but we do know that time and space are among the **all things** made by him. Time and space are neither substances, attributes, nor entities; they are rather relations of finite existence. "And, Thou, Lord, in the beginning has laid the foundation of the earth; and the heavens are the works of thine hands: they shall perish; but thou remainest; and they all shall wax old as doth a garment; and as a vesture shalt thou fold them up, and they shall be changed : but thou art the same, and thy years shall not fail" (Heb. 1 : 10-12).

4. The Immutability of God

Immutability when predicated of God and his attributes means that his nature is unchanged and unchangeable and not subject to any modification from without or within. Mutability is the characteristic of all created beings whose history involves development, maturity, and decline, but the Supreme Being is eternally changeless in himself and in all his purposes toward his creatures. He is the unchanging and unchangeable God. "And God said unto Moses, I AM THAT I AM" (Ex. 3 : 14). "God is not a man, that he should lie; neither the son of man, that he should repent : hath he said, and shall he not do it? or hath he spoken, and shall he not make it good?" (Num. 23 : 19). "For I am the LORD, I change not" (Mal. 3 : 6).

As each perfection of God's character is necessary to and crowns the other perfections, so his immutability insures the continuation and enhances the beauty of all his excellencies. It might be supposed that in his relation to his creatures his purposes might be modified by their actions, but God's nature and purposes are, and must be, independent of created beings. Passages of Scripture have been produced as evidence of his change of purpose in view of certain outward circumstances, but these passages are merely accommodated to our finite modes of thought. Indeed, some at least of the passages referred to would indicate that it is because God is immutable that he changes his relationships. In the case of fallen man the relationship of displacency replaced what had been complacency toward man. If this were not so, it would rather indicate that God was mutable. All these changes of relationship are the result of his immutable purposes and decrees. To suppose that God would act in a specific case and afterwards change his mind would be to ascribe not only humanity to him but also infirmity. The decree to create and to effect the incarnation of Christ, though bringing God into new relations with mankind, made no change in the purpose of God, since his decrees are eternal.

It has been asserted that it is vain to pray to God since this would effect no change in his purpose toward us, but this objection is easily removed if we consider that God commands and encourages men to pray for certain blessings and, further, produces in men the desire to pray for these blessings; and he does grant their requests according to his will. We may be assured in view of his gracious character revealed in Scripture that he will fulfil all his promises and that he will never disappoint the confidence his own Word has inspired. "For the mountains shall depart, and the hills be removed; but my kindness shall not depart from thee, neither shall the covenant of my peace be removed, saith the LORD that hath mercy on thee" (Isa. 54 : 10).

5. The Wisdom of God

The wisdom and knowledge of God are inseparably united. His wisdom appears in the infinite intelligence and in the faultless execution of his purpose. "His infinite knowledge comprehends all things in heaven and earth by one intuitive glance of his infinite mind; but his infinite wisdom directs all these things to the proper ends for which he has given them their being."[14] God's knowledge is intuitive, immediate, simultaneous, and complete, embracing all things actual and possible in their essences and modes. The ancient Egyptians symbolized the Deity by an eye to intimate that all things are open to his inspection. "Neither is there any creature that is not manifest in his sight: but all things are naked and opened unto the eyes of him with whom we have to do" (Heb. 4 : 13). The wisdom of God is that perfection of his nature whereby he selects the fittest means to accomplish the best possible ends.

Theologians have discussed God's wisdom under the headings of creation, providence, and redemption. The wisdom of God in creation has respect to the whole of reality and its component parts, and the adaptation of means to ends in the organization and preservation of natural forces, which have operated ceaselessly for untold centuries, and which are calculated to lead men to admire and reverence the manifold wisdom of the Creator and to

14. **Fisher's Catechism** (Edin. 1805) p. 33.

exclaim with the Church: "The heavens declare the glory of God; and the firmament sheweth his handywork" (Psa. 19 : 1). "Thou art worthy, O Lord, to receive glory and honour and power : for thou has created all things, and for thy pleasure they are and were created" (Rev. 4 : 11).

Providence is God's natural and moral government of the universe by his own immediate and invisible agency and by the instrumentality of second causes. His wisdom is shown in the ordering of all things according to his divine and eternal plan and in the number and variety of the contrivances he has created for the preservation and well-being of his creatures. The narratives and miracles recorded in Scripture in the history of nations and individuals through the centuries abound with evidences of the invincible methods he has used, and give accounts of the agents he has appointed to control and subserve the actions of men for his own glory and the good of the Church.

The plan of redemption gives us the most glorious manifestation of the wisdom of God. The restoration of lost sinners in accordance with all the perfections of God through the incarnation and satisfaction of his own Son is the greatest instance given of the divine wisdom, and so we read that Christ crucified is "the power and wisdom of God"; while an apostle is so transported that he exclaims: "O the depths of the riches both of the wisdom and knowledge of God! how unsearchable are his judgments, and his ways past finding out! For who hath known the mind of the Lord? or who hath been his counsellor?" (Rom. 11 : 33, 34).

6. The Power of God

The testimony of Scripture sets before us a God of infinite power to whom nothing is impossible and whose power is defined by his peerless perfections, rendering it impossible for him to lie or to work contradictions, as this would imply a defect in the divine nature. We do not, however, confine his power to what he actually performs since he possesses an infinite reserve of power, which transcends the most exalted conceptions of men or angels. Hence, all believers will agree that "these are parts of his ways: but how little a portion is heard of him? but the thunder of his power who can understand?" (Job 26 : 14).

God's infinite power is admitted by all who acknowledge his existence, but some have denied this power either directly or by implication. Some have limited his power to what he actually performs while others, beset by the deepest mysteries which harass the human mind, question his power to prevent or control the entrance or progress of sin. But there is no restriction to God's power, and he can save and sanctify all whom he will in spite of the opposition and malignity of his creatures, for his power controls all their actions. That God is the Creator and Controller of all things and can work with means, without means, and against means is a truth that must be held fast by all believers.

7. The Will of God

The will of God and the power of God are called attributes of sovereignty. His power expresses the effective energy of his nature as the only source of causation. His will denotes primarily the attribute of self-determination, by which he acts in accordance with his eternal power and Godhead. It has been said that God's will is limited by his perfections, but it is better to say that God's will is not limited in any sense, for his perfections ensure that he will not do that which is incompatible with his nature.

The word **will** as applied to God is susceptible of various meanings in accordance with the Hebrew and Greek terms used. The precise meaning must be ascertained from an examination of the word in its context. A critical view of the various passages in which this term occurs will evince its several important meanings such as the perfection of his moral nature, his absolute will which cannot be resisted, his purpose, the effect of his purpose, his secret and revealed will, his decretive and preceptive will, his wish or desire.

Theologians distinguish between the decretive and preceptive will of God. By the former he decrees whatsoever comes to pass, and by the latter he indicates the duties he enjoins upon his creatures. His decretive will is always effective, but his preceptive will is often disobeyed. A distinction has also been made between the secret and revealed will of God. His secret will or purpose is known only to himself; his revealed will is made known to man. It appears that God's decretive will includes many things which he forbids in his preceptive will. The word **will**, however, is used here in two different senses. The decretive will defines his purpose; the preceptive will is his command or what he wishes us to do. God's secret will simply means God's hidden decree. His revealed will is that which he has declared to us.

Some have a difficulty with these terms, since it appears to them that there is a contradiction somewhere. The truth is that we are not capable of entering into this subject, and so we create difficulties for ourselves which we cannot solve. We can, however, see no contradiction in the idea that God commands sinful men to obey the law while he knows very well they will not obey. Indeed, it would be a contradiction to suppose that if God has given man a law for his obedience, he would do anything less than command obedience. That God knows sinful man will not obey this law until a change takes place in his inner self must be self-evident. Some theologians have maintained that his decretive will is contrary to his preceptive will, but this arises either from the confounding of terms or else from failing to realize that there can be no contradiction in the divine nature.

8. The Holiness of God

The holiness of God renders him inapproachable in his perfections, separating him in the infinite majesty and glory of his nature from all the creatures he has made. "Who is like unto thee, O LORD . . . glorious in holiness" (Ex. 15 : 11). "Holy, holy, holy, is the LORD of hosts: the whole earth is full of his glory" (Is. 6 : 3). The holiness of God also sets before us his intellectual and moral splendour whereby he delights in purity and hates iniquity. "Ye shall be holy; for I am holy" (Lev. 11 : 44). Considerations of God's holiness fill us with awe and oppress us with a sense of sinfulness and utter unworthiness. This should lead us to repentance and adoration.

The root meaning of the word **holy** is to cut or separate; therefore, holy persons and things were separated from a common to a holy use. Such a separation must involve the possession of spiritual and moral excellence. God's holiness consists in his absolute separation from sin, the infinite purity of his perfections, his delight in purity, and his utter antagonism to sin. God is said to be a consuming fire to impress upon us his abhorrence of sin and his delight in purity, and hence we are commanded to "serve God acceptably with reverence and godly fear" (Heb. 12 : 28); and as he commands us to be holy as he is holy we may believe that the holiness of the redeemed must be of a similar kind and that he imparts to them a reflection of his holiness as the light of the sun sheds its radiance on the earth below.

Theologians generally adopt the view that holiness is not a specific attribute but the crowning excellence of his perfections. Dr Dick and Dr Dabney say that holiness is a complex term signifying the general character of God as resulting from his moral attributes. "His moral attributes are the special crown; his intelligence and will are the brow that wears it. His holiness is the collective and consummate glory of his nature as the infinite, morally pure, active and intelligent spirit" (Dabney); and Hodge says, "Infinite moral perfection is the crown of his Godhead; holiness is the total glory thus crowned."

The holiness of God is set forth in Scripture with exceeding clearness and when properly presented serves to impress us with the majesty and glory of the Divine Being. The moral law, originally given to man, or rather concreated with him, and inlaid in the very constitution of his spiritual and moral nature, was designed to confirm him in perfection and purity. The purity of the law itself in its nature and extent is an evident proof of the holy nature of God while the moral government of the world, setting forth the evils of disobedience and the rewards bestowed upon the righteous, confirms the evidence of God's holiness.

It is the economy of redemption, however, that the holiness of God is especially proclaimed to us: in the provision of a Perfect Saviour, who by his unparalleled sufferings and obedience purchased salvation for his people. There is also the consideration that, while the immediate design of the Atonement was to put away sin, the ultimate design was the restoration of men to that purity from which

they had fallen (Dr Dick); and, finally, the purity with which
salvation is connected is not a mere assent to the doctrines
of the Cross but is chiefly rooted in the heart and so per-
meates itself through the whole life enlisting all the faculties
in the service of God. Christ "gave himself for us, that he
might redeem us from all iniquity, and purify unto himself
a peculiar people, zealous of good works" (Titus 2 : 14).

9. The Justice of God

The moral attributes of justice, goodness, and truth are the
most important and most glorious perfections of God, and
these three concur in his consummate attribute of holiness
(Dr Dabney). God's justice has been defined as absolute
and relative. The former is the instrinsic righteousness of
his nature, and the latter is the exercise of his justice
towards his creatures. The distinction between his holiness
and his justice is that holiness is the opposition of his
nature towards sin and his justice the external visible display
of that opposition (Dr Ridgeley). Dr Shedd understands
justice to be a mode of his holiness. The Hebrew and Greek
words corresponding to righteousness contain the idea of
conformity to a standard (Dr Berkhof). Theologians have
generally discussed this subject under the headings of **rectoral**
and **distributive** justice. Distributive justice is both remunerative and retributive. For the sake of convenience, however,
the justice of God may be considered under the heads of
rectoral, remunerative, and retributive justices.

(1) **God's Rectoral Justice.** This aspect of God's justice
proclaims him to be the moral Governor of the world, who
reveals a just law to mankind with promises of reward to
the obedient and threats of punishment to the disobedient.
"Justice and judgment are the habitation of thy throne:
mercy and truth shall go before thy face" (Ps. 89 : 14).
"For the LORD is our judge, the LORD is our lawgiver, the
LORD is our king; he will save us" (Is. 33 : 22).

God's justice is intimately related to his own law, which
corresponds to the righteousness of his nature. This law
is that "imperial standard of moral excellence imposed upon
mankind from without and from above them by the supreme authority of a personal moral governor over personal
moral subjects" (Dr A. A. Hodge). The law of God is

summed up into love of God and our neighbor: this has
hardly ever been denied by any who professed to believe in
God. The law, however, to be authoritative must be enforced
by proper sanctions, and therefore rewards and punishments
are annexed to it. Justice requires that obedience be rewarded
and disobedience punished in accordance with the principles
of righteousness.

A consideration of the justice of God in the light of our
non-conformity tends to oppress us with feelings of terror;
hence, attempts have been made, in defiance of the declarations of Scripture, to deprive God of this attribute or to
give it another meaning. Even theologians of standing have
attempted to prove that justice is optional with God and
that "the divine law is a product of the divine will and
therefore at the option of God is relaxable alike in its
preceptive and penal elements" (Hugo Grotius, quoted by
Dr A. A. Hodge). But the declarations of Scripture and
the economy of redemption set forth the determination of
God to visit every sin with punishment according to its
desert. The Word of God teaches that Christ suffered the
penalty of sin in the room and stead of his elect people
and so fulfilled all the claims of the law which God's
righteousness demanded. Perhaps the basic passage bearing
upon this subject as it relates to man's redemption is to be
found in the Epistle of Paul to the Romans. "For all have
sinned, and come short of the glory of God; being justified
freely by his grace through the redemption that is in Christ
Jesus: whom God hath set forth to be a propitiation through
faith in his blood, to declare his righteousness for the re-
mission of sins that are past, through the forbearance of
God; to declare, I say, at this time his righteousness: that
he might be just, and the justifier of him which believeth in
Jesus" (Rom. 3 : 23-26).

(2) **God's Remunerative Justice.** God's remunerative justice is revealed in the distribution of rewards to both men
and angels. "Verily there is a reward for the righteous:
verily he is a God that judgeth in the earth" (Psa. 58 : 11).
"Who will render to every man according to his deeds: to
them who by patient continuance in well doing seek for
glory and honour and immortality, eternal life" (Rom. 2 :
6, 7). God's remunerative justice is an expression of divine

love, dealing out its bounties, not on the basis of strict merit, but according to promise and agreement. (Luke 17 : 10; 1 Cor. 4 : 7) (Dr Berkhof).

(3) **God's Retributive Justice.** God's retributive justice or punitive justice is concerned with the infliction of penalties because of sin and is an expression of the divine wrath. "Cursed be he that confirmeth not all the words of this law to do them" (Deut. 27 : 26). "The soul that sinneth, it shall die" (Ezek. 18 : 20). "The wages of sin is death" (Rom. 6 : 23).

10. The Goodness of God

The goodness of God has been defined as that perfection of his nature which disposes him to communicate happiness to his creatures. Dr Shedd says that goodness is not the attribute by which God **is** good, but by which he **does** good. As good in himself, God is holy; as showing goodness to others, he is good; and his goodness is that transitive attribute issuing forth from the Divine nature, which designs the welfare and happiness of the universe. This attribute, according to Dr Dick, completes our ideas of an all-perfect Being, and is the foundation of the trust, love, and hope with which he is regarded by man. "God's goodness," in the words of Dr Dabney, "is the generic attribute of which the love of benevolence, grace, pity, mercy, and forgiveness are the specific actings." Theologians have usually considered this perfection under the headings of love, mercy, and grace.

(1) **The Love of God.** God's love is that affection which disposes him to delight in his creatures and in their well-being. This love has been resolved into the love of **benevolence** and the love of **complacency.** By the former is meant that love of God to his sinful creatures which leads him to provide for their well-being; the latter denotes that love with which he delights in his people on account of their spiritual excellence. God's **benevolent** interest extends to the irrational and rational creation. "Thou openest thine hand, and satisfiest the desire of every living thing" (Psa. 145 : 16). "The young lions roar after their prey, and seek their meat from God" (Psa. 104 : 21). "He maketh his sun to rise on the evil and on the good, and sendeth rain on the just and

on the unjust" (Matt. 5 : 45); and to further their likeness
to him, his own children are commanded to imitate God's
benevolence; "Love your enemies, bless them that curse you,
do good to them that hate you . . .; that ye may be the
children of your Father which is in heaven" (Matt. 5 : 44, 45).
God's love of **complacency** expresses his delight in his people
because of their spiritual excellencies and loving services
to him. "The LORD taketh pleasure in them that fear him,
in those that hope in his mercy" (Psa. 147 : 11). "If ye keep
my commandments, ye shall abide in my love; even as I
have kept my Father's commandments, and abide in his
love" (John 15 : 10).

"Since God is absolutely good in himself, his love
cannot find complete satisfaction in any object that falls
short of absolute perfection. He loves his rational
creatures for his own sake: or, to express it otherwise,
he loves in them himself, his virtues, his work, and his
gifts. He does not even withdraw his love completely
from the sinner in his present sinful state, though the
latter's sin is an abomination to him, since he recog-
nizes even in the sinner his image bearer. John 3 : 16;
Matt. 5 : 44, 45. At the same time he loves believers
with a special love, since he contemplates them as his
spiritual children in Christ. It is to them that he communicates himself in the fullness of his grace and
mercy. (John 16 : 27; Rom. 5 : 8; 1 John 3 : 1)." (Dr
Berkhof—**Systematic Theology,** p. 71).

(2) **The Mercy of God.** The mercy of God has been
defined as an aspect of the goodness of God shown to
those who are in misery, irrespective of their merits. The
Hebrew, the Septuagint, and the New Testament words
denote compassion or tender mercy. It has been suggested
that the etymology of the Gaelic word **trocair** (mercy)
brings before us two ideas, "love" and "death". If we
accept this meaning, mercy connotes love meeting with
death. God's mercy contemplates the misery of his creatures
and makes provision for their relief. "The LORD, The
LORD God, merciful and gracious, longsuffering, and
abundant in goodness and truth, keeping mercy for thousands, forgiving iniquity and transgression and sin" (Ex. 34 :

15. Dr Berkhof, **Systematic Theology,** p. 71.

6, 7). "It is of the LORD'S mercies that we are not consumed, because his compassions fail not" (Lam. 3 : 22). "For I will be merciful to their unrighteousness, and their sins and their iniquities will I remember no more" (Heb. 8 : 12).

(3) **The Grace of God.** The grace of God denotes his unmerited love to those who have forfeited his favour and are under the judicial sentence of condemnation. Mercy views man as a sufferer: grace considers him as a sinner. The words **grace** and **mercy** are, however, sometimes used interchangeably. The grace of God embraces those who are unworthy and ill-deserving and is the source of all spiritual blessings: "In whom we have redemption through his blood, the forgiveness of sins, according to the riches of his grace" (Eph. 1 : 7); "That in the ages to come he might shew the exceeding riches of his grace in his kindness toward us through Christ Jesus" (Eph. 2 : 7); "For ye know the grace of our Lord Jesus Christ, that, though he was rich, yet for your sakes he became poor, that ye through his poverty might be rich" (2 Cor. 8 : 9).

The work of creation affords proof of God's goodness if we attend to the fact that God, in giving life to the different orders of creation, provided a fit habitation for them and made every conceivable provision for their well-being and happiness. In connection with this part of the subject, Dr Dick writes:

"When we say that God does anything for His glory, if we affix any distinct sense to our words, we must mean that He does it for the manifestation of His perfections. There is no inconsistency therefore in maintaining that goodness was the motive of creation, for this is only to say that God purposed to display the benevolence of His nature in giving being to other beings besides Himself. It is true that creation has eventually served to glorify all His perfections in the great scheme of providence of which fallen men are the objects; but considering it by itself and in its high intention, we are authorised to assert that its primary design was the diffusion of happiness." (Dr John Dick, **Lectures in Theology,** Vol. 1, p. 431).

16. Dr John Dick, **Lectures in Theology,** Vol. I, p. 43.

That the goodness of God has been misunderstood and abused by men professing to worship the one God of the Scriptures is notorious in the annals of modern theology. The love of God has been dealt with as if this were the only attribute worthy of consideration, so that the other perfections of his nature, such as wisdom, justice, and truth, have been held in the background or altogether omitted to make way for a sentimental conception of a loving God, who loves everybody, punishes no one, would banish evil if he could, and provides a redemption that in its nature and consequences is wholly inadequate to meet the requirements of Jehovah or the pleas of the human conscience when oppressed by the burden of sin. When Scripture asserts that God is love, we are also to remember that God is light and that God is a consuming fire; and the Word of the Lord makes it abundantly clear that the most glorious display of justice, as well as goodness, is manifested in the bitter sufferings of the Lord Jesus Christ.

The manifestation of God's goodness and love is set forth in exceeding brightness and glory in the Incarnation and Satisfaction of Christ, and any question as to the goodness of God to mankind finds its answer in the purchase price of our redemption. "For God so loved the world, that he gave his only begotten Son, that whosoever believeth in him should not perish, but have everlasting life" (John 3 : 16). This expression of God's love at such an infinite cost and in accordance with the attributes of wisdom and justice is eminently fitted to draw forth our gratitude and devotion. "We love him, because he first loved us" (1 John 4 : 19).

> "Redemption is not an act of omnipotence alone, nor of love alone. It is not an act of creation but an act of moral administration; and hence it exhibits a provision and combination of means, illustrative of the riches of His wisdom . . . And reflecting upon the character of our Saviour, we must be sensible that by appointing Him to die for us, He has given us a higher demonstration of love than if the whole system to which we belong had been offered up as an atonement for our sins." (Dr Dick. Vol. 1, p. 446).

In reply to those who find difficulty in reconciling the goodness

17.   Dr John Dick, **Lectures in Theology,** Vol. ?, p. 431.

of God with the existence and prevalence of evil in the world, it might be pointed out that on this subject men have not considered with sufficient attention the fall of man, and have failed to take into account that man, being placed under a moral administration of a righteous governor, must suffer penalties as a rebellious and disloyal subject if the provisions of law and justice are to be maintained. At the same time, the permission of sin is an unsolved mystery and we must accept the available evidence of the manifold goodness of God; it is by faith that we can rest assured that God is good and doeth good. "And we know that all things work together for good to them that love God, to them who are the called according to his purpose" (Rom. 8 : 28).

11. The Truth of God

That God, as the living and true God, is distinguished from lifeless and false idols and that his communications and promises to mankind are consistent and faithful must be inferred from the perfection of the Divine nature. That he will execute his threatenings upon those who flagrantly disobey his commands must also be deduced in the same way. The Word of God, however, explains at large the nature and results of God's truth and faithfulness.

That the Word of God is true must be accepted; otherwise we should have no confidence in its Author. The Scriptures being self-consistent, their historical features being confirmed by collateral evidence, and the doctrines contained in them agreeable to the dictates of sound reasoning, we must conclude that those facts transcending reason are equally true. The highest evidence for the truth of the Word of God is his own testimony, which is received by faith. We are told that "All scripture is given by inspiration of God, and is profitable for doctrine, for reproof, for correction, for instruction in righteousness: that the man of God may be perfect, throughly furnished unto all good works" (2 Tim. 3 : 16, 17).

God's truth as it relates to his promises and threats is either absolute or conditional. The destruction of nations, individuals, and false systems, because of their continued opposition to God, will surely be executed in due time, where it has not already been brought to pass in the history of man. "He, that being often reproved hardeneth his neck, shall suddenly be destroyed, and that without remedy" (Prov. 29 : 1). "For the nation and kingdom that will not serve thee shall perish; yea, those nations shall be utterly wasted" (Is. 60 : 12). God's conditional threats are explained on the ground that a condition of repentance is implied as in the case of the threatened destruction of Ninevah (Jonah 3 : 14). In the case of Hezekiah, we may suppose that according to his physical condition he was at the point of death but that the period of his life was extended through the power of God. (Is. 38 : 1).

Gods promises are absolute or conditional. The absolute promise of God to provide a Saviour and to save and sanctify sinners is independent of their conduct and has been accomplished in the face of the greatest opposition by those who afterwards became the greatest beneficiaries of his grace. His conditional promise in the case of admission to the Promised Land of a certain generation of people was withdrawn from some because by their disobedience and ingratitude they had forfeited all claim to the inheritance; and, hence, it is written "that they could not enter in because of unbelief" (Heb. 3 : 19).

The promises and invitation of the Gospel have presented problems to some people, mainly because they have not sufficiently considered the character and purposes of God. When God commands men to believe and obey, we must understand he does this because obedience and faith are agreeable to him, for he loves righteousness and hates iniquity and because, in the nature of the case, sinners ought to fulfil his commands. That sinners are unable to obey his commands must be ascribed to the depraved condition of their nature. (It surely must be of the utmost importance that we make a candid study of the statements of Scripture before we build up metaphysical theories as to how God should conduct himself in dealing with sinful man). The promise of salvation is not made to those who hear the Gospel but to those who believe it; and to maintain that to be sincere God must bestow power to believe upon all men who are invited to avail themselves of salvation is not only philosophically unsound but is in flat contradiction to the plain statements of Scripture. If, however, we assert that God has given power to all men to accept his overtures of mercy, it surely must strike us as peculiar that in the whole compass of the sacred writings we find no hint that unregenerate men are able to believe or obey but rather the reverse.

That God is true in his character and communications and faithful to all his promises is a source of confidence and joy to all who put their trust in him. "For the mountains shall depart, and the hills be removed; but my kindness shall not depart from thee, neither shall the covenant of my peace be removed, saith the LORD that hath mercy on thee" (Is. 54 : 10). "If they break my statutes, and keep not my commandments; then will I visit their transgression with the rod, and their iniquity with stripes. Nevertheless my lovingkindness will I not utterly take from him, nor suffer my faithfulness to fail" (Psa. 89 : 31-33).

CHAPTER IV

THE DOCTRINE OF THE TRINITY

I. OLD TESTAMENT PROOFS
    1. Passages referring to the Son
    2. Passages referring to the Holy Spirit

II. NEW TESTAMENT PROOFS

III. THE ONTOLOGICAL TRINITY
    1. The Persons of the Trinity
    2. The Personal Properties
    3. The Economic Relations
    4. The Person of the Son (1) His Consubstantiality, (2) The Eternal Sonship
    5. The Holy Ghost

The doctrine of the Trinity is based upon two propositions: first, that God is one; and secondly, that the Father is God, the Son is God, and the Holy Spirit is God. These truths are so plainly stated in the New Testament that they may be accepted by any intelligent reader, but the doctrine itself is so mysterious that it must be received by faith in that God who has revealed himself. The real mystery that confronts us lies in the relations in which the Persons subsist within the divine essence. These relations we cannot fathom but we can formulate statements which show that the truth stated is not contrary to reason and that it is based upon Scripture.

The two main errors relating to this subject are: first, the emphasis laid upon God's unity to the exclusion of the Trinity, and secondly, the emphasis laid upon the Trinity to the exclusion of the Divine unity. The Sabellians emphasised the unity of God to such an extent that they ignored the personal properties of the Trinity and substituted the doctrine that the persons were mere names or manifestations of the one God. The Tritheists urged the Trinity of God and developed the conception that there were three Gods. Other heretical sects either denied the

personality of one or both Persons of the Son and the Holy
Spirit or maintained that these Persons were inferior to God.

I. OLD TESTAMENT PROOFS

As the doctrine of the Trinity is of fundamental importance
our opponents would have us prove it from the Old Testament, but they should not compel us to assert that it is so
clearly revealed there as in the New Testament, as this
would not agree with the genius of a progressive revelation,
nor would it be in line with the revelation of other doctrines
of fundamental importance, such as the atonement which
was gradually developed. When we maintain, however, that
the doctrine can be proved from the Old Testament we
must take notice of two extreme positions, first, the idea
that the Old Testament doctrine of God is not only mono-
theistic, but monadic, that is, that God revealed himself
solely in one Person as well as nature; and secondly, the
idea that we have a clear revelation of the Trinity in the
Old Testament. The view taken here is that the doctrine
being fundamental is of necessity revealed, but obscurely so
in the Old Testament.

Calvin says, "God while he declares himself to be but
one, he proposes himself to be distinctively considered in
three persons, without apprehending which we have only a
bare and empty name of God floating in our brains without
any idea of the true God." (14a John Calvin, Institutes
1:13:2). The same writer points out that as God afforded
a clearer manifestation of himself at the advent of Christ,
the three also became better known.

It would indeed seem strange, if the Old Testament
conception of God were monadic, why we find so many
instances in which distinctions appear that relate not to
qualities of being but to persons and agents. "In the
beginning **God** created the heaven and the earth" (Gen. 1 : 1)
"and the **Spirit** of God moved upon the face of the waters"
(Gen. 1 : 2) "And God said let **us** make man in **our** image
after our likeness" (Gen. 1 : 26). We are thus near the
beginning of written revelation directed to distinctions in
the nature of God, obscure to be sure, but we could hardly
expect anything further at this stage of a progressive self-

revelation of God. There are, besides, a considerable number of references and passages in the Old Testament which would preclude us from adopting the extreme view that there was no revelation of the Trinity in the Old Testament Scriptures.

1. Passages referring to the Son

The Angel Jehovah passages have been adduced by some commentators as pointing to Christ since this angel is referred to distinctively, and in the same context identified with God. This is shown in the encounter between the angel and Hagar where the angel is identified with God (Gen. 16 : 13). The reference to Balaam and the ass seems to lead to the same conclusion (Num. 22 : 22). The angel that came from Gilgal to Bochim is identified with God who brought Israel from Egypt into the promised land (Judges 2 : 1). There are also a number of other instances in which men and angels who were identified with God appeared to the Old Testament people (Gen. 18 : 13; Gen. 32 : 30; Ex. 3 : 2-4); Judges, 13 : 21, 22). Having the New Testament in our hands it is not difficult for us to believe that Christ temporarily assumed the form of a man or an angel; but how much was understood of the Triune nature of God by the Old Testament saints we cannot tell.

Passages such as Psa. 2 : 7; Psa. 45 : 6; Prov. 8 : 30 and Isaiah 9 : 6 have also been adduced by divines as referring to Christ. That Psalm Two speaks of Christ is plainly allowed. Psa. 45 : 6 has also been adduced as another proof although an alternative reading has been suggested. Calvin objects to this alternative reading but maintains that there is no obscurity in Isa. 9 : 6 which introduces Christ as God crowned with supreme power. With regard to Prov. 8 : 30 some commentators will not commit themselves to the notion that this verse refers to Christ. Dr Pye Smith says this cannot be proved but Dr John Harris says the notion cannot be disproved. Dr Ridgeley has no hesitation in applying this verse to our Lord.

2. Passages referring to the Holy Spirit

There are two questions to be dealt with here. The first is what proofs are available in the Old Testament to point to the personality of the Holy Ghost, and then, what proofs can we marshal that the Holy Ghost is God. There are several passages which point to the Spirit of God as a Person and which also prove that he possesses absolute Deity with the Father. As to his Personality, Gen. 1 : 2 refers to an activity as moving; Gen. 6 : 3 speaks of a striving; Psa. 104 : 30 of a creating; Isa. 61 : 1 of a setting apart; and Isa. 63 : 10 of being vexed. There are a considerable number of other passages which could be referred to. The objection that these passages are figurative or metaphorical would make nonsense of sober truths and narratives where the context clearly sets forth the writer's meaning. The following passages may be cited which prove the Deity of the Holy Ghost. The work of creation is referred to in Gen. 1 : 2. Note also 2 Sam. 23 : 2, 3 where the Spirit of the Lord is identified with the God of Israel. Isa. 6 : 9 makes it plain that it was the Lord who spoke to Isaiah who is here called the Holy Ghost.

II. NEW TESTAMENT PROOFS

The evidence to the Deity of Christ presented in the New Testament is shown in many passages either by direct assertion or by necessary inference. There are some passages however which stand out by themselves and can be grasped by any honest reader. John 1 : 1 has been hopelessly juggled in order to deprive it of its true meaning but the Greek construction undoubtedly points to the Deity of Christ. All the attempts made to manœuvre the words "God blessed for ever" in the last clause of Rom. 9 : 6 which refers to Christ, are a violation of Greek grammar. "God was manifest in the flesh" (1 Tim. 3 : 16), refers without doubt to Christ. "The church of God which he has purchased with his blood" (Acts 20 : 28). The meaning here can only be that God the Son, purchased the church with his own blood.

The objectors to the Deity of Christ are not willing to discuss these texts if they can avoid it but will produce other passages which prove that Christ is finite. This is fully granted in respect of his human nature. If, however, passages such as Matt. 19 : 7, John 14 : 28, and John 17 : 21 prove that Christ is merely a creature, them these passages are opposed to others such as John 5 : 17; John 10 : 30, and John 10 : 36. We maintain there is no opposition since Christ is both human and divine.

The passage in John 14 : 28, "For my Father is greater than I" refers to his person in his mediatorial office. But it could also refer to his present state of humiliation in contrast with the state of glory, which he was soon to enter. When we quote the text "I and the Father are one" (John 10 : 30), the objector will state that this is a oneness in respect of likeness or purpose and he will compare it to John 17 : 21, "That they also may be one in us". That the objector does not understand the meaning of John 10 : 30 is proved by the action of the Jews who threatened to stone Jesus because they understood his meaning to be that he claimed to be God (John 10 : 33).

"My Father worketh hitherto, and I work" (John 5 : 17). We can see from the context that the Jews understood Jesus to claim for himself equality with God. That he did not deny their inference is proved by the verses following where he claimed equal power (27) an honour (23) with the Father. The worship due to God is predicated of Christ in Math. 28 : 19 and in 2 Cor. 13 : 14. In these two passages the Father, the Son, and the Holy Ghost are placed upon an equality. In respect of personality they are distinguished, but in respect of honour, glory and grace, they are one.

III. THE ONTOLOGICAL TRINITY

The Ontological Trinity refers to the intra-divine relations relations within the Divine essence while the Economic Trinity expresses the relations of the Trinity to created beings. Whether these terms are sufficiently accurate or not, the distinction itself is important, since, in dealing with this topic, we should try to make a distinction between what God is in himself and what he is to us.

1. The Persons of the Trinity

Neither the word **Trinity** nor the word **unity** is to be found in Scripture. The word **Trinity** came into use in order to defend the true doctrine against heretics, who professed to believe the plain statements of Scripture but denied their true meaning. The word expresses precisely the truth we hold. It means tri-unity or three in one and sets forth the doctrine that there are three distinct Persons in the same numerical or specific essence. The word **numerical** signifies one in number and the word **specific** when used in this connection signifies the same species or nature.

That there is a distinction of Persons may be observed from the consideration of many passages of Scripture. Christ speaks of the Father and Himself (John 5 : 17, John 6 : 44, John 8 : 42) and of the Spirit and Himself (John 16 : 7, 8, 14), and the Father speaks of the Son (Matt. 17 : 5, Mark 9 : 7). The three Persons are spoken of together (Matt. 28 : 19, 2 Cor. 13 : 14).

It is, however, one thing to acknowledge that there are three Persons of the same nature, and equal in power and glory, but it is another thing to attempt to explain these distinctions in our endeavour to defend the truth against objectors. And it is well for us to remember that this is a mystery, not in the sense of something which was hidden and now revealed, but a mystery incomprehensible.

The word **Person** brings before us the idea of an **I - thou** relation, and we tend to confuse it with a human person. The word **Person** here is more than a manifestation, influence, or a role sustained for a time; yet it differs from our conception of a human person. When we view this subject we find that the Persons though distinguished are not separate and that the whole essence is not outside of them or behind them but that the whole essence is in each Person, for the personal distinctions referred to are within the one Divine essence.

Calvin says: "What I denominate a Person is a subsistence within the divine essence, which is related to the others and yet distinguished from them by an incommunicable property. By the word **subsistence** we mean something different from the word **essence**."[18] Fisher on **The Shorter Catechism** says that a Person in the Godhead means "a complete, intelligent, and individual substance which is neither a part of nor sustained by any other, but is dis-

18. Calvin, **Institutes**, I : XIII : 6.

tinguished by an incommunicable property in the same individual essence."[18a]

2. The Personal Properties

It has also been stated that the Persons have not a distinct nature or essence of their own since the same Divine essence is one and common to them all, the Person though distinct being inseparable from the Divine nature or the other Persons. Perhaps these distinctions convey little information to us, but they will help to convince us that there is no contradiction in stating that the essence may be one and the distinctions within the essence three.

The Persons are distinguished by personal and incommunicable properties. A **personal** property is peculiar to one of the Persons and incommunicable, but an **essential** property is common to them all. The personal property of of Father is to beget the Son. The personal property of the of the Holy Spirit is to proceed from the Father and the Son. For example, we could not say that the Father is begotten by the Son or that the Holy Ghost was begotten by the Father. The peculiar property of the Father is paternity; of the Son, filiation; and of the Holy Spirit, procession. We are assured from Scripture that there are such properties and relations, but what they are we know not. The following passages of Scripture do prove these truths: John 1 : 14, 16; John 3 : 16, 18; John 5 : 18; Rom. 8 : 32; 1 John 4 : 9 with John 15 : 26; Rom. 8 : 9; Gal. 4 : 6.

3. The Economic Relations

We should also remember in dealing with this subject that there is an order referred to in relation to created beings. Although all three concur in all works of creation, providence, and redemption, some acts are predominantly referred **to the Father,** such as creation and providence, the councils of redemption, election and calling; **to the Son** are referred the work of salvation through his manifestations to the Church in the Old Testament, the incarnation, the work of obedience and suffering, the resurrection, and the gathering together of the Church under his own Headship — all

18a. Fisher, **Shorter Catechism** (Edinburgh, 1805) p. 47.

this is done **for** the Church; **to the Holy Spirit:** all gifts and graces, regeneration, sanctification, and perfection — all this is done **in** the Church.

In terms of order the Father sends the Son, and the Father and Son send the Spirit to complete the work of salvation. The terms First, Second, and Third Persons are currently used in this economic order. The word **subordination** is used in dealing with this subject, but it is unfortunate that this word has been so used in connection with the intra-divine relations. If the Father, the Son, and the Holy Spirit are the same in substance, equal in power and glory, the word **subordination** has no place in this category. Probably one of the best statements that have been made on the Ontological Trinity in this regard is to be found in the Second Helvetic Confession. Two statements in it are noteworthy, one guarding against the temptation to define the eternal generation, and the other excluding any intra-divine subordination. "We believe and teach that God is one in essence (Deut. 6 : 5; Exod. 20 : 2, 3, etc.), and three in persons: Father, Son, and Holy Ghost. The Father hath begotten the Son from eternity; **the Son is begotten in an unspeakable manner;** the Holy Ghost eternally proceeds from both, and is to be worshipped with both as one God. There are not three Gods, but three persons, consubstantial, co-eternal, **distinct as to person and order, yet without any inequality** [italics mine]. The Divine essence or nature is the same in the Father, the Son, and the Spirit (Luke 1 : 35; Matt. 3 : 17; 28 : 19; John 1 : 32; 14 : 26).[19]

4. The Person of the Son

(1) **His Consubstantiality.** If we take it for granted that Christ is one of the Persons of the Trinity from the Scriptural evidence that there are distinctions within the Divine essence and that there is an **I - thou** relationship, we now deal with the doctrine of Christ's consubstantiality. This just means that he possesses the same numerical essence as the Father. It would, of course, be possible to say that he is the same in substance or of a similar substance while still leaving room for a doctrine of Tritheism or a subordination of the Son.

19. **Second Helvetic Confession** (Bullinger, 1566).

However, the use of this word in theological language excludes both the one and the other. In the Nicene controversies some Arians held that the Son was of a different substance — **heteroòusios;** the semi-Arians, and perhaps some orthodox among them, said the Son possessed a similar substance — **homoiòusios.** The true Trinitarians, however, preferred to use the word **homoòusios** to indicate that the Son was possessed not only of the same substance, but of one and the same substance. We may think that the terms used here serve no useful purpose, but the history of doctrine shows that some, while they professed to agree with the words of Scripture, refused to acknowledge the truth that the Son possessed the same numerical essence or substance as the Father. The whole of the argument regarding the consubstantiality of Christ is simply that he is the possessor of the whole Divine essence as the Father and the Spirit. "I and my Father are one" (John 10 : 20); "The Father is in me, and I in him" (John 10 : 38); "He that hath seen me hath seen the Father" (John 14 : 9); "That all men should honour the Son, even as they honour the Father" (John 5 : 23). The whole Divine essence belongs to the Father and to the Son and to the Holy Spirit.

(2) **The Eternal Sonship.** A complete review of this subject would necessitate a survey of the history of doctrine as well as a discussion of the titles predicated of Christ, such as the **Logos,** the **Son of man,** and the **Son of God.** The Logos doubtless refers to the revelation of God in and through Jesus Christ while the Son of man must have in view his human nature and representative character. The Son of God, at least in some texts in the New Testament, undoubtedly requires the sense that Christ possesses the same nature as the Father. Whether, however, his Sonship is prolated, derived, or communicated is another question. The further question meets us here as to whether the Sonship of Christ is economic or ontological: that is, whether his Sonship is Messianic or Trinitarian. Objections to his Trinitarian Sonship have been made by some who acknowledge his absolute Deity because in their view a Trinitarian Sonship would be a subordinate Sonship.

It has been already stated that there are three distinctions within the Divine essence and that these three are distinguished by peculiar properties. The peculiar property of the Father is to beget the Son and of the Son to be begotten of the Father. In other words, the relation between these two persons is that of Father and Son. Divines, therefore, have dealt with this subject under the heading of the Eternal Sonship. Unhappily, theological confusion has arisen here as it has in the discussion of the Persons because it has been conceived that the word **Person** as the word **Son** connotes the same or similar ideas as these words convey in human relationships thereby giving the impression that the Father must be prior to the Son in nature or in dignity. And, therefore, some of those who object to the Eternal Sonship do so because they believe that the doctrine reduces the Son to a subordinate position. I think it is generally admitted that the relationship between the Father and the Son is a profound mystery; yet men have tried to explain the terms of it by those of human relationships.

If we deny that Christ's Sonship is eternal, we must maintain that it came into being before or after the creation of the world. We must otherwise say that his Sonship is eternal. Some have, as Origen, spoken of the generation of the Son as a sovereign act of God; others speak of it as a necessary act and an eternal act. It has also been spoken of as the generation of the Person rather than the generation of the nature. A number of these statements, which have been derived from speculations by the Nicene fathers, have doubtless given some ground for criticism of the doctrine of the Eternal Sonship. We should distinguish, however, between criticism of the doctrine and criticism of the explanations of the doctrine, in some cases where attempts were made to explain what cannot be explained.

A reading of theological debate on this subject will show us that a number of great divines have accepted the doctrine but have been unable to accept some of the explanations. John Calvin himself was accused of denying this doctrine because he disagreed with the Nicene speculations about the eternal generation; yet Calvin explicitly asserts the doctrine. B. B. Warfield points out that Calvin's assertion of the **auto theos** of the Son marks an epoch in the doctrine of the Trinity because the current modes of stating it were not sufficiently guarded. Dr John Gill — who is quoted with approval by Rev. J. C. Philpot, who himself preached vehement sermons against opposers of the Eternal Sonship — says: "I know it is represented by some, who otherwise are sound in the doctrine of the Trinity, that the divine nature is communicated from the Father to the Son and Spirit, and that he is **fons Deitatis,** the fountain of the Deity, which I think unsafe phrases, since they seem to imply a priority in the Father to the other two Persons; for he that communicates must, at least, in order of nature, and according to our conception of things, be prior to whom the communication is made." Dr Dick makes the statement: "It occurs to me, that, after all this learned talk about communication, origin, principle, fountain, cause, nothing more is meant than what we all acknowledge that the nature of the Son, is the very same with the nature of the Father, which certainly is necessary to preserve the unity; but such terms are unhappily employed to express it. Bishop Horsely, who is of the same opinion, with Bishop Bull and the fathers, might well call the subordination of the Son mysterious, for a subordination among equal persons, a subordination of one who is truly God is indeed a mystery, a thing perfectly unintelligible."[19a]

Dr Cunningham points out that while Scripture sets before us the doctrine that the Father, the Son, and the Holy Ghost are one God, they are distinguished from each other so that they might be marked out by the personal pronouns of **I, Thou,** and **He,** and that when it is added that they are distinguished by their personal properties, we are to understand that the peculiar distinguishing property of the Father is to beget the Son and of the Son to be begotten of the Father, and of the Holy Ghost to proceed from the Father and the Son from all eternity. This, says the doctor, constitutes the substance of the doctrine which has been held by the Church in all ages under the name of the Eternal Sonship. This doctrine, that there was a generation of begetting by which the Father in some sense communicated the Divine nature, essence, or substance, and the Son, of course, derived or received it from the Father so as to be even as God, a Son and begotten, is held by Cunningham

19a. Dr John Dick, **Lectures on Theology** Vol. 2, p. 68.

to be clearly the doctrine which the Nicene fathers intended to teach and which has been generally received ever since by the most orthodox churches. The use of the word **subordination,** says Dr Cunningham, has been generally avoided by orthodox writers, as it is fitted to suggest ideas inconsistent with the Deity of Christ.[19b]

The substance of the doctrine which has always been recognised by the Church is: that there is in the Divine essence an internal and eternal relation which is in some manner analogous to the relation between father and son among men. This follows from the names **Father** and **Son** referring to what is termed the First and Second Persons of the Trinity. This relation involves the idea of sameness of nature, and this is the only idea essential to our receiving of the doctrine as the truth of God. The Father, the Son, and the Holy Spirit are the same in substance, equal in power and glory. The ideas of generation and begetting, therefore, as these terms apply to the Father and the Son, must exclude concepts of human modes of father and son relations, and to attempt to give a nearer or more definite explanation of the Eternal Sonship is to intrude into matters above the level of our knowledge. If we speak of a necessary act of generation or the communication of person or essence, great care must be taken to exclude ideas of priority or subordination. It is, of course, proper to say that the eternal generation refers to an eternal and necessary relationship to the Father. After all, the only ideas we can form of a communication of essence is that all the perfections of the Divine essence are equally and eternally predicated of the Father, the Son, and the Holy Spirit. It is true that Scripture affords us more information about the relation between the Father and the Son than the notion of sameness of substance and equality of power and glory.

The New Testament, and especially the writings of the Apostle John, sets forth the intimacy of the relation in terms of oneness of sovereignty, of glory, of purpose, of love, joy, and fellowship; but these manifestations of the intra-divine relations do not permit us to define the mode of the Eternal

19b. Principal Cunningham, **Historical Theology** (Edinburgh, 1870) p. 296.

Sonship of our Lord in terms which are neither intelligible to ourselves or to others.

5. The Holy Ghost

The doctrine respecting the Person of the Holy Ghost was formulated in the heat of Trinitarian controversy. The Nicene Second General Council held at Constantinople in 381 A.D. described the Holy Ghost as the "Lord and Life-giver, proceeding from the Father, and with the Father and the Son to be worshipped and glorified, who spake by the prophets." The Latin or Western Church in 589 A.D. added the word **filioque** (and the Son), meaning that the Holy Spirit proceeds from the Father and from the Son. The Greek or Eastern Church refused to accept this position and so the Eastern and Western Churches separated. The peculiar property of the Holy Ghost, therefore, is to proceed from the Father and the Son, but what this procession means we are unable to conceive. And the current mode of stating this position is that it is a communication from the Father and the Son. Whatever the communication means, it must co-exist with equality of nature. Some have defined this communication by saying that generation as well as procession is simply that the Divine essence is predicated of the Son and the Holy Spirit. The reader will notice that no specific explanation has been given for **generation** and **procession.** The truth is that no explanation can be given though attempts have been made to distinguish between the one and the other. To state, however, that the Son is **begotten** and that the Spirit **proceeds from the Father and the Son** is based upon Scriptural declarations. Fisher, on **The Shorter Catechism** shows us that the proofs of the procession of the Spirit are to be found in Scripture. He is called "the Spirit of his Son" (Gal. 4 : 6); "the Spirit of Christ" (Rom. 8 : 9). The Spirit is said to receive all things from Christ (John 16 : 14, 15); to be sent by him (John 15 : 26), and the Father is said to send him in Christ's name (John 14 : 26).

Speculation upon this mysterious subject is unsafe, and although we recognise that orthodox church councils found it necessary to issue creedal statements as against heretics, attempted distinctions based upon the Divine intellect and will are neither Scriptural nor beneficial. The dignified and guarded statement of the Westminster divines on this subject is worthy of imitation. "In the unity of the Godhead, there be three persons, of one substance, power, and eternity; God the Father, God the Son, and God the Holy Ghost. The Father is of none, neither begotten nor proceeding; the Son is eternally begotten of the Father; the Holy Ghost eternally proceeding from the Father and the Son."[20]

It is not too clear to some why the Spirit is called the Holy Spirit or the Holy Ghost. It is probably easier to state why the Son is called the Son and the Father, the Father. Some have dealt with this subject on economical grounds by saying that he is the author of holiness throughout the universe. It is better, however, not to say that he is called the Spirit or the Holy Spirit because he is holy or because he is spirit but because he proceeds from the Father and the Son. Some of the Scholastics who used the word **spiration** instead of procession referred the title to his mode of existence as emanating or breathed from the Father and the Son. Others have maintained that the term **Spirit** refers to the Hebrew and Greek terms **ruach** and **pneuma,** which like the Latin word **spiritus** are derived from roots which mean to breathe.

Once we have proved that the Holy Ghost is a Person, it will not be difficult to set forth his Deity from passages of New Testament Scriptures, for the Spirit is nowhere spoken of in such lowly terms as are ascribed to Christ though he is spoken of as sent by the Father and the Son. If we compare Heb. 3 : 9 with Exodus 17 : 7 and Acts 28 : 25 with 2 Sam. 23 : 2 and Isa. 6 : 9, we shall have no difficulty in finding that the name Jehovah is applied to him. Divine attributes are ascribed to him as in Matt. 12 : 28, John 16 : 13, Rom. 8 : 11, 1 Cor. 3 : 16, 1 Cor. 6 : 11, 1 Cor. 12 : 11, 2 Thess. 2 : 13; 1 Pet. 1 : 2, Rev. 1 : 4. Objections may be made to some of these passages as not being sufficiently pertinent to this subject, but there are further considerations that may be convincing, such as the place given to the Holy Ghost in the economy of redemption. All spiritual gifts are ascribed to him; Divine attributes are ascribed to him; blasphemy against him is declared to be

20. Westminster **Confession of Faith, II : III.**

unpardonable; believers are to be baptized in his name; the resurrection of the dead is attributed to him; and he is worshipped equally with the Father and the Son.

The Deity of the Holy Spirit is confirmed by the fact that, while all Divine operations are usually referred to God, some works are predominantly ascribed to one Person where the others have no concurrence but by approbation and consent. The works of nature are ascribed to God the Father; the work of redemption to God the Son; and the works of grace to God the Holy Spirit. He prepares Christ for his mediatorial work; he inspires Scripture; he forms and purifies the Church by regeneration and sanctification; and he teaches and guides the Church into all truth. Christ himself refers to him as his equal when he declares that he will take his place upon earth and when he calls him another Comforter.

CHAPTER V

THE DECREES OF GOD

I.   THE DECREES IN GENERAL
II. EFFICACIOUS AND PERMISSIVE DECREES
III. OF SPECIFIC DECREES
IV. THE ORDER OF DECREES
V.   OBJECTIONS TO THE DECREES
VI. REFLECTIONS ON THE DECREES

I. THE DECREES IN GENERAL

It has been said that no subject in theology has produced more discussion than the divine decrees. Not only the theologian but almost every philosopher, and even pre-Christian thinkers, have brought this subject under review. The decrees in general and especially the decrees of pre-destination and election are extremely objectionable to the sinful human mind, not only because of their condemnatory aspects but because they have been misrepresented and thrown out of focus by their advocates as well as by their objectors. The subject is said to be too mysterious (and some parts of it appear to some to be in conflict with what we know of the goodness of God), and therefore many believe discussion of it should be avoided, except perhaps in the theological arena. One great difficulty seems to be that the nexus between God's sovereignty and human responsibility cannot be perceived by the human mind. The doctrine itself is plainly taught in Scripture and we think it can be relieved of some of the misconceptions that have been attached to it. Mysterious as these decrees are every believer should know that God has a plan for the universe, and the decrees embody that plan before its execution. "The decrees of God are his eternal purpose, according to the counsel of his will, whereby, for his own glory, he hath foreordained whatsoever comes to pass."[21]

21. **Shorter Catechism, Q.7.**

Men do not object to the decrees generally but they shrink from a consideration of the eternal decree which bears upon the final doom of impenitent men.

The decrees or rather the decree of God is manifold and comprehends not only the general features of his plan but the perfection of all its details including all the means and circumstances which he uses to accomplish his purposes. These decrees are eternal and immutable and are all inter-related and positioned in their respective places within the orbit of God's all comprehensive purpose. The attention paid to particular decrees while ignoring others is calculated to produce a fractional and segmentary view of God's purpose for the universe.

II. EFFICACIOUS AND PERMISSIVE DECREES

Some decrees have been called efficacious and others permissive. The efficacious decree respects the good and the permissive decree the evil. Since God has foreordained whatsoever comes to pass we must allow that all decrees are efficacious in the sense that the result comes to pass. It is commonly held that some of the decrees are merely permissive, but the proper way of stating the matter is that God decrees to effect some events and decrees to permit other events. The difference between the effective and the permissive decree is said to be, that in the former case God decrees to work in the agent to will and to do, but in the permissive decree he does not so work in the agent. I am not sure, however, that we are capable of understanding all the elements in this explanation. Perhaps it is better to say that in the permissive decree God, who is the First Cause, works indirectly through second causes. It is much easier for us to understand the effective decree, than the other, partly, at least, because Scripture gives us more information regarding the former. The permission of sin is an awful mystery and we can only say that God permits moral evil because in some way it is adapted to his eternal purpose. The statements of Scripture such as Exod. 9 : 12-16 and Rom. 9 : 17-22 must not lead us into positions which would imply that God is the author of sin. The following elements in the permissive decree appear to conform to

Scripture. 1. The decree to sustain the sinful human agent in his voluntary operations. 2. The decree not to hinder these operations. 3. The decree to control these sinful operations within the manifold purpose of God.

III. OF SPECIFIC DECREES

1. Predestination

The decrees of God are his eternal purposes — but predestination is often used to point out the counsel of God respecting fallen man. This decree includes the election of some and the non-election of the rest. The word **election** used in this discussion is admittedly used in different senses in Scripture. Saul, David, the Levites, Israel were elected (1 Sam. 10 : 24; Psa. 78 : 70, 71; 1 Chron. 15 : 2; Deut. 7 : 6). The word is also used of Christ's choice of men to be apostles (Luke 6 : 13). This, however, includes their election to spiritual life. God's choice of the Jewish Church (Acts 13 : 17) and the choice made by God for special service (Acts 15 : 7). It is also used to mean that God has chosen some sinners to everlasting life. The following passages place the matter beyond doubt. "For many are called, but few chosen" (Matt. 22 : 14). "For whom he did foreknow, he also did predestinate to be conformed to the image of his Son (Rom. 8 : 29). "Even so then at this present time there is a remnant according to the election of Grace (Rom. 11 : 5). "According as he has chosen us in him before the foundation of the world" (Eph. 1 : 4).

2. Election

The doctrine of election means that God has chosen some rather than others. Why he has done so we have no means of knowing, although we should naturally suppose that these were better than others. What Scripture teaches is, that God's choice was not based on the goodness or relative goodness of the elect or upon a foreknowledge of their faith, but because it pleased him to do so (Rom. 9 : 11).

3. Reprobation

The doctrine of reprobation is unconceivably solemn. It would be so even if only one millionth of the race were involved, and they were all Judases. Calvin says "It is an awful decree, I confess, but no one can deny that God foreknew the future final fate of man before he created him, and that he did foreknow it because it was appointed by his own decree." This particular doctrine appears to be relieved of some of its awfulness by the distinction made between God's sovereign act and his judicial act in dealing with sinful humanity. There is first a negative act, that is the non-election or passing by of sinners called **preterition,** the leaving of men in the natural state of sin. There is further the positive act of God, proceeding from his justice, in ordaining men to wrath because of their sin. This is called the decree of **condemnation.** Preterition is a sovereign act of God proceeding from his will: condemnation is a judicial act, and proceeds from his justice. It will be seen from this view of the subject that God only condemns men on account of their sin. This is different from the horrible interpretation of some who do not hesitate to say that God created man to damn him. God created man to glorify Himself. And this is man's chief end.

IV. THE ORDER OF DECREES

The theological scheme of supra-lapsarianism is that God views man as creatible and the object of salvation or condemnation, the order being: 1. The decree to elect, 2. The decree to create, 3. The decree to permit to fall, 4. The decree to provide salvation for the elect. The sub-lapsarian scheme views man as created and fallen, in the following order. 1. The decree to create, 2. The decree to permit to fall, 3. The decree to elect, 4. The decree to provide salvation for the elect. Both of these theories contain the same truth; the difference lies in the scholastic order of the decrees. Dr Dabney says that both schemes are illogical and contradictory to the facts and should never have been formulated, since neither part precedes another in God's eternal decree; but he adds that sub-lapsarianism is more Scriptural and more honouring to God. Dr Twisse, though himself a supralapsarian says the order of decrees is a mere **logical nicety;** and he remarks that "God doth not ordain any man to damnation before the consideration of his sin, but that every one that is damned is damned for his sin and that wilfully committed and contumaciously continued in them that come to ripe years."

The view of Dr Camero (1620 A.D.), called hypothetic universalism, is as follows: 1. The decree to create, 2. To permit man to fall, 3. To provide salvation for all, 4. But foreseeing that if men were left to themselves none would believe he elected some to whom he decreed the grace of faith. According to Dr A. A. Hodge, this is an attempt to weld Calvinism and Arminianism.

The Arminian order of the decrees is: 1. The decree to create, 2. God foreseeing the fall decreed to provide salvation for all men, 3. He decreed absolutely to save believers and condemn unbelievers, 4. God foreseeing that some would believe and that some would not believe, elected the former to salvation. This order denies the absolute foreordination of certain persons, and instead asserts that God eternally predestinated some whom he foresaw would believe.

V. OBJECTIONS TO THE DECREES

The most common objections to the decrees are: that they are unjust; that they make God the author of sin; that they dispense with the use of means; that they interfere with man's free agency; and that they reduce the number of the saved. In dealing with these objections it is necessary that we distinguish between those who oppose the human proofs presented on the side of the decrees, and those who deny that the Word of God teaches this doctrine. For example the Arminians are agreed that God is just, etc., but they assert that he would not be if the Bible taught the doctrine that Calvinism upholds. There are others who hold that the Word of God teaches this doctrine but they do not agree with the interpretation placed upon by the Calvinists. We have also to contend with those who discount or modify Scripture statements dealing with this and other subjects on the assumption that the Bible is fallible. Such objectors maintain that the Apostle Paul disagrees with other Biblical writers. This leaves the whole range of theological doctrine on any subject whatsoever under the control, not of the Holy Spirit as the author of Scripture, but in the hands of any individual or company of individuals to construct any doctrine they please without any reference to a supreme standard of faith and morals.

Some of the objections raised against this doctrine are not seriously made but men are so perplexed about the problem that they suppose argument should provide a solution and they are of the opinion that if the doctrine is true it does not harmonise with what we already know of God's goodness and man's misery. It should be a lesson to us that the Apostle Paul when anticipating such objections to this same doctrine in the ninth chapter of Roman's refuses to reply to the objectors but refers everything to the sovereignty of God.

Predestination has been discussed as an intellectual problem in all its aspects by theologians and philosophers but our concern should be to treat it as a practical doctrine bearing upon the condition and destiny of ourselves and the church of God. The contrary position whether based upon fate, chance, or human effort, does not make man's salvation any easier. According to ordinary standards human effort is conditioned by man's environment and condition; and the total result is the moving of the problem from one position to another. The Gospel scheme which is accepted by all true Christians shows that the natural man possesses no spiritual life and that the production of that life is brought about in the first instance by the creator of our natural life. God's justice and goodness are so clearly displayed in giving his beloved Son over to the sufferings and death of the Cross that sinners might be saved, as to challenge any question of the perfection of his attributes; while on the human side the offer of salvation through Christ Jesus is so clearly proclaimed to the most abandoned sinners who repent and believe the Gospel that we are impressed with the strongest convictions that the divine decrees place no obstacle in the way of sinners.

Having written a few words as a mere preface to an important doctrine, I conclude it by three quotations which deal with some aspects of this subject. The Confession of Faith and Shorter Catechism.

"The decrees of God are his eternal purpose, according to the counsel of his will, whereby for his own glory he hath foreordained whatsoever comes to pass (S.C. No. 7). The doctrine of this high mystery of predestination is to be handled with special prudence and care, that men attending to the will of God revealed in his word and yielding obedience thereby may from the certainty of their effectual vocation, be assured of their eternal election. So shall this doctrine afford matter of praise, reverence and admiration of God and of humility, diligence and abundant consolation to all that sincerely obey the Gospel."[22]

VI. REFLECTIONS ON THE DECREES

Dr Dabney says that since, according to the Confession of Faith, the doctrine of this high mystery of predestination should be handled with prudence and care, in the preaching of it the proportion should be observed which obtains in the Bible and that no polemical zeal ought to tempt ministers to obtrude it more often. To press it prominently on inquirers or those already confused, or to urge it on one inclined to scepticism or one devoid of sufficient christian knowledge is unsuitable and imprudent, and when taught it should be in the mode which usually prevails in Scripture viz., a posteriori, as inferred from its result, effectual calling. When thus taught the doctrine gives ground to humility, inspires confident hope, and opens the fountains of love and gratitude.[23] Dr Shedd says the doctrine should not be preached out of season or out of logical order. It supposes, he says, some maturity in Christian experience. The teacher does not put to the beginner the 47th proposition in geometry. The doctrine of election is more encouraging to the preacher than the opposite theory. It is more probable that a sinner will repent if this depends upon the power of the Holy Spirit and not on his own. It is more probable that the world of sinful men will come to repentance if this event devolves wholly upon God. If the success of the Holy Ghost depends upon the assistance of the sinner He may not succeed. But if this success depends wholly upon Himself, He is certain to succeed.[24]

22. Westminster Confession of Faith, 3 : 8.
23. Dr Dabney, Systematic Theology, p. 246.
24. Dr Shedd, Dogmatic Theology, Vol. 1, pp. 460-461.

CHAPTER VI

THE WORKS OF GOD

I. CREATION

1. Theories of Creation

The theological works on this subject usually deal with the various theories of the origin of the world, such as the dualistic, the emanation, and the evolution theories.

(1) **The Dualistic Theory.** This theory maintains that both God and matter are eternal. Plato, while holding that matter was eternal, thought that God framed it into suitable forms to reflect his own perfect and infinite ideas.

(2) **The Emanation Theory.** Here the world is identified with God and creation is considered as an outflowing of the Divine Being.

(3) **The Evolution Theory.** Those who hold this view have defined creation as a series of gradual progressive changes in matter effected by means of resident forces inherent in matter itself. Evolution is either eternal or temporal. The advocates of the former say that matter is eternal, and they ascribe the origin of life to spontaneous generation. But what is subject to change cannot be eternal. Those who say that evolution is temporal must also find it difficult to prove that crude matter can originate life and personality.

Theistic evolution acknowledges the existence of God

and affirms that he works according to the laws of nature but that in some instances, as in the original creation, he originates life and afterwards allows the principles of force to complete the work of creation. This excludes God's immanence and his continual activity. These creationists who acknowledge God's immanence and activity in all his works but who hold to the doctrine of the gradual evolution of the world through untold ages to its present condition, and who represent the Scriptural account of the creation as partly literal and partly symbolical must be charged with inconsistency because they refuse to accept creation in its absolute sense. They do this on the assumption that absolute creation conflicts with the discoveries of science; neither creation, however, nor the formation of matter in the first instance necessarily required ages of time for its completion any more than Adam required time to be full grown since he was not born but made.

2. The Creative Act

The precise idea of creation is not to be ascertained merely by a consideration of the term used in the beginning of God's written revelation. The term **created** is used in the absolute sense to declare the bringing into existence of the matter out of which the heaven and the earth is composed. The first verse in Genesis informs us that God brought the universe into being. The subsequent verses refer to the steps taken to complete the work of creation. These successive parts of the work having been completed, we are told that "God saw everything that he had made, and, behold, it was very good. And the evening and the morning were the sixth day. Thus the heavens and the earth were finished, and all the host of them" (Gen. 1 : 31 - 2 : 1). Some philosophers, while accepting an absolute creation first, say that this is against reason but not contrary to faith. It is proper to say, however, that creation is not **against** reason but **above** reason and is to be accepted by faith in the power of God, and this is just what the author of the Epistle to the Hebrews asserts (Heb. 11 : 3).

3. The Date of the Creation

It is useless to attempt to state the age of creation. Some

place it at 4,000 years before Christ. Certain scientists in order to mystify the common people mention a loose figure of millions of years. They reason this out by an investigation of natural phenomena which sets the clock of time back into the remotest ages. Creation, however, with its subsequent omnipotent feats must be placed in the category not of the natural but of the supernatural. According to the common chronology which modern researches have not yet been able to disprove the age of man is about 6,000 or 8,000 years. In order to harmonise the text with geological discoveries and other data the first and second chapters of Genesis have been subjected to unfair criticism. According to one account the description of the chaos mentioned in Gen. 1 : 2, proceeded from the fallen angels who laid God's beautiful creation waste. This theory must be regarded as speculation since it is not warranted by the text, seeing that verse 31 has been placed where it is and not between verses 1 and 2. "And God saw everything that he had made, and, behold, it was very good, And the evening and the morning were the sixth day" (Gen. 1 : 31).

It has also been stated that the chaos referred to might have continued for a vast period of time before the Creator commenced the six days work. It would be far safer for theologians not to commit themselves to the date of creation, but to content themselves with pointing out that we have here a plain historical narrative of God's creation of the universe and the earth, with the successive steps taken to bring about its completion at the end of six days.

"If man evolved over billions of years, why is it that complex language sprang into being so suddenly about only 5,000 to 6,000 years ago? Why is it that even in the writings of evolutionists one finds the admission that the earliest written language goes back to about 3,500 B.C.? The **World Book Encyclopædia** says: 'The earliest records we have of human history go back only about 5,000 years' . . . There is no evidence of man's existence before then." **(Good Health,** Nov. 1968, from Mrs D. Bowers, Selsdon, Surrey).

4. The Six Days

Another view which seems to harmonize with the discoveries

of science and geological speculation is that the six days mentioned in the first chapter of Genesis denote great periods of time. The word **day**, however, occurs in a chapter dealing with a series of historical events which are to be understood in their primary and historical sense. This use of the word is confirmed by the phrases, "evening and morning", and the declaration that God rested on the seventh day. The command given in Exodus to rest on the seventh day because God made heaven and earth in six days and rested on the seventh must also confirm us in the view that the days of creation were literal days.

We should remember that the discoveries of science are no part of theology and cannot add to its value nor subtract from its truth though they may serve to convince sceptics and confirm believers in the consistency of God's Word. We may also bear in mind that in this period of the history of the race science has advanced several theories which have not yet been satisfactorily demonstrated.

In dealing with the question as to whether the days of creation are to be regarded as literal twenty-four hour days, or long periods of time, Rev. J. Vos states:

"The conclusion reached was that the literal view is preferable though neither view is without some difficulties. We now wish to call attention to a remarkable article on this subject which was published in the January 1954 issue of HIS, a magazine of the Inter-Varsity Christian Fellowship. The article, which appears on page 6 of the January issue is entitled CREATION AND DELUGE, by Dr Henry M. Morris, a professional civil engineer and scientist. Following a very striking presentation of the evidence Dr Morris argues strongly in favour of the literal interpretation of the creation days. He holds that the literal interpretation is the only one which really fits the Biblical data, adding that all theories which attempt to harmonise the Genesis account with the doctrines of evolutionary geology require so much juggling of the plain sense of the account as in effect to amount to its rejection." (Blue Banner, April 1954; see also article favouring the literal days of creation by Rev. Vos in the same issue).

5. The Creation of Angels

The word **angel** in Scripture is used in different senses and is applied to various persons and agencies, but it is chiefly applied to spiritual and supernatural intelligences. Angels possess invisible and spiritual natures, and even when they appeared to men under human aspects, we must understand that these forms were assumed temporarily in order to establish communication with human beings. The supposition that angels were created before the world was brought into being can hardly be maintained from the poetic reference to them in Job 28 : 7. We are told in Scripture that they are a numberless host, possessing superhuman wisdom and power; and we may reflect that some of the greatest problems which have baffled the wisest intellects may present no difficulty to the good angels.

It is noteworthy that angels have appeared to men at critical periods in the history of the Church and especially in connection with the history of our Lord. Scripture represents them as serving God in various capacities and ministering for those who shall be heirs of salvation. As to the details of this ministry, we have to confess the limitations of our knowledge, which requires that we be cautious in accepting some of the eccentric views of the past on this subject. It has been said that on occasions the angels prompt God's people to good deeds, that there is a guardian angel for each believer, and that every saint is transported to paradise by angels. But some of these views are not sufficiently clear to warrant our drawing positive conclusions, and caution is required lest we appear to encroach on the work of Christ and the Holy Spirit. However, one is reminded that there is a ministry of angels to the heirs of salvation: and so we should not neglect this teaching of Scripture.

A subordination of rank among the angels seems to be indicated by the different designations given to some of them, but we may conceive that these refer to office and not to rank. Some of the titles mentioned, such as "Archangel", may be attributed to Christ himself. The words "Michael" and "Gabriel" are supposed by many to designate high dignitaries among the angels. Others believe that these titles refer to the Son of God. Though the latter view has been frowned upon by some theologians, others have supported it by reasons possessing some weight. The opinions of theologians on this subject must be considered as their theologisms unless they produce a full and satisfactory proof from the sacred text. An examination of the Old Testament canon will evince that in a number of references where the word **angel** is used it cannot apply to angels in the ordinary sense but to the Angel of the Covenant, Christ himself. The references to cherubim and seraphim in Scripture seem to convey the idea that these were different from other angels although most of the reformers held that these also were angels. Principal Fairbairn, the eminent typologist, and others, were of the opinion that the cherubim are ideal representations of redeemed and glorified saints. Others since their day maintained that this position was untenable, but Fairbairn's theory, based upon the examination of various passages of Scripture, has much to recommend it.

6. The Evil Angels

Whatever mystery attaches to the fall of some of the angels, we have reason to think that a number of them revolted simultaneously against God and so fell from the estate wherein they were created. That they are numerous we have no reason to doubt, and whatever degrees of subordination may exist among them we are assured that they are led by an evil archangel called Satan.

These fallen angels, though doomed to perdition, are still allowed to oppose the designs of God and seduce his creatures so that there is a continual conflict between them and the children of God. They are permitted to attack and deceive men, and some think they possess the power to afflict them in body and soul; but whatever the extent of their power we know that they are kept under control by God. We believe that their usual method of attack is by deception and persuasion. We are to remember, however, for our comfort that the devil is a creature and that he is neither omnipotent nor omniscient, and though he sometimes appears to possess the secrets of our hearts, this is not so since God only possesses the power to search the heart of man. "For thou only knowest the hearts of the children of men" (2 Chron. 6 : 30).

II. PROVIDENCE

We read in Scripture that when the work of creation was completed it was pronounced very good, and that God rested on the seventh day from all the work which he had made. We are not to think, however, that God left the world and its inhabitants to themselves. The doctrine of providence teaches us that he preserves and governs all his creatures and all their actions.

For the sake of convenience a distinction has been made between providence and grace; but strictly speaking there is none, for God's work of providence includes the preservation and governing of all his creatures and all their actions, whether these operations relate to the works of nature, the events of history, or to the well-being of his Church. A convenient distinction is to make common providence refer to man's temporal welfare and special providence to his spiritual welfare.

According to the **deistic** interpretation of providence, the Creator, having completed the work of creation and having imparted various powers to the world and its inhabitants, left them to continue their existence in accordance with the funcions allotted to them. This theory appears to derive its strength from the views entertained as to the inherent forces of nature and the powers bestowed upon human beings. These forces and powers are observed to function in certain fixed ways, called by some the uniformity of nature. According to this scheme, the world is a machine which God has made and put into motion, leaving it to proceed under its own power.

The **Theistic** interpretation of providence agrees with the deistic in acknowledging that God has imparted to the world of nature and man inherent properties after their kind, which are made subject to general laws but maintains, in opposition to the deists, that the Creator continues to preserve and control all that he has created and made in accordance with the laws of nature and the particular needs of their existence.

Various theories have been propounded as to the mode of God's operation in preserving and governing mind and matter, but we are as profoundly ignorant of God's **modus operandi** in providence as we are of the operations of the New Birth. "The wind bloweth where it listeth, and thou hearest the sound thereof, but canst not tell whence it cometh, and whither it goeth: so is every one that is born of the Spirit" (John 3 : 8).

In the material world God immediately works in and through material properties and laws. In the mental world God immediately works in and through the properties and faculties of mind . . . The best illustration of the mode in which God operates in providence is found in the action of the human soul upon the body . . . The soul as an ego and a whole exists in every part of the body, and operates immediately at every point of the body: yet as in an entity other than the body, and controlling it . . . "In him we live and move and have our being". (Dr Shedd, **in loc**).

We hear much about the laws of nature and the inherent forces in the physical world and the various ways in which bodies act and re-act to one another, but if we examine the subject more closely, we are constrained to admit that however familiar we are with the terminology used we are at a loss to know what these laws and forces are. Some theologians maintain that matter is passive and that its disposition into certain forms and relations still leaves matter inert and devoid of power until God exercises his power immediately to produce effects. Others contradict this view, and say that to deny all properties of action to material things seems too difficult for ordinary minds; but it has been suggested that God controls the powers he bestows upon matter so that they will act under certain conditions.

The operations of God in the preservation and governing of rational beings is the most important part of this subject and perhaps the most difficult; and in a discussion of the providence of God in relation to the evil actions of men, various expedients have been suggested to harmonise intelligently the absolute sovereignty of the Creator and the responsibility of the creature in accordance with the great truth that God is not the author of sin. It has been pointed out that the various phrases used in Scripture, such as the

hardening of the heart, the blinding of the eyes, the deliver-
ing of men to their own lusts, cannot mean that God
influences the mind, forces wickedness into it, or confirms
its proud and rebellious disposition; but rather, that God
withholds his grace, leaves men under the power of their
own evil minds, and does not prevent them from being
exposed to temptation. It is evident, however, that this
subject surpasses our finite intelligence, and that we cannot
define with any accuracy the boundary between the actions
of God and the actions of rational creatures. It becomes
us to believe, however, that the Creator preserves and
governs all his creatures and all their actions, and that all
their sins proceed immediately from themselves.

What has been said of the providence of God in nature
and in the history of man applies with equal force to the
operation of grace in the human soul. We are commanded
to "Work out our own salvation with fear and trembling.
For it is God that worketh in us both to will and to do
of his good pleasure" (Phil. 2 : 12-13). In regeneration God
implants a holy principle from which all gracious affections
and exercises proceed. This is the new creation which
brings with it inherent powers and gracious activities.
Nevertheless, these are unable to function of themselves,
for it is God that worketh in us analogous to his modes of
operation in nature (this analogy, however, fails if we are
to conclude that matter possesses no inherent energy, but
it would hold in the case of the natural man in respect of
his utter lack of spiritual power) so that believers depend
upon the preserving and governing of the Holy Ghost
within them. Notwithstanding, while seeking the support
and guidance of his grace, they must actively co-operate as
free agents in the spirit of faith and under a profound
sense of personal responsibility. We are, therefore, taught
here that in addition to the new creation there is needed the
continual influence of the Holy Spirit for our preservation
and growth in grace.

III. MIRACLES

The word **miracle** is generally used to denote an extraordinary event, the causes of which are unknown or are

apparently contrary to the ordinary laws of nature. Strictly speaking, the difference between a miracle and an ordinary event consists in the manner in which omnipotence is exercised. "A miracle differs from an ordinary event not because it requires a greater exertion of Divine power but a different exercise of it" (Dr Shedd). In an ordinary event the hand of God is concealed, but in a miracle it is openly displayed. The gradual destruction of nations because of their wickedness follows the ordinary mode of God's moral administration, but the destruction of the antediluvians by flood and the destruction of the Sodomites by fire were miracles of Divine judgment in which God's power and wrath were openly shown. The miracles of Moses in Egypt were imitated by the magicians, but the plague of lice assumed such a terrifying aspect that the magicians were constrained to acknowledge an extraordinary manifestation of Divine power. The miracle of Elijah at Carmel performed in the presence of all Israel was an extraordinary event and an evident manifestation of God's power: "Then the fire of the LORD fell, and consumed the burnt sacrifice, and the wood, and the stones, and the dust, and licked up the water that was in the trench. And when all the people saw it, they fell on their faces: and they said, The LORD, he is the God; the LORD, he is the God" (1 Kings 18 : 38, 39).

We are not to think, however, that miracles are common, for God usually adheres to the ordinary course of nature and wishes us to have confidence in its uniformity and to regulate ourselves thereby. We may conclude that miracles are performed by God only when the ordinary means are inadequate, or to demonstrate his omnipotence by showing us that he can work with, without, and against means if he so pleases. It is clear that God purposed to give the Babylonians a demonstration of the exceeding greatness of his power and to show them the vanity of their false gods when he delivered the three young men, who chose to die rather than disobey their Lord. The manner of their deliverance exceeded the ordinary power of means to accomplish it so omnipotence was called into exercise to deliver them from the effects of the fiery furnace.

Hume argued that miracles are established by human

testimony, which is sometimes unreliable. And a miracle, says he, is a violation of the laws of nature; experience, however, teaches us that the laws of nature are uniform; and the testimony of some witnesses does not induce a rational belief in miracles. The substance of this argument is that miracles cannot be proved as they contradict experience; but it has been replied that the evidence of testimony is as reliable as the evidence of sense or experience, and this in itself would overturn the argument against miracles. We ourselves were not witnesses of the miracles performed by Christ or his messengers, but we are assured of their reality through the testimony of a number of witnesses who produced adequate evidence that such miracles took place.

It is maintained that a miracle is a violation or suspension of the laws of nature; but the correctness of this view is open to question, since in the case of miracles these laws still continue to operate without deviation. In the case of the miracle performed by Elisha when he recovered the axehead, no law of nature was interfered with. The law of gravity still continued to operate and tended to draw the iron to the bottom. This law still continued to operate not only in all other places, but in this particular location, only here a stronger force overcame the laws of gravity, and the axehead rose to the surface as though it were a piece of wood.

The significance of miracles in the history of the Church of God is that there were signs and evidences of the Being and power of God and that he gave some of his servants power to perform miracles to establish their commission and vindicate their claims. This is exemplified in the miracles of Moses, Joshua, Samuel, and other prophets and judges. The claims of Christ and his Apostles to be messengers of God, commissioned and authorised by him, were received upon the basis of the miracles performed by them and the prophesies fulfilled in them, or uttered by them and afterwards fulfilled. "If I do not the works of my Father, believe me not. But if I do, though ye believe not me, believe the works: that ye may know, and believe, that the Father is in me, and I in him" (John 10 : 37, 38).

CHAPTER VII

THE WORD OF GOD

I. NATURAL AND REVEALED RELIGION

II. THE NECESSITY OF SCRIPTURE

III. THE GENUINENESS OF SCRIPTURE
1. The Old Testament
2. The New Testament

IV. THE AUTHENTICITY OF SCRIPTURE
1. The Old Testament
2. The New Testament

V. THE INSPIRATION OF SCRIPTURE

VI. THE CANON OF SCRIPTURE

The topics relating to this subject are included under the heading of Bibliology, which deals with the genuineness, authenticity, inspiration, and canonicity of the Scriptures. Its importance is admitted by all Christians who acknowledge that "The Scriptures principally teach what man is to believe concerning God and what duty God requires of man."[25] Some of the questions asked by enquirers who profess to seek information on this theme are: How are we to know that God has given a written revelation of his will? If he has, is the Bible such? Granting that the Word of God is the only and complete written revelation given to us by him, how are we to be assured that it is infallible and inerrant?

I. NATURAL AND REVEALED RELIGION

Theology has been divided into natural and revealed religion. Natural religion consists of the knowledge of God which is obtainable by the powers of reason unassisted by

25. **Shorter Catechism.**

any special revelation from God. The materials of this knowledge are obtainable by a consideration of the works of creation and providence. The works of creation include the whole of what men call reality, together with man himself; and the works of providence include not only the changes occurring in nature which we ourselves observe, but also those changes observed by others which we learn of through their testimony.

A distinction has been made by theologians between a general and a special revelation, the former being the revelation given of God in nature, and the latter, the revelation given in his own Word. It should be noted here that special revelations were made to men when no written revelation was available, such as those made to Noah and Abraham. Some theologians distinguish between a general and a special revelation by saying that in the former God meets with the natural needs of mankind and in the latter he meets with their spiritual needs. Rationalists and deists, who have asserted that a supernatural revelation is unnecessary, were themselves indebted to its writings and influence. Deists maintain that a supernatural revelation is not necessary since natural religion gives sufficient knowledge for all practical purposes. Some of these would concede that a supernatural or written revelation merely enforces or confirms what man already knows concerning God.

II. THE NECESSITY OF SCRIPTURE

Scripture itself declares that man in his original state possessed an adequate knowledge of God, but after the fall when man lost communion with his Creator, it became necessary, if he were to be restored, that a supernatural revelation be given to him. In this new revelation much more was required than a knowledge of his duties to God, since the restoration of the Church necessitated a revelation and provision of mercy as well as a revelation of law. This makes the fundamental difference between the Christian religion and all others. The Gospel of Christ contemplates man as lost and undone and so reveals the mercy of God through a Mediator, providing a suitable remedy through the Atonement of Christ and the sanctifying influence of the Holy Ghost, producing what the best teachings of Plato, Seneca, Buddha, and Confucius have failed to effect by their ethical systems and golden rules: a radical and renovating change in the heart and life of all who cordially accept Jesus Christ as their Lord and Saviour. "For I am not ashamed of the Gospel of Christ: for it is the power of God unto salvation to every one that believeth; to the Jew first, and also to the Greek" (Rom. 1 : 16).

III. THE GENUINENESS OF SCRIPTURE

When it is said that a book is genuine, the meaning is that it has been proved to be written by the person whose name it bears. When it is said that a book is authentic, the meaning is that its contents are true. A book may be genuine which is fictitious; on the other hand, the contents of a book may be true though attributed to another than its real author. The Word of God is both genuine and authentic.

1. The Old Testament

The genuineness of the Old Testament has been proved by a variety of evidence sufficient to convince any reasonable inquirer. The authorship of the various books has been attested by Jewish and Christian writers of all ages and by heathen authors who had no interest in proving their genuineness. The five books of Moses, called the Pentateuch, have been attributed to Moses by the unanimous testimony of the Jewish and Christian Church. Those who have attempted to discredit this testimony have spent their strength largely on incidental matters, such as names, numbers, and minor circumstances, but they have hardly ever ventured to cope with the fundamental facts of the literary criticism involved. Some of the difficulties they have referred to are easily disposed of; others will be cleared up through the researches of archæology and cognate studies. The Pentateuch, which is the basis of Old Testament history, has been attested as the writing of Moses by Christ himself; and those who refuse to hear his testimony are not likely to be convinced by the most compelling evidence.

The various authors of the remaining Old Testament books are in some cases directly named; in others, they are more or less clearly determined by scholarly examination and judgment. According to tradition the book of Joshua is his own work. It comprises a period of about thirty years from the death of Moses to that of Joshua. While there is no certain evidence that Joshua was the author of this independent work, the materials provided by a contemporary and an eyewitness are probably those of Joshua with additions made by a later writer. The authorship of Judges is not certainly known though some have concluded that it is the work of Samuel; and to this may be added the book of Ruth. The two books of Samuel are also claimed to be the work of Samuel himself except the latter part, which was added by the prophets, Gad and Nathan. And if the books of Samuel were not compiled by Samuel, Gad, and Nathan, we must conclude that they were subsequently composed from historical annals by Jeremiah or Ezra, or possibly by previous scribes. The books of Kings form only one book and according to Jewish tradition is the composition of Jeremiah, while the books of Chronicles are ascribed to Ezra or to some other writer whose interests were more priestly than prophetic. Part of the book of Ezra is certainly his own work; the same may be said of the book of Nehemiah. Esther is said to be the work of Mordecai; on the other hand, it may have been extracted from the records of Persia. The book of Job is supposed to belong to the age of Genesis and composed by Job or Moses. The Psalms contain the poetical compositions of King David, but some were written before or after his time. The books of Proverbs, Ecclesiastes, and the Song of Solomon have been admitted by common consent to be the works of King Solomon. Since, however, we cannot be certain of some of these particulars, we may expect that alternative authors may be cited by some critics. As to the works of the prophets, there is no uncertainty, since their names are prefixed to their writings and attested by satisfactory proofs. Had any real doubt existed as to the genuineness of most of these books, it is extremely probable that convincing evidence would have been produced before now to challenge their genuineness and to point out their true writers.

2. The New Testament

The four Gospels have been attested as genuine by the unanimous voice of the Christian Church. The Acts of the Apostles is ascribed to Luke, the writer of the third Gospel. The Epistles have been divided into two classes, the Pauline Epistles and the Catholic Epistles. Eusebius, who lived in the Fourth Century, divided the books of the New Testament into three classes: those **received** by the Church, those **doubted,** and those considered **spurious.** He distinguished the spurious productions from the true by their style, which was different from that of the Apostles, and by their sentiments, which were heretical. He also maintained that the spurious writings were not quoted by ecclesiastical writers. Clement, a fellow-labourer of Paul; Barnabas, a companion of Paul; and Ignatius and Polycarp all quote from the Gospels. The various catalogues drawn up during the first few centuries evidence that the writings were genuine, and even the testimonies of Cerinthus, a heretic, Celsus and Porphyry, enemies of Christianity, and Julian the Apostate are in favour of the genuineness of the New Testament books. A further confirmation of their genuineness is the caution which was exercised in acknowledging them as belonging to the canon. Several of the books, though acknowledged by the majority of Christians, were under suspicion for some time until, upon the fullest investigation, they were finally acknowledged.

IV. THE AUTHENTICITY OF SCRIPTURE

1. The Old Testament

The authenticity of truth of the Old Testament may be established without the aid of the New Testament. Many of the principal facts of its history are supported by heathen writers, while the historical allusions and geographical references have been verified by subsequent researches. A considerable number of the prophesies of the Old Testament have already been fulfilled, while all the information given to us is in accordance with well-known facts. The books themselves have produced an untold influence upon the hearts and destinies of mankind, a sufficient proof of their supernatural elements. And whatever objections have been made as to the integrity of the sacred text, the most eminent scholars are assured that the Old Testament is substantially the same as it existed in the days of our Saviour, and that its readings are supported by the most valuable versions. Christ and his Apostles refer to their writings as being authentic and quote from almost all of them. "If they hear not Moses and the prophets, neither will they be persuaded, though one rose from the dead" (Luke 16 : 31). "And beginning at Moses and all the prophets, he expounded unto them in all the scriptures the things concerning himself" (Luke 24 : 27). "Search the scriptures; for in them ye think ye have eternal life: and they are they that testify of me" (John 5 : 39).

2. The New Testament

The authenticity of the New Testament is proved by the impeccable character of its Founder, the purity of its ethics, the miracles performed by him and his Apostles, the prophecies fulfilled in them or referred to by them, and the testimonies given of the facts described in the New Testament by the enemies as well as by the friends of Christianity.

V. THE INSPIRATION OF SCRIPTURE

Revelation, inspiration, and illumination, have been distinguished from one another. Revelation is an objective communication from God, such as the Scriptures of the Old and New Testaments. Inspiration is the Divine influence exerted upon the writers of Scripture guiding their faculties to communicate truth, whether that truth was new or previously known. Illumination consists in the influence of the Holy Ghost, which communicates no new revelation but leads true believers to a discernment of the truth and efficacy of God's Word.

All the views set forth, under whatever names, may be reduced to three. 1. Those who advocate a partial inspiration of the Bible are those who believe that some parts are God's Word, and so inspired, and that other parts are man's word, and so not inspired. Whatever arguments are advanced to support this theory, those who maintain it deny that the Word of God is infallible and inerrant. We disagree with the above manner of statement though we admit that in one sense Scripture is the Word of God and in another sense the word of man, since God employed human authors to give written communications of his will. 2. Others acknowledge the infallibility of the whole Word of God but deny the writers were inspired to communicaate the words of Scripture as well as the matter. In order to maintain this theory it is asserted that the writers were left to select their own words. This distinction, however, has no foundation in Scripture and is calculated to produce a disposition at variance with the reverence due to the Word of God.

3. The theory that we maintain is that there are no degrees of inspiration and that the words as well as the matter are inspired. Whether these matters were a new doctrine, a known doctrine, a fact of history or chronology, an event, or the statements of good or evil men; the writers were guided infallibly, not only in the selection of matter, but also in the choice of words. It should be noted that the advocates of verbal plenary inspiration have nothing to say about the Spirit's agency upon the writers. They simply affirm that all Scripture, the whole of Scripture, is inspired, the words as well as the matter. The classic deliverance in proof of the verbal plenary inspiration is 2 Timothy 3 : 16. The text according to its literal and obvious meaning refers not to the writers but to the Word itself and plainly states that every Scripture is God-breathed, that is, inspired by God, and this is opposed to any other theory of inspiration. According to Turrettin "The sacred writers were so moved and inspired by the Holy Ghost both in respect of thought and language that they were kept from all error and their writings are truly authentic and divine."

VI. THE CANON OF SCRIPTURE

The canon of Scripture, or the supreme rule of faith and life admitted by Protestants, consists exclusively of the Scriptures of the Old and New Testaments. The evidence for the canon of Scripture is closely identified with the evidence of its genuineness and authenticity. The proof that all the books contained in the Bible are truly the Word of God is based mainly on the testimony of history.

The formation of the Old Testament canon was a gradual process extending over several centuries from the days of Moses until the period of Malachi. Moses ordered the Pentateuch, of the first five books of the Bible, to be placed in the side of the Ark (Deut. 31 : 26); it was probably this book of the Law which was discovered in the temple in the reign of Josiah. The collection and formation of the Old Testament books, according to the voice of antiquity, was the work of Ezra, who about 457 B.C. collected and arranged the sacred books. Some critics believe his successors continued this work until it was completed about 300 B.C.

The Old Testament canon was attested by Christ and his Apostles as being the Word of God: Mark 14 : 49; Luke 24 : 44; John 5 : 39; 2 Tim. 3 : 15, 16. However, we must not think that the canon of Scripture was settled by the authority of the Church nor need we possess information as to when, or by whom, these books were collected or acknowledged by the testimony of the Church to be the inspired Word of God. All we have to prove is that these books were the production of inspired men who were commissioned to reveal his will to the Church of God

The historical evidence for the Old Testament is complete and conclusive. The Septuagint, or Greek version, contains all the books of the Old Testament, and Josephus, the historian, refers to the same catalogue of books. The exclusion by Protestants of the books commonly called the Apocrypha is based upon the fact that the canonicity of these books was denied by the Jews to whom were committed the oracles of God; that they were written in Greek and not in the Hebrew of the Old Testament; that the writing were posterior to Malachi, after which it is generally conceded that the spirit of prophecy ceased until the advent; that no part of them is quoted by Christ or his Apostles; and that they contain erroneous and immoral statements contrary to the inspired statements of the Old Testament.

The evidence for the New Testament canon requires an examination of all the books contained in it, the testimony of contemporaries of the inspired men who wrote it, and ancient manuscripts of these books. Most of the books in the New Testament were acknowledged by the early Christian writers, and we have the fullest evidence extending back to the Apostolic Age and their successors. All these books were written by Apostles except those by Mark and Luke. These two men, however, were associated with the Apostles, and it is presumed that Mark wrote his Gospel under the direction of Peter, and Luke under the direction of Paul. Several of the New Testament books though admitted as canonical by some were doubted by others, the point of dispute, however, being whether or not they were written by the men to whom they were generally ascribed. These books — The Epistle to the Hebrews, The Epistle of James, The Second Epistle of Peter, The Second and Third Epistles of John, and The Revelation — were ultimately acknowledged as belonging to the canon about the Fourth Century.

It is well known that the Jews copied and preserved their manuscripts with the greatest care, and all those available from the tenth to the fourteenth centuries showed that the various readings hardly ever interfered with the meaning of the text. The Samaritan Pentateuch, or the five books of Moses which were inherited by the Samaritans from the ten tribes, and the early translations of the Scriptures in other languages, such as the Greek Septuagint (285 B.C.), the Peshito or Syriac version (100 A.D.), and the Latin Vulgate (385 A.D.), all confirm the correctness of the Old Testament Scriptures.

The correctness of the New Testament text is also confirmed by the Vatin and Sinaitic manuscripts of the fourth century. The Vatican contains all the New Testament books except the Epistles to Philemon, to Titus, to Timothy, to the Hebrews, and The Revelation. The Sinaitic contains the Gospels, all the Epistles, and The Revelation.

Most of the positions maintained on this subject must be investigated and corroborated by extended proofs. The discussion of these investigations and the proofs are to be found mainly under the heading of exegetical theology.

II. MAN

CHAPTER VIII

THE DOCTRINE OF MAN

The first section in theology is concerned with the doctrine of God. The second is called anthropology or the doctrine of man in relation to God. Theological anthropology is wholly derived from Scripture, the perusal of which provides a true account of man's primal and lapsed state. The discussion of this subject is confined to man's pre-lapsarian and post-lapsarian state and does not include an account of man's recovery by grace, since the latter subject is dealt with under the heading of soteriology, or the doctrine of salvation.

MAN IN HIS ORIGINAL STATE

I. THE NATURE OF MAN

1. Dichotomy

Dichotomy is the view that man consists of two parts or complete entities; namely, a material body and an immaterial soul. Various attempts have been made by philosophers to define the elements in man's nature, such as the personality, the ego, the soul, and the spirit. The teaching of Scripture is that the first man consisted of two different substances and two only. "And the LORD God formed man of the dust of the ground, and breathed into his nostrils the breath of life; and man became a living soul" (Gen. 2 : 7). "Then shall the dust return to the earth as it was: and the spirit shall return unto God who gave it" (Ecc. 12 : 7). "And fear not them which shall kill the body, but are not able to kill the soul: but rather fear him which is able to destroy both soul and body in hell" (Matt. 10 : 28).

The idea that **soul** and **spirit** do not denote two entities is in thorough agreement with the testimony of self-consciousness. Man is conscious of a difference between body and soul but not between soul and spirit. Some say that the spirit signifies the principle of life and action, and the soul the principle of thought and affection. Others say that the spirit emphasises man's rationality, and the soul the animating principle. The whole difficulty about these theories is that the proofs offered are not convincing and that, indeed, the subject transcends our intelligence. In some cases the words **soul** and **spirit** are used interchangeably; in others, the context seems to indicate a preference. Even if distinctions are made, it would be unwise to hold a theory that makes the soul and the spirit two different substances. According to Dr Hodge, the word **pneuma** (spirit) designates the one soul emphasising its quality as rational. The word **psyche** (soul) designates the same soul emphasising its quality as the vital and animating principle of the body.

2. Trichotomy

This view is that man is composed of three elements: body, soul, and spirit. This account of man's nature is a revival of the old Platonic idea that man consists of a rational spirit, an animal soul, and a material body. The theory was revived in the Church in an attempt to give additional information about man's constitutional nature. The theory that man is a trinal being is very captivating on several accounts, and there is a good deal to be said for this view. An animal, for example, possesses a soul and a body. The difference between an animal and a man is that man is a rational being. Therefore, the soul is the principle of animal life, the spirit of rational life, and the body of material life. The theory, however, has not been stated in these plain terms, but the idea emerges that the spirit emphasises the

God-consciousness of man and the soul his self-consciousness. Others say that the soul comprises the life of man in its animal, intellectual, and moral framework. The soul, therefore, is the seat of personality and possesses all the principles necessary to a definition of human nature. The spirit, however, is the faculty of God-consciousness, which in the fall became dead or dormant. In regeneration this principle is quickened so that man can hold communion with God.

One objection to this reasoning is that the highest spiritual exercises are predictated of the soul as well as the spirit (Matt. 26 : 38; Mark 8 : 12; John 13 : 21). The trichotomists lay great stress on such texts as 1 Thess. 5 : 23 and Heb. 4 : 12. "And I pray God your whole spirit and soul and body be preserved blameless unto the coming of our Lord Jesus Christ" (1 Thess. 5 : 23). If we are to make a sharp distinction between soul and spirit on the basis of this text, we could well maintain a similar distinction between heart, soul, and mind in the statement where Christ tells men to love God with all their heart, and all their soul, and all their mind (Matt. 22 : 37). But the heart, soul, and mind are not several different principles or entities; rather the meaning is that we are to love God with all the spiritual force of our being. "For the word of God is quick, and powerful, and sharper than any twoedged sword, piercing even to the dividing asunder of soul and spirit, and of the joints and marrow, and is a discerner of the thoughts and intents of the heart" (Heb. 4 : 12). The plain meaning of this passage is that all the inner recesses of our being are exposed to view. Emphasis has been laid by the trichotomists on the words, "dividing asunder of soul and spirit, and of the joints and marrow." The statement is supposed to indicate the separation between soul and spirit, and joints and marrow. There is, however, another aspect of thought here, which is in agreement with cognate expressions in Scripture, suggesting the idea of **penetration** and not **separation.**

Although the advocates of this view have provided some interesting and important information on this subject, they have failed to make a good case for trichotomy on the basis of Scripture. For example, there is no evidence to prove that the result of man's fall was merely the loss, depravity, or dormancy of the spirit. Man's fall affected every part of his nature, and he is not only depraved in all the faculties and members, but he is totally depraved in all these. The trichotomists' explanation of the operations of grace in regeneration is equally faulty, since the true effect is a renovation not only of the spirit but of the whole man.

II. THE ORIGIN OF THE SOUL

The three main theories which profess to give an account of the origin of the soul are pre-existence, traducianism, and creationism.

1. Pre-existence

According to this scheme the souls of men existed in a previous state. This was Plato's idea, and it has been worked out by Origen, a theologian of the third century, who believed that men sinned in a previous existence. All these souls were later united to the body. This view professed to give some explanation for man's fallen state, since this had been brought about by sins committed in a previous existence. This theory was never favoured by the generality of Christian theologians, and it is now obsolete.

2. Traducianism

The position of this school is that the souls of men are propagated along with their bodies and are derived from the parents by ordinary generation. This theory prevailed in the early Church and is still favoured by the Lutherans. It was also held by eminent theologians of the past. Reformed theologians such as Dr Shedd and Dr Strong have made a strong case for this view.

It is admitted by traducians and creationists that God is the Creator of the soul as well as the body and that the substance of the body is traduced or brought forth by the parents. The traducian, however, maintains that the substance of the soul and the body was created by God in the beginning and transmitted through the parents by ordinary generation. This is just saying that the whole human nature, consisting of soul and body, was incorporated in our first parents and afterwards individualised into a series of persons.

The arguments in favour of traducianism are various, such as Scriptural representations to the effect that God created man in the beginning and left him to propagate the species (Gen. 1 : 28; 2 : 7; 5 : 3). For example, Adam begat a son in his own likeness; though this phrase would seem to refer primarily to the soul. It has also been said that God does not now create, but this is a moot question. The scheme derives its strength from the evidence of moral depravity, and the mental and physical peculiarities of Adam's descendants; and consequently it appears to give a more understandable explanation of the transmission of sin from the parents to the children. The fundamental objection is, that in relation to the human nature of Christ it seems to imply that he partook of our fallen nature and was therefore sinful. This objection has been parried by the reply that the human nature of Christ was sanctified by the Holy Ghost and therefore rendered impeccable.

Creationists object to traducianism because it would seem to involve a materialistic division of the soul and because it teaches that God only works mediately. This does not allow for immediate creation, such as the creation of the soul from nothing, and the new creation, when man is immediately regenerated by God's Spirit. And these objections and others have been rebutted by the opposite parties, and we must conclude that a dogmatic view on this subject is difficult to maintain.

3. Creationism

The teaching under this heading is that God creates each soul separately and unites it to the body at the appointed time. Creationism accepts the fact that the substance of the body is derived from the parents and affirms that God immediately creates every human soul and unites it to the body. The greatest problem to be faced here is the transmission of sin. The creationist admits that while God creates each soul in a pure state, he withholds from it those spiritual influences which constitute spiritual life as a just punishment for Adam's first sin. It has been objected that according to this view God is made indirectly responsible for sin, since he places the soul into a situation which will inevitably involve it in transgression. In other words, if

God creates the soul in a pure state, how are we to account for its sinful condition. The creationist replies that the descendants of Adam are not constituted sinners through being brought into contact with the body but through having sin imputed to them on the ground of Adam's first sin, which is laid to their account the moment they come into being.

The difference between creationism and traducianism is not considered of serious importance by theologians as the Scriptural arguments on either side cannot be held conclusive. The conclusion we arrive at is that this mystery is not capable of solution. Most Reformed theologians, however have been creationists. Augustine hesitated between both views all his life. Thomas Aquinas considered traducianism as being heretical. Luther was a traducianist while Calvin was a creationist and considered the other view as "and ancient figment". Turretin says that "some are of the opinion that the difficulties pertaining to the propagation of original sin are best resolved by the doctrine of the propagation of the soul (animal traducianism): a view held by not a few of the fathers, and to which Augustine seems to incline. And there is no doubt that by this theory all the difficulty seems to be removed; but since it does not accord with Scripture or with sound reason, and is exposed to great difficulties, we do not think recourse should be had to it."[27] The most powerful advocate of traducianism is Dr Shedd, who argues for its truth from Scripture, systematic theology, and physiology. Dr Shedd defends the weak part of traducianism in relation to Christology by affirming that the human nature of Christ was sanctified by the Holy Ghost. And he makes the best of the argument that traducianism is the most Scriptural and rational explanation for the fallen condition of mankind.

III. THE CREATION OF MAN

We are informed by Scripture that man was made in God's image and after his likeness. Attempts have been made to

27. Francis Turretin (1623-8) **Institutis Theologiae Elencticae.** A valuable work but unobtainable in English. Indeed only parts of his Latin have been translated into English.

distinguish between the "image" and the "likeness", but they both refer to the same idea though perhaps from different points of view. The Romanist says that the image consists in man's spirituality, freedom, and immortality. He also adds that even in unfallen man there was a tendency for the lower passions to rebel against the higher faculties of reason and conscience; and so God **after his creation** endowed man with the supernatural gift of original righteousness. This supernatural gift was lost when man sinned. There is some diversity among Protestant divines as to the exact meaning of the term "image". Some hold that man lost the image in which he was created when he fell. Others deny this and say that the image was essential to man's nature and that he retained the image even in his postlapsarian state.

The Reformers generally distinguish between the image in a comprehensive and restricted sense. The latter consists in those spiritual qualities with which man was created, such as knowledge, righteousness, and holiness. The image of God in a comprehensive sense consists in the spirituality, rationality, and immortality of man. It is only when we view God's image in this comprehensive sense that man can, since the fall, still be called the image-bearer of God in accordance with the testimony of Scripture, such as Gen. 9 : 6 and James 3 : 9. These texts and others cannot be construed otherwise, since they apply to man as man without any reference to his restoration or holiness. On the other hand, the restrictive term is applied to the restored believer in such passages as Eph. 4 : 24 and Col. 3 : 10.

IV. THE COVENANT OF WORKS

The Westminster Shorter Catechism states that "Man's chief end is to glorify God, and to enjoy him for ever". When man was created, he was fitted by the constitution of his nature to fulfil the end of his creation. And even if we were not told that man was created in God's image, we might still be warranted in drawing the conclusion that he was perfect in soul and body, since we are informed that "God saw everything that he had made, and behold, it was very good" (Gen. 1 : 31).

The basis for the idea of a covenant of works is to be found in the commandment given to man after he was placed in the Garden of Eden. "And the LORD God commanded the man, saying, . . . But of the tree of the knowledge of good and evil, thou shalt not eat of it: for in the day that thou eatest thereof thou shalt surely die" (Gen. 2 : 16, 17). We have here all the elements of a covenant: namely; the parties, God and man; the promise implied, life; the condition, perfect obedience; and the penalty, death.

It has been objected that the word **covenant** is not used here; but in studying Scripture we do not merely read the words; rather we try to understand the meaning conveyed by them. It has also been said that this was merely a command imposed upon Adam, who had no alternative but to accept its terms. It is true, of course, that this was a unilateral covenant, and surely nothing different could be expected in any relations between the Creator and the creature; but the objection fails to take into account the moral excellence of our first covenant-head and the reward promised upon obedience. It has also been objected that though a penalty is mentioned, no reward is indicated. Surely to this it is sufficient to say that not to die is to live. Besides, if we are permitted to reason upon this subject, it would be unreasonable to suppose that a gracious sovereign would enter into terms with his subject without offering a reward for obedience. And we may gather from Scripture that such a reward was not merely a continuance of life but a condition of infallible and eternal blessedness. We shall also find additional evidence in various passages of Scripture for this view of covenants between God and man. "We shall therefore keep my statutes, and my judgments: which if a man do, he shall live in them: I am the LORD" (Lev. 18 : 5). "If thou wilt enter into life, keep the commandments" (Matt. 19 : 17). "For Moses describeth the righteousness which is of the law, that the man which doeth those things shall live by them" (Rom. 10 : 5). "And the law is not of faith: but the man that doeth them shall live in them" (Gal. 3 : 12).

There are also the parallels drawn between Christ and Adam. Christ, the Saviour of his people, was made under the law and fulfilled its precepts to procure life for his people according to a bi-lateral covenant agreement; and in the fifth chapter of Romans the parallel is drawn between Christ and Adam as the respective heads of their people. The truth set down in the latter part of this chapter can only be understood on the assumption that Adam and Christ were both covenant heads. Further confirmation on this point is that man's relationship to God is both natural and covenantal. When man was created original righteousness was concreated with him, and he found it easy and agreeable to serve the Lord though no promise of continuance of life or blessedness was yet given to him; yet he was liable to punishment if he disobeyed God. This seems to be the state in which we find man before he was placed in the garden, after which the Edenic statute was declared to him. If we find it possible to view the matter in this light, we may suppose that man's natural relationship to God stood on a very insecure footing though he enjoyed fellowship with God. Therefore, the subsequent covenant relationship was a gracious covenant, offering, not only a continuance of Divine favour, but a condition and state of eternal blessedness upon condition of perfect obedience for a probationary period. And this convention was to be entered into by a voluntary agent — for his own interest and that of his posterity — who was created in a state of moral perfection and was therefore able to carry out the terms of this covenant.

The curious question has been debated as to whether or not the covenant of works is still in force. The answers given have been that the covenant is in force in the sense that it demands perfect obedience and that death is pronounced against those who sin and that life is promised upon obedience. But in another sense the covenant is not in force, because none is now able to render perfect obedience and because Christ has fulfilled its condition on behalf of his people. The covenant has in this sense been fulfilled in the Second Adam and therefore abrogated in the Gospel of Christ.

CHAPTER IX

MAN IN A STATE OF SIN

I. THE FALL OF MAN

According to theologians the first great mystery, which refers to this subject, is the existence of sin in a God-controlled system; the second great mystery is the existence of sin in a perfect moral agent. All the wonderful explanations given to solve these great mysteries leave us just where we were before. The existence of sin is something we know and feel; its origin we cannot understand. That God has permitted sin when he could have prevented it, we cannot deny; and that, therefore, it was right of him to do so, we must not question. But why it was right for God to permit sin, we cannot tell.

Adam in his pre-lapsarian state was not only innocent but positively holy so that the whole inclination of his heart was to obey God's will. We further learn that the command not to eat of the forbidden fruit was moral-positive and not moral-natural. This means that the thing forbidden was not sinful in itself but became so because it was forbidden by God. It has been pointed out that this moral-positive form of the command was the best trial of man's obedience.

Some attempted explanations of the first sin are: that the holy nature of Adam contained principles morally indifferent, such as a natural desire for knowledge, admiration, and appeasement of appetite and that these desires became sinful when exercised contrary to God's will; and that Satan in tempting our first parents worked on these natural desires until belief in God was extinguished. It has also been shown that our first parents were inexperienced in the assaults of temptation and that they were assailed by a vastly superior intelligence, who used one of the lower animals as his instrument.

Our first parents were not charged with sin merely because they desired the fruits of the trees but because this particular tree was forbidden by God by a positive mandate as a test of true obedience to him in a matter that was not in itself sinful but which was forbidden by God's authority. But Eve lusted after a forbidden knowledge as Achan coveted the spoils of Jericho. Sin began with doubt, advanced to unbelief, and ended in actual disobedience. According to Dr Hodge, doubt, unbelief, and pride were the principles at work in the first sin. The emphasis, however, must be placed upon unbelief, which resulted in disobedience. It was a tree desired to make one wise. This desire was a covetous one, and the term so used is repeated in the tenth commandment of the Decalogue, "Thou shalt not covet." Dr Shedd says that "according to St. Paul, Adam was seduced by his affection for Eve, rather than deceived by the lie of Satan. He fell with his eyes wide open to the fact that if he ate he would die. But in loving his wife more than God he worshipped and served the creature instead of the Creator."[28] Whether or not this whole quotation is according to St. Paul, it is certain that Scripture says that "Adam was not deceived, but the woman being deceived was in the transgression" (1 Tim. 2 : 14). The point that has been noted in this connection is that Eve, affecting to decide this matter for her-

28. Dogmatic Theology, vol. 1, 176.

self and her husband, soon gave proof of her inferiority when assailed by a more powerful adversary, who undoubtedly must have known her inequality of shrewdness, intellect, and purpose, in comparison with her husband. In any case, the text quoted above must be taken comparatively, it being hardly proper to say that Adam sinned merely because of his affection for Eve. It is preferable to say that "Adam was not first deceived, nor indeed at all immediately deceived by the serpent but only enticed and deceived by the woman, who was the tempter's agent: so as that she was both first in the transgression in order to time, and also principal of it, contributing to the seduction and trangression of man; which ought to be a consideration to keep the woman humble, in a low opinion of herself, and that lower order wherein God hath fixed her."[29]

Our first parents were tempted and sinned inwardly before they ate of the forbidden fruit. This is just saying that sin is a product of the heart. In his original state Adam possessed, not only an innocent or indifferent disposition, but an actual bias towards holiness. And the moment he began to incline toward sin, he became sinful and the subsequent steps in his fall are simply parts of his first great sin. This does not, however, mean that temptation constitutes sin. The Saviour was tempted but did not sin, and in the prophecy referring to him he is spoken of as refusing the evil and choosing the good (Isa. 7 : 16). It is also possible that a believer may be tempted without sinning. Christian in the Valley of Humiliation speaks of whispering suggestions of grievous blasphemies by wicked ones so that he thought they proceeded from his own mind (**Pilgrim's Progress**).

The consequence of the first sin was that man lost his original integrity, such as his knowledge, righteousness, and holiness. But this does not imply that his constitutional nature was changed, since he still retained his intellectual, emotional, moral, and volitional faculties; but he became totally depraved in all his members and faculties and thus incapable of willing or performing any good action. This state and condition was not gradual but immediate. Sin deprived him of that union and communion with God, which

29. Matthew Pool. 1 Tim. 2 : 14.

constitutes the spiritual life of man. This change in his relation to God carried with it condemnation and death and produced feelings of guilt and shame. The full execution of the sentence of death was not, however, put into immediate operation, since provision was made in the covenant of grace for man's restoration.

II. THE DOCTRINE OF IMPUTATION

The history of mankind is a record of the universality of sin. The human conscience everywhere acknowledges that man's nature is depraved; and philosophers and theologians of all ages have wrestled with the problem of the origin of sin in the human race. Some, having no solution to offer, refer the matter to the sovereignty of God; others say that man is born with a depraved nature which he has derived from an animal ancestry. The Word of God not only emphasises the guilt and universality of sin, but it also provides some explanation as to its origin when we are told that "by one man sin entered into the world, and death by sin; and so death passed upon all men, for that all have sinned" (Rom. 5 : 12). We have no doubt but that this man was Adam and that the sin he committed was his first sin. If this is admitted, then we have two plain truths set before us : that sin, and death by sin, entered into the human family through the first sin of Adam and, that all men have sinned. This might mean that all men are corrupt; or that all men are somehow involved in the sin of Adam and that they are therefore punished for their own sin. If we accept the latter statement as true, we are bound to maintain that sin is charged or imputed to men because they are sinners in virtue of their own individual acts, or in virtue of their connection or union with Adam as their first father and head. Various theories have been brought forward to account for the precise connection between the sin of Adam and that of his posterity.

1. Imputation Defined

The term **imputation** means to impute, esteem, reckon, or charge to one's account as the ground of punishment or justification. This is the sense in which the word is used in

Scripture. David speaks of God imputing righteousness without works and of God not imputing sin. Faith was imputed to Abraham for righteousness. "God was in Christ, reconciling the world unto himself not imputing their trespasses unto them" (Rom. 4 : 6, 8, 9; 2 Cor. 5 : 19). These phrases must mean that righteousness was charged to the account of sinners and that they were treated as righteous, and that sin was not charged to their account; whether or not David and Abraham were personally righteous or sinless, they were reckoned so by God, and they were treated as righteous.

If we accept this explanation of imputation, we may conclude that men have Adam's sin imputed to them; that is, they have it charged to their account and they are exposed to punishment. But then this may mean an arbitrary charging to men's account of sins for which they are not responsible. This, however, would be an unjust procedure, and we must understand the term to mean that God charges Adam's sin to men because they are responsible for his sin. And there are only two ways in which they become responsible; that is, by personal sins, or in virtue of their union with Adam. It should be remembered in this connection that the word **sin** or **guilt** is used in several senses : a wrong action, a depraved moral nature, or a legal responsibility for the action of another. It is in the last sense that the word is used here in reference to the participation of the race in Adam's first sin. It is, therefore, not maintained that the sin was antecedently and personally theirs or that they are charged with being corrupt but that they are held responsible for Adam's sin and exposed to punishment. In precise language men are deserving of punishment and under condemnation because they are involved in Adam's first sin. The phrase, "for that all have sinned" (Rom. 5 : 12), does not mean that all men actually sinned or that all are corrupt but that they are all united to Adam and therefore involved in his transgression though they have not antecedently or personally sinned. This seems rather complicated and appears to be unjust; and illustrations do not solve the problem although we find general principles enumerated in Scripture and history which show that individuals and nations are involved in the sins of others. For example, in war innocent subjects suffer because of the actions of their leaders, yet there is a general agreement that the proceeding is just because subjects are involved in the destinies of their nations for weal or woe.

Our Saviour was innocent and owed nothing for himself; yet as the Mediator of his people he voluntarily bore the blame for the sins of the Church and bore, not only the punishment, but the sin itself, that is the demerit, though he was personally innocent. The only way in which this can be explained is by considering the union between Christ and the Church. What he suffered is imputed to them as if they had suffered and his obedience is imputed to them as if they had obeyed. They have not antecedently or personally suffered or obeyed, but they are involved in the obedience of their Surety.

This is the doctrine taught in Romans 5 : 12-19. Christ and Adam are represented as the two covenant heads. "For by one man's disobedience many were made sinners, so by the obedience of one shall many be made righteous" (Rom. 5 : 19). It is through the sin of Adam that men were **made sinners**. This cannot mean that they were depraved or had personally done wrong, and it must therefore mean that they were involved in his sin in every sense in which he was, except that his sin was not antecedently and personally theirs, and that consequently they are blamed for his sin and are under condemnation. To be **made righteous** must therefore mean that those referred to are involved in the obedience of Christ in every sense in which he was except that his obedience was not antecedently and personally theirs but his.

2. Theories of Imputation

Several theories have been propounded to account for the relation between Adam's sin and his posterity, but they are so unsatisfactory and unscriptural as to be undeserving of notice. Origen (200 A.D.) found an explanation for man's sinfulness in the personal sins of mankind in a pre-temporal state. Pelagius (409 A.D.) denied any real connection between Adam and his race. Arminius (1590 A.D.) and some of his followers refused to acknowledge the idea of a real union between Adam and his posterity and their views broadly are that man is responsible for his own acts of sin and nothing else.

(1). **The Federal Theory.** The federal or covenantal school maintains that our union with Adam is both natural and federal, or covenantal : natural, as Adam is the father and root of the whole human family, and federal by Divine constitution as a party to the covenant of works in which he represented his posterity. It is this federal or representative union which is the ground of the imputation of sin to them. The evidence for this view is found in the transactions recorded in the third chapter of Genesis and in the principles set forth in Rom. 5 : 12-19 and 1 Cor. 15 : 21, 22. The regulative principles governing this covenant and its results are also to be found in other passages of Scripture. Those who acknowledge man's fallen condition must accept this view of the matter or provide a better explanation.

(2). **The Realistic View.** According to this view — which is based upon the views of Tertullian (200 A.D.) and Augustine (400 A.D.) and defended by Dr Shedd, Dr Strong, and others — the whole human nature was created in and with our first parents; and their descendants are not separate substances but manifestations of the same general substance of human nature. Adam's sin, therefore, is charged to his posterity because they actually sinned as he did, and thus they are responsible for their own sin. This makes for a more rational explanation for the sin of Adam and our involvement in it, but it is exposed to several difficulties, for it **appears** to give a materialistic conception to the human person and deprives him of a separate personality; besides, it does not explain why Adam's descendants are responsible for his first sin only. Indeed on this view we have committed all the sins which our progenitors have committed and will be held responsible for them. It has also been pointed out that since Christ shared the nature that actually sinned, he would be deeply involved in the sin of Adam. In any case, the question of liability is almost as great here as on the federal view. According to the realistic view generic humanity sinned, and according to the federal view the head sinned and the members are responsible. But even on the realistic view we cannot posit an antecedent personal sin of the individual, for generic humanity must be distinguished from the individual. In both cases there is no antecedent and personal sin of the individual and so the nexus between Adam and his posterity is not much closer on the realistic view than it is on the federal view.

When, however, we come to deal with the question of the union of Christ with his people, we cannot discover any realistic union but rather a union of representation. Adam is the covenant head of one family, and Christ is the Covenant Head of the other. Our relation to Christ is therefore a covenantal relation. In the realistic view it is difficult to discover our precise relation to Christ, for we must maintain that sin was imputed to him not because he was inherently or actually sinful but because he suffered in our room and place and his righteousness is imputed to us although we are inherently and actually sinful. He had no inherent sin, and we had no inherent righteousness. But our sins were charged to his account and he suffered on that account; his righteousness moreover, was imputed to us and put to our account for justification. "For he hath made him to be sin for us, who knew no sin; that we might be made the righteousness of God in him" (2 Cor. 5 : 21).

3. Conclusion

The federal view, which makes the violated covenant with Adam the cause of our guilt and corruption, is not free from difficulties; and when to this is added the doctrine of creationism, the difficulties are greater. But, nonetheless, if we are to give a reasonable explanation of the question, we think that the federal theory is more Scriptural and less open to objection than the realistic view.

It has been said that the federal view is defective, since it is said there is no specific mention of a covenant or a covenant head. This, however, makes the transactions in the third chapter of Genesis and the principles regulating the headship of Christ and Adam in Rom. 5 : 12-19 and 1 Cor. 15 : 21, 22 exegetically impossible on any other interpretation. Besides this, the idea of a covenant added to the natural headship of Adam seems to make the problem of human guilt easier to understand.

It has also been objected that God regards and treats men as sinners when they are not sinners. Such a criticism coming from a realist evinces a failure to see all the angles of the problem. The realist accepts the view that men are condemned because they sinned in Adam as an organic whole; but, in this case, the condemnation affects those individuals who sinned before they had a being and were, therefore, free from antecedent or personal sins. Besides, the federalist says that God regards and treats men as sinners, not because they happened to be in Adam, but because they are sinners in virtue of their involvement in the sin of their covenant head. It is also argued that God holds men responsible for the violation of a covenant which they had no part in establishing, but this bears with equal weight against the realist. Were there no explanation given of the sin of the human family, there is ample evidence to prove that the greatest benefits inherited by lost sinners arise from a covenant of grace which they had no part in establishing. As the first is a Divine constitution, so is the second.[30]

The simple account of the doctrine of imputation is that wrong-doing is charged to our account because it is really and properly ours. But wrong-doing may be charged to our account even when it is not antecedently and personally ours, for we may in several ways be responsible for the wrong-doing of another; and if this is proved in law we are held responsible and so punished. This is so in the case of the imputation of Adam's first sin. We are in covenant with him and so held responsible for his violation of its terms. The imputation of sin to Christ, if not of a precise nature in the circumstances of it, is the same essentially. He being in covenant with his people is held responsible for sins not antecedently and personally his own. He died for our sins according to the Scriptures. The imputation of Christ's righteousness to believers proceeds in the same manner. They being in covenant with him are held to be in law partakers of his righteousness. His obedience is charged to their account. This obedience is really and truly theirs, though not so antecedently and personally. Therefore, his obedience is reckoned as theirs.

---

30. **Systematic Theology** 1953, pages 612-616, Dr Strong.

III. ORIGINAL SIN

1. The Meaning of the Word, Sin

Many ingenious explanations have been given of the nature of sin, such as: that it is a necessity of finiteness, a process in man's evolution, the result of natural impulses in man's moral nature, mere ignorance, or a misfortune in man's nature for which he is not responsible.

All these explanations and others fail to take into consideration the real moral evil inherent in sin apart from its consequences. The standard of judgment here is the will or law of God, whether enshrined in Scripture or impressed upon man's conscience, making a rational agent responsible for his disposition and actions. And whether we make the measure of man's responsibility obedience to God's law or perfect love to God, sin is a defect in man's moral nature which constitutes disconformity or transgression of that law that requires the performance of all the duties the creature owes to the Creator.

The root meaning of the Hebrew and Greek terms used in Scripture to express **sin** is to err from a rule or law. Sin is not being or not doing what God requires. We need not say, however, that sin is a substance or the property of a substance. A property belongs necessarily to a substance while an accident may or may not belong to a substance. "Sin," says Calvin, "is an adventitious quality or accident, rather than a substantial property originally innate."[31] Sin is the presence of evil in man and a positive quality of his being, but it is not an entity in itself, for it requires an agent who is responsible for his state, dispositions, and actions. Dr Shedd quaintly remarks that under and within the permissive will of God **sin is man's creation;** he makes it out of nothing.[32] According to Scripture sin is lawlessness (1 John 3 : 4). Sin is not a new positive quality infused into the soul but a disordered state of its principles leading it to positive desires contrary to the law of nature and the revealed will of God and issuing in actual sin. Sin is therefore lust or concupiscence. "Then when lust hath conceived, it bringeth

31. **Institutes.** XI : 1.
32. **Christian Doctrine** 1888, Vol. 1, page 16.

forth sin: and sin, when it is finished, bringeth forth death" (James 1 : 15).

It is a common saying that sin consists in overt acts against the law, but the truth is that sin is a state and disposition, which must be distinguished from its consequences and penalties. Sin is a moral evil against the law of the Creator and has its being in man's heart. It is an old heresy that still obtains a hearing in some schools of thought that man's nature is not sinful but that sin consists in acts of the will. Some will say that although habits and dispositions are of a sinful character, they cannot strictly be called sin for real sin consists in an act of will. Scripture, however, gives another intrepretation of the matter. Concupiscence, or a sinful disposition, is set forth in clear terms as sin. "I had not known sin, but by the law: for I had not known concupiscence, except the law had said, Thou shalt not covet" (Rom. 7 : 7). "The motions of sin" and "the law of sin" and "sin that dwelleth in me" are called sin although no overt act is spoken of. Besides, Scripture clearly asserts that the habitual state of the soul is sinful when not conformed to the law of God. Sins are said to "reign in the mortal body" and the unregenerate are the "servants of sin." This evil tendency is called "flesh," "blindness of heart," and a condition of "being past feeling" (Rom. 6 : 12, 13, 17; Gal. 5 : 17; Eph. 4 : 18, 19; James 1 : 14,15).

If we consider virtue as simply obedience to law, and vice as a failure to come up to this standard, we are liable to adopt a mechanical view of moral values. The natural man too often considers obedience and love to God, even when rightly revealed to him, as the command of an imperious Creator who wishes to hamper his individual freedom and activities. But the source of this feeling is an evil heart of unbelief and disobedience. The objective law of God is contrary to the moral character of the sinner; but when that law is transplanted into his heart by the Holy Spirit, the conscience is restored and the heart is burdened with a true sense of indebtedness to God and a real love to his Person so that the freed slave not only obeys the Lord from the heart but finds warm and loving affections in those devotional and practical exercises that lead to moral and spiritual excellence.

2. Sin as Guilt

Original sin is called so because it is derived from the original parents of the race and because it is the root of all other sins. The two elements in sin are guilt and depravity. Guilt is spoken of in a two-fold sense. What is called **potential guilt** is the intrinsic ill-desert of sin. This is of the essence of sin and part of its sinfulness and would continue to be true even if there were no punishment. The sinner when he sins deserves to be punished whether he is punished or not. On the other hand, **actual guilt** relates to the punishment and is not of the essence of sin. It is a relative state, which exposes a sinful person to the penalty of sin. Actual guilt or the punishment due to sin may be removed by transference either personally or vicariously. This distinction, which is of considerable importance in the controversies of theology, must be further explained. Sin in itself is evil and makes the person who sins wicked. This is of the essence of sin and is called **reatus culpae;** it is also deserving of punishment and called **reatus poenae.** The former cannot be transferred from one person to another; the latter can. These terms have been criticised for their want of accuracy. We are concerned only with the ideas suggested by them.

3. Original Sin

"The sinfulness of that estate whereinto man fell, consists in the guilt of Adam's first sin, the want of original righteousness, and the corruption of his whole nature, which is commonly called Original Sin; together with all actual transgressions which proceed from it."[33] According to this definition there are three elements in original sin; namely, **guilt, the absence of holiness,** and **a corrupt nature.**

(1) **Guilt.** The guilt of Adam's first sin means that his sin was immediately charged to the account of his posterity, not because he is their natural father or merely because **he** sinned, but because they were involved in the covenant made with Adam, and consequently as his posterity comes into existence this sin is imputed to them and they are blamed for it and suffer the punishment.

(2) **The Want of Original Righteousness.** Man before his

33. **Shorter Catechism.** 18.

fall was not only innocent and free from sin, but he was positively conformed in his heart and actions to the law of God. His posterity do not possess this righteousness and are therefore sinners by defect — there is in them a want of conformity to the law of God.

(3) **A Corruption of Nature.** The corruption of man's whole nature is what is commonly and properly called original sin or hereditary depravity. This is in some respects the most serious element in man's nature as fallen and the source of all his actual transgressions. He not only does not bring into the world any moral or spiritual excellence, but his nature is indisposed towards, and averse to, the requirements of the law. In the words of Scripture, the **carnal mind** is enmity against God." From this corrupt nature proceeds all actual transgressions. Actual transgressions are commonly taken to mean overt or outward acts of sin, but strictly speaking, actual sin does not only consist in these only but in the inward sins, such as unbelief, lust, pride, and hatred. There is, therefore, an evil principle in the faculties of the soul which leads to sinful thoughts and actions. Before the fall man possessed original righteousness, but since the fall he does not possess it. The original righteousness referred to is not simply freedom from sin but positive conformity in heart and life to the law of God. The Reformers held that when Adam sinned against God, he lost the true knowledge, righteousness, and holiness which constituted him a perfect creation. And when men come into existence they are deprived of this original righteousness because of Adam's first sin and become depraved.

IV. SIN AS TOTAL DEPRAVITY

Even when we consider sin to be a negative or privative quality or principle in fallen men, we must not forget that not to love God is to be indifferent to his claims or to hate him, and not to obey him is to disobey him. This disposition follows from the essential activity of the soul and the essential nature of virtue, so that moral indifference in a rational person is impossible. But when it is said that man is totally depraved, it means that he is totally depraved in all his faculties, although we are not required to believe that man is as sinful as he can be. For example, we must not compare Nicodemus with the saved thief though both required to be born again since they possessed no spiritual life. We are informed that before the flood "God saw that the wickedness of man was great in the earth, and that every imagination of the thoughts of his heart was only evil continually" (Gen. 6 : 5). This statement alone sets forth the inveterate and deep-seated nature of sin. Not only all his thoughts but every imagination of the thoughts of his evil heart was evil continually. Even the flood-judgment did not change man's evil heart, for we are told after the flood that "the imagina-tion of man's heart is evil from his youth" (Gen. 8 : 21). Isaiah says that "we are all as an unclean thing, and all our righteousnesses are as filthy rags" (Isa. 64 : 6). "There is none that doeth good, no, not one" (Rom. 3 : 12). "The carnal mind is enmity against God" (Rom. 8 : 7). "So then they that are in the flesh cannot please God" (Rom. 8 : 8). "And you hath he quickened, who were dead in trespasses and sins" (Eph. 2 : 1).

Total depravity does not mean that man is as depraved as it is possible for him to become or that he has lost all the use of his understanding, conscience, and will or that he cannot distinguish between right and wrong, or that he can-not exercise domestic or civil virtues or the external duties of religion. But it does mean that all his faculties have been impaired by sin and that there remains no recuperative quality in his soul. This position would be better understood if men realised that the sin of Adam, and the sin of every fallen man, disrupts the union with God, which is the source of spiritual life. This union, being the essence of spiritual life and blessedness, is restored by the life-giving influence of the Spirit of Christ, "for as the Father raiseth up the dead and quickeneth them even so the Son quickeneth whom he will" (John 5 : 21). "The hour is coming, and now is, when the dead shall hear the voice of the Son of God: and they that hear shall live" (John 5 : 25).

V. TOTAL INABILITY

The doctrine of total inability has been assailed by Pelagians, Socinians, and Arminians, and doubtless it will be spoken against and misunderstood until the end of time. Some have denied the doctrine because they have misunderstood it; others, because they believe that man possesses some power to believe and repent. A number who have considered the statements of Scripture on this subject have been swayed by other considerations, for they find passages in the Word of God which seem to teach that man possesses some power to believe the Gospel. Because God invites and commands men to believe and repent, they reason that God will never command men to do what they cannot do. The answer to this is that if it is man's duty to obey, love, or believe in God, he should be informed of his duty. This information does not necessarily intimate any power in man to obey. Surely man may be brought to see that it is his duty to obey God even if he finds that because of his sinfulness, he is incapable of doing so. But further, men will fail to find one passage in Scripture which asserts that fallen man of himself is able to love God. On the other hand, we have the explicit testimony of Scripture that man cannot believe. "No man can come to me, except the Father which hath sent me draw him" (John 6 : 44). "For without me ye can do nothing" (John 15 : 5). "For by grace are ye saved through faith; and that not of yourselves: it is the gift of God" (Eph. 2 : 8).

The doctrine of the full and free invitation of the Gospel has been brought in here because men think it unreasonable and unscriptural that sinners should be invited to be partakers of its blessings when they are unable to accept its overtures. The truth is that some sinners do avail themselves of these overtures. If we ask **How?,** we are told that they receive power to do so. And although the nexus between God's sovereignty and man's responsibility cannot be explained, it can be rendered less exceptional than some of the opponents of this doctrine represent it. It is clear from Scripture that all the graces necessary to salvation are outside the sinner's power and are God's work and gift for "it is not of him that willeth, nor of him that runneth, but of God that sheweth mercy" (Rom. 9 : 16). Further, God never tells sinners that they are able to free themselves from the bondage of sin or that he expects them to implant spiritual life into themselves, nor does he say that anyone can atone for his own sin. Besides, there is no intimation in Scripture that God expects sinners to repent or believe while they are in a state of sinful bondage. Furthermore, when God commands and invites men to do those things which cannot be performed without his special grace, he sometimes supposes them to have a principle of spiritual life within them; or if this is not so, he imparts spiritual life on occasions when he commands men to believe or repent. There is really nothing in Scripture which would contradict this view, but Scripture rather confirms it. In some cases the invitation is addressed to those who have been regenerated and who are now called to make further progress in grace. Why one man who has heard the Gospel many times and has not believed it, does afterwards believe the same Gospel must be accounted for by the fact that on previous occasions he was unable because he was in a state of spiritual bondage, while later he was able, because by the effectual power of the Spirit he was enabled to embrace Jesus Christ offered to him in the Gospel.

VI. LIBERTY AND ABILITY

In theological works various explanations have been offered in an attempt to explain this subject. There is the greatest difference between liberty and ability. **Liberty** consists in the power to choose or to refuse according to our inclinations. But this choice will be in harmony with man's character. A man who is essentially evil or totally depraved, while he chooses freely, is bound to choose the evil and not the good. And even if his reason and conscience prompts him to desire the good, his essential wickedness will not allow him to rise above the level of his character. People are sometimes confused when they hear that man is in bondage to sin while, at the same time, he possesses liberty. But the bondage consists in his inability to choose that which is good. Indeed to speak of man's **will** is to assert that he possesses freedom of choice.

Ability, on the other hand, when referred to the natural man, means that he has power to change his subjective state; that is, to make himself prefer what he does not prefer. Though man is as free since the fall as he was before it, he has lost all ability to obey the will of God. "Because the carnal mind is enmity against God; for it is not subject to the law of God, neither indeed can be" (Rom. 8 : 7).

VII. NATURAL AND MORAL ABILITY

A distinction has also been made between natural and moral ability. By **natural ability** is meant that man possesses all the faculties to obey as a man possesses feet to walk. By **moral ability** is meant the moral state of these faculties or that disposition in man which leads him to obey God's will. This distinction is considered to be of some considerable importance in assessing the measure of man's responsibility. It is said, for example, that man possesses all the physical or metaphysical faculties to obey God and that these faculties are not interfered with, from without, to prevent his performing the obedience required. On the other hand, it is pointed out that these faculties have been morally injured and consequently man is not able to obey. This solution, however, does not go to the root of the matter, for it seems unreasonable to tell a man who has two paralysed legs that he possesses natural ability to walk but not physical ability. To go further into the matter, we may say that man possesses a **will,** but he has no ability to **will to obey** God, and the reason he does not obey is because he cannot will to obey. The fact, however, that he possesses a will must be distinguished from the supposition that he possesses no will, for if he possessed no will then he would not be responsible. In other words, the natural man possesses a will but he is not willing to obey God.

VIII. MODERN IDEAS OF SIN

Some people consider sin as an unfortunate disease or imperfection for which man is not responsible. Because he is sinful, he is to be pitied but not punished. But fallen man possesses reason and conscience and knows the true from the false and the right from the wrong, and he is self-determined in the choice of evil. Modern ideas suggest that sin is a matter of opinion, since different people have different ideas about right and wrong. This view would do away with reason, conscience, and law, and indeed few sane people would consider the removal of or interference with their persons or property as being anything else but wrong. Sin is not merely crime; it relates to God's authority and law. Sin is transgression of that law whether written in Scripture or inscribed in man's heart, for the works of the law are written in men's hearts and they cannot ignore the claims of the law. It is true, of course, that some acts are neither good or evil. The appetites of hunger and sex are in themselves indifferent, but when they are exercised in defiance of the law of nature and the revealed will of God as in gluttony, drunkenness, and immorality, they are subject to God's condemnation; and we are told that the adulterer, the drunkard, the idolater, and the pleasure lover shall not inherit the kingdom of God.

The modern Pelagian does not believe in original sin and therefore does not believe that man is born in sin. Hence, he does not believe that man must be born again, but he does believe that man should practice all the social virtues and engage in spiritual exercises. This he supposes man to be quite capable of doing through his own efforts. According to materialistic views, man inherits brute instincts which become sinful when they manifest themselves in actions. Cultured man, however, condemns these impulses and says that they are sinful when yielded to. Sinfulness, therefore, consists in the control of the lower instincts over the higher nature of man. There is little or no place here for the grace of God or the influence of the Holy Ghost. Man is still climbing out of his lower environment and will ultimately arrive at perfection when he is able to extinguish his animal instincts.

Principal Cunningham remarks that the decay of true religion has always been accompanied by a large measure of error on this subject and that there are tendencies in every age to underrate the injurious effects of the fall of man. And he points out that even when God may have been pleased to bless the labours of those who hold erroneous views on man's fallen state, this has not been done because of the error they hold, but in spite of it and because of the truth they hold along with it. It should be remembered in dealing with this subject that we ought to distinguish between the **actual condition** of fallen man as set forth in Scripture and the **origin and causes** of this condition, since it is reasonable to suppose that we may possess considerable information as to our own corrupt nature even if we cannot account for the causes which have brought it about. The knowledge of our moral and spiritual condition and the knowledge of the remedy to meet with this condition is of the greatest importance. It is interesting and instructive to notice in Paul's classic to the Romans that he first deals with man's moral condition before God (Chapters 1, 2, 3). This he follows by setting forth the remedy for sin (Chapters 3, 4, 5). Afterwards, he reverts to the entrance of sin into the world and its relation to Adam and Christ (Chapter 5), while in Chapters 8, 9, 10, and 11, he discusses the subjects of election and reprobation in connection with Israel. And it would be well if our order and emphasis were closer to his in setting forth the Gospel of Jesus Christ.

CHAPTER X

THE COVENANT OF GRACE

Introduction

Man is a creature under law to God, and he is therefore under obedience exclusive of any notion of promise or reward. It seems that this was man's original condition before God entered into a covenant with him in the Garden of Eden. The transactions in Eden, therefore, though a sovereign administration, must be considered under the notion of a covenant. The parties are God and man; the requirement is obedience; the penalty is death; and the reward is a continuance of life and eternal blessedness. That a promise of life is implied though not stated must be evident from other passages of Scripture. "The man which doeth those things shall live by them " (Rom. 10 : 5). "The commandment . . . was ordained to life" (Rom. 7 : 10). "If thou wilt enter into life, keep the commandments" (Matt. 19 : 17).

It is also certain that this covenant was made with Adam as the representative of his posterity (Rom. 5 : 12), "Wherefore, as by one man sin entered into the world, and death by sin; and so death passed upon all men, for that all have sinned." That Rom. 5 : 12-21 refers to two covenant heads, Christ and Adam, representing their posterity cannot be denied by any unbiassed reader. Objections have been made to calling these transactions "covenants," and the procedure has been deemed inequitable, but it is quite another matter to give better explanations of the passages referred to in dealing with this subject.

I. THE COVENANT OF GRACE

Since man by the fall lost communion with God, provision must be made, if a remedy is to be provided, to relieve him and his seed of the responsibility of sin, to reinstate him in God's favour, and to enable him to hold communion with God. Such a remedy, we are assured from Scripture, envisaged the fall, and was therefore planned in the eternal councils. The origination, execution, and administration of this remedy has been usually dealt with under the caption of **the covenant of grace.**

The reality of such a covenant between the Father and the Son may be gathered from such passages as Psa. 89 : 3, "I have made a covenant with my chosen," and Isa. 53 : 10, "If his soul shall make a propitiatory sacrifice he shall see a seed which shall prolong their days; and the gracious purpose of Jehovah shall prosper in his hands" (Bishop Lowth's Translation); "I the LORD have called thee in righteousness, and will hold thine hand, and will keep thee, and give thee for a covenant of the people, for a light of the Gentiles" (Isa. 42 : 6); "I have glorified thee on the earth: I have finished the work which thou gavest me to do" (John 17 : 4). The covenant of grace was formed in eternity and contracted between the Father representing the Godhead, and Christ representing his elect people; and God the Spirit was to administer the terms of the covenant in the sanctification of his people, or, as the Shorter Catechism puts it, "The Spirit applieth to us the redemption purchased by Christ, by working faith in us, and thereby uniting us to Christ is our effectual calling."[34] The condition of this covenant upon the part of the Son included his suffering and obedience in the room and stead of his people. The promises, upon fulfilment of the conditions, included his exaltation,

34. **Shorter Catechism.** 30.

his universal dominion, his administration of its provisions, and the complete salvation of all for whom he acted.

II. THE WORD, COVENANT

The Hebrew word for **covenant** in the Old Testament is **berith**. It is difficult to get at the precise meaning of the word. This must be gathered from the representations of Scripture. The word itself may denote a mutual voluntary agreement or a disposition or arrangement imposed by one party upon another. When the parties are equal, such as the Father and the Son, there is a mutual voluntary agreement; but when the parties are unequal, the covenant assumes the form of a disposition, since God is the Sovereign, who imposes his own arrangements upon his creatures. In any reference to a covenant of grace between God and man in the Old Testament, we must assume that the word **berith** is a sovereign disposition imposed by God upon man. We must not, however, in framing such a definition, exclude the idea of mutuality or consent; since men can only partake of the blessings of the covenant by the exercise of faith and the voluntary partaking of the duties required by the covenant. The exercise of these graces, nevertheless, must be conceived of as being part of the sovereign administration of the covenant of grace.

The word **diatheke** in the New Testament in reference to God's dealings with his church is translated covenant and means disposition and arrangement, the only difference in meaning between the Hebrew and the Greek idea being that the latter covenant idea reached its consummation in the actual sufferings and obedience of Christ. And the Apostle Paul, or the writer to the Hebrews, in dealing with this subject brings in the notion of a last will or testament, which secures to the beneficiaries the benefits of the covenant through the death of the Testator (Heb. 9 : 16, 17). While, however, the covenant of grace appears to be set forth in this precious testamentary aspect of it in the passage mentioned above (and even this has been queried), it would appear that in some, if not all, of the other passages where the word **testament** is used, the word **covenant** would have been better. Although we find in Scripture that a covenant of grace was made with Christ for the salvation of his people, we cannot fail to see that God is represented as making a covenant of grace with men. Yet we are not to think that this is a different covenant but rather the administration of the same covenant through which God "freely offereth unto sinners life and salvation by Jesus Christ, requiring of them faith in him, that they may be saved."[35]

III. THE COVENANT OF REDEMPTION

In developing the covenant idea some theologians have made a distinction between the **covenant of redemption** and the **covenant of grace.** The covenant of redemption, they say, was formed in eternity between the Father and the Son for the salvation of elect sinners. The covenant of grace they consider as being made by God with elect sinners on condition of faith. In this covenant of grace Christ is not one of the parties but the Mediator who on behalf of his people guarantees all the conditions demanded of his people. Others maintain that there is only one covenant, the covenant of grace, but that it should be considered under two aspects; that is, a covenant **made** with Christ and administered in the Gospel. The distinction is not important but it makes for simplicity to consider the covenant of grace as one. "It appears more simple to regard as the foundation of all God's dealings with mankind, of whatever class, only two great contrasted covenants of works and of grace: the **former** made by God at the creation of the world with Adam, as the federal head and representative of all his posterity (of the promises, conditions, penalty, and issue of that covenant, I have spoken under a former head — see Chapter XVII); the **latter** or covenant of grace formed in the counsels of eternity between the Father and the Son as contracting parties, the Son therein contracting as the second Adam, representing all his people, as their mediator and surety, assuming their place, and undertaking to apply to them all the benefits secured by this eternal covenant of grace, and to secure the performance upon their part of all those duties which are involved therein."[36] Dr Dabney distinguished between the covenant of redemption and the covenant of

35. **Westminster Confession,** VI and III, 7-3.
36. Dr A. A. Hodge. **Outlines,** page 370.

grace as against Dr John Dick, who holds to the one covenant. Dr Dabney pursues the subject with some keenness,[37] yet he himself later in his discussion uses the following words: "And first, we urge the general consideration that the Bible never speaks of more than two covenants, that of the law of Works and of Grace."[38] Dr Dabney, however, is speaking against dispensationalists and uses these words in a different connection; yet he seems to stress the existence of only two covenants, the covenant of works and the covenant of grace.

The distinction between the covenant of redemption and the covenant of grace was maintained by Dr Owen, Charnock, Flavel, and others. That the covenant made with Christ and believers is the same covenant has been maintained by Boston, Erskine, Dick, and several others.

"The truth is," as Dr Dick has remarked, "that what these divines call the covenant of grace is merely the administration of what they call the covenant of redemption, for the purpose of communicating its blessings to those for whom they were intended; and cannot be properly considered as a covenant because it is not suspended upon a proper condition." The Westminster Assembly in this section appear to describe what was then usually called the covenant of grace, as distinguished from the covenant of redemption. But, though they viewed the covenant under a two-fold consideration, as made with the Surety from everlasting, and as made with sinners in time, they certainly regarded it as one and the same covenant. "The covenant of grace," say they, "was made with Christ as the second Adam, and in him with all the elect as his seed."[39]

IV. THE ADMINISTRATION OF THE COVENANT

The covenant of grace is one under all dispensations and administrations. The Head of the covenant is Christ; and he is the Mediator. The faith of God's children is the same in all ages and the blessings are the same: justification by faith,

---

37. Dr abney. **Systematic Theology,** page 432.
38. Ibid, page 454.
39. Dr Shaw. **Confession,** chapter VII.

the sanctification of heart and life, and everlasting life. Some have viewed the covenant in the Old Testament as being merely national, bestowing only temporal blessings. A critical study of the Scriptures does, however, evince that the Gospel church in the New Testament is a continuation and development of the Old Testament church. And Paul in his Epistle to the Galatians speaks of the Gospel that was preached to Abraham (Gal. 3 : 8). Paul in writing to the Romans speaks of the faith of Abraham and the blessing of forgiveness to David (Rom. 4 : 3, 5, 6, 7) not to speak of the faith of the patriarchs mentioned in Hebrews and their desire for a better country, that is, an heavenly (Heb. 11 : 16).

1. The Covenant Made with Adam

It has been maintained with some force that the first revelation of the covenant of grace is to be found in Genesis 3 : 15. Here we have the elements of a covenant, which, though obscurely set forth, contains a promise of grace and a promise of victory over sin.

2. The Covenant with Noah

The covenant with Noah as the second natural head of the race, though of a generic nature and promising natural blessings to mankind, rested upon the covenant of grace (Gen. 9 : 9). Even previous to the deluge there was some revelation of this covenant, since we read of the preaching of Enoch and Noah and the strivings of the Holy Ghost (Gen. 6 : 3, 2 Pet. 2 : 5, Jude 14). We also read in Hebrews of the faith of some of these antediluvians, and we are warranted in believing that they had some acquaintance with the substance of the covenant of grace.

3. The Covenant with Abraham

The covenant with Abraham brings into prominence the gracious character of God's covenant. This is brought out again and again in God's dealings with this patriarch and is confirmed by such passages as Romans 4, Galatians 3, and Hebrews 11. "And the Scripture, foreseeing that God would justify the heathen through faith, preached before the gospel unto Abraham, saying, In thee shall all nations be blessed" (Gal. 3 : 8).

4. The Sinaitic Covenant

The Sinaitic covenant was essentially the same as that established with Abraham, but a continuation and development of it, embracing the nation rather than the family. And while the outward frame of this covenant had a legal aspect in virtue of the moral law and its complicated sacrifices and services, it was essentially a covenant of grace. The moral law was set forth as the standard of righteousness, and was made a condition of God's favour and of all national blessings, yet it was grafted on a covenant of grace in a similar manner to which the covenant of grace bears upon God's children under the Gospel. The preface to the ten commandments teaches that because God is the Lord and Redeemer, the people were bound to keep all his commandments. This is agreeable to the preface itself: "I am the LORD thy God, which have brought thee out of the land of Egypt, out of the house of bondage" (Ex. 20 : 2).

V. THE NEW COVENANT

The covenant revealed in the New Testament is substantially the same as that in the Old. The God of the Old Testament is identical with the God of the New: his character is unchanged, his law is the same, and the plan of salvation in all its principles and arrangements stresses the covenant relationship between God and his people, who are commanded now as then to love him and keep his commandments (Deut. 6 : 5, 17; John 14 : 15). The truths set forth in the old economy, veiled under rites and ceremonies, had respect not only to the spiritual condition of the people but to the design of that progressive revelation which ordained the coming of the Saviour in the fulness of time. "But before faith came, we were kept under the law, shut up unto the faith which should afterwards be revealed" (Gal. 3 : 23). "But when the fulness of the time was come, God sent forth his Son, made of a woman, made under the law" (Gal 4 : 4). Christ was promised in the Old Testament, and his sufferings and death and the benefits of his passion were set forth in the Mosaic sacrifices and services. The actual coming of Christ as the Mediator of the Covenant dispensed with these rites, since the promise was now fulfilled. The new covenant is, therefore, the old in essence but the new in fulfilment and administration.

The contrast referred to by the New Testament writers and made so much of by some theologians may be considered from two points of view. First, these writers wished to produce the strongest impression upon their readers that the old rites and ceremonies were to be dispensed with at the advent of a better priest, a better sacrifice, and a more spiritual and liberal economy (Heb. 8 : 6, 7). Secondly, the writers were arguing against self-righteous Jews who based their salvation upon the observance of these rites while they failed to see that the rites and ceremonies typified the priesthood of the Saviour.

Some of those who are called the dispensational writers, though they have brought to light some interesting and profitable subjects of discussion have tended to ignore the unity and perpetuity of the covenant. The less extreme ones indeed admitted that the promises of salvation were made to Abraham and his seed; that the Gospel was preached to Abraham (Gal. 3 : 8); and that the Old Testament saints were saved by faith. Yet they became so wedded to their conception of numerous dispensations that they looked upon the Mosaic economy as a system of absolute bondage, which was relieved only by the advent of the Saviour. The truth however, is that not only did the saints enjoy the grace of salvation under the Mosaic economy, but the dispensation itself was governed and regulated as a covenant of grace. Christ pointed out to the Jews that eternal life was to be obtained in the Scriptures which spoke of himself. "Search the Scriptures; for in them ye think ye have eternal life: and they are they which testify of me." "For had ye believed Moses, ye would have believed me: for he wrote of me" (John 5 : 39, 46). The Galatian Epistle asserts that the covenant made with Abraham was not made void nor suspended by the Mosaic law (Gal. 3 : 17); and it would be nothing less than legalism to hold that being kept under the law until faith came meant to be kept under its condemning power until the coming of Christ (Gal. 4 : 23). The Apostle speaks of the heir being a child under governors until the time appointed of the father, until the coming of Christ, that we might receive the adoption of sons. This is just saying that the children of the covenant were in relative bondage to the rites and ceremonies of the Mosaic economy. These were dispensed with in the fulness of time by the Saviour who was prefigured in them (Gal. 4 : 1-7).

Some orthodox writers have underestimated the benefits of the Old Testament and refer to this period as one of intolerable bondage and terror. But the expressions of hope, gratitude, and joy uttered by some of the Old Testament saints will not support this theory. These spiritual benefits of a high order were not only enjoyed by Abraham, the father of the faithful, but by some less eminent saints, who were saved and sanctified by the same grace and whose hearts and lives gave evidence that they enjoyed as much and loved as much as their brethren of the New Testament period. And in viewing the problem of the comparative obscurity of God's provision of grace, we must not forget the piety of those who embraced the promises by faith. A crude illustration may help us here, for we can conceive of a skilful and cautious captain who can pilot his craft in foggy weather with as much confidence as another possesses on a clear day.

The differences between the old covenant and the new has been variously treated. These differences have been considered under four particulars. In respect of **evidence,** the Old Testament reveals Christ who was to come; in the New he did come. In the Old Testament the truth was obscure, being veiled under the ritual and sacrifices; but it is now clearly revealed in the Gospel of Christ. In respect of **worship,** the old covenant was encumbered with rites and ceremonies; the new is more simple, more spiritual, and more intimate. In its **extent,** the Old Testament saints were mainly confined to one nation, but the Gospel now embraces the whole world. In its **duration,** the old covenant was preparatory and temporary; whereas the new dispensation will continue unaltered until the consummation of all things.

VI. THE COVENANT AND THE LAW

The law, or the ten commandments, was the basis of God's covenant with Israel, revealing his will to his people and regulating the whole of the worship and services of the

Mosaic economy, while its universal and timeless principles of righteousness were designed to set the spiritual and moral standards for all the successive generations of the world. It is called a testimony to indicate the authority and will of God; it was also a standing witness against the sins of the children of the covenant. By its prohibitions and requirements it testified to the holiness of Jehovah and was the standard of holiness required of his people. The law, however, was not a mere legal instrument of instruction and condemnation, since it contemplated God as the Deliverer of his people; and he therefore expected and enjoined their homage and loving obedience. This is intimated in the preface to the law. "I am the LORD thy God, which have brought thee out of the land of Egypt, out of the house of bondage" (Ex. 20 : 2).

This law in its external aspect, though holy and just and good, was antagonistic to the sinful nature of the people, and hence if they were to realise their relation to God as his redeemed people, provision must be made to meet its claims and to guarantee its fulfilment in the people themselves. We, therefore, find that in the process of time its claims were actually fulfilled in the obedience of Christ. The covenant, however, made provision, not only to instate its beneficiaries into it, but to enable them to exercise the loving obedience which the law required. The aim of the law was to instruct and command **from without** while the covenant qualified the Church to perform that obedience **from within.** The consummating purpose of the covenant being to establish his people in communion with himself, God the Holy Spirit implants the law within their hearts. This simply means that God creates in the hearts of his people a disposition which leads them spontaneously and lovingly to render the obedience required. All this is provided in the covenant. "A new heart also will I give you, and a new spirit will I put within you: and I will take the stony heart out of your flesh, and I will give you an heart of flesh. And I will put my spirit within you, and cause you to walk in my statutes, and ye shall keep my judgments, and do them" (Ezek. 36 : 26, 27). "For this is the covenant that I will make with the house of Israel after those days, saith the Lord; I will put my laws into their mind, and write them in their hearts: and I will be to them a God, and they shall be to me a people" (Heb. 8 : 10). This is the consummation of the covenant and brings its blessings to the highest level possible: for his law is in their hearts and he is their God and they are his people.

VII. THE CONDITION OF THE COVENANT

According to the Confession of Faith: "The Lord was pleased to make a second **covenant,** commonly called the Covenant of Grace: whereby he freely offereth unto sinners life and salvation by Jesus Christ, requiring of them faith in him, that they may be saved."[40] Holding the view, as we do, that God's covenant to man is an administration of grace and promise, and consequently unilateral, still we do not exclude the idea of mutuality and consent upon the part of the beneficiaries. And we must take into account the truth that God comes to man and graciously establishes his covenant with him and that he must believe in order that he may enter into it. While we are bound to hold that God himself fulfils all its conditions in the case of the elect, it is of the utmost importance in preaching the Gospel to insist that faith is indispensible to the enjoyment of the benefits of the covenant (John 3 : 16, 36; Acts 8 : 37; Rom. 10 : 9). It is therefore quite proper to call faith a condition so long as we recognise that it does not signify a meritorious or procuring cause of salvation. It is a condition of order, or an instrument or means to obtain an interest in the Gospel. Since the word **condition** has, however, been abused, the word **instrument** seems preferable.

"No human wit can evade the fact, that God proposes to man a something for him to do, which, if done, will secure redemption: if neglected will ensure damnation, and that something is in one sense a condition. But of what kind? Paul everywhere contrasts the condition of works, and the condition of faith. This contrast will be sufficiently established, and all danger of human merits, being intruded will be obviated, if it be observed that faith is only the appointed instrument for receiving free

40. **Westminster Confession,** VII-III.

grace purchased by our Surety. It owes its organic virtue as such, to God's mere appointment, not to the virtue of its own nature. In the Covenant of Works, the fulfilment of the condition on man's part earned the result: justification by its proper moral merit. In the Covenant of Grace, the condition has no moral merit to earn the promised grace, being merely an act of receptivity. In the Covenant of Works, man was required to fulfil the condition in his own strength. In the Covenant of Grace, strength is given to him to believe from God."[41]

III. THE PERSON AND WORK OF CHRIST

THE DOCTRINE OF THE PERSON AND WORK OF CHRIST

Soteriology, or the doctrine of salvation, includes the execution and application of the redemption of the Church and embraces within it the doctrine of Christ's Person and work (Dr Hodge and Dr Strong). Dr Berkhof says that soteriology treats of the communication of the blessings of salvation and excludes Christology, or the doctrine of the Saviour, which precedes it. Christology stresses what Christ does for his people and soteriology what the Spirit of Christ does in his people. If we accept the classification suggested by Dr Berkhof, we discuss: 1. The doctrine of the Person and work of Christ. 2. The doctrine of the Spirit's work. The first heading is Christology and the second, Soteriology.

41. Dabney. **Op sit.** page 438.

CHAPTER XI

JESUS CHRIST, THE SON OF GOD

I. CHRIST THE MESSIAH

In stating the position that the promised Messiah has already come and that Jesus Christ the Son of God is that Person, we prove that the Old Testament prophecies relating to the advent and work of Christ have been fulfilled. In one word, the phophecies of the Old Testament as against the Jews is that the Messiah has come and that he is Jesus Christ the Son of God. In proving this truth, we take for granted the following concessions on their part: (1) that they acknowledge the truth of the Old Testament Messianic prophecies, (2) that they acknowledge that these writings were in existence long before Christ appeared, and (3) that the Messianic prophecies relate to a Saviour who was to come. Though Jewish believers acknowledge these truths, they deny that the prophecies refer to Christ or that they have been fulfilled.

In arguing against unbelievers who refuse to accept the truth of the prophecies or who maintain that the prophecies are not sufficiently specific to limit the application to Christ, endeavours are made to point out the true meaning of these prophecies showing their correspondence to the events referred to in the life of Christ. These proofs are to be found in a considerable number of passages which are distinct and specific and cannot be applied to anyone else. A diligent enquirer will find a strong body of prophetical truth and a series of predictions commencing early in the writings of the Old Testament and extending over a long period of time, which, with increasing clearness and cumulative force, point individually and collectively to their accomplishment in the Person of our Saviour.

II. MESSIANIC PROPHECY

Genesis 3 : 15: "And I will put enmity between thee and the woman, and between thy seed and her seed; it shall bruise thy head, and thou shalt bruise his heel." This is the first Messianic prophecy, and has been called the first Gospel promise or the **Prot. Evangelium.** Notwithstanding the obscurity of this passage when taken by itself, it embodies a sentence against the tempter and a promise of deliverance for fallen men. The seed of the woman is referred to in the promise made to Abraham: "And in thy seed shall all the nations of the earth be blessed" (Gen. 22 : 18). This passage is quoted by Paul as referring to Christ. "Now to Abraham and his seed were the promises made. He saith not, And to seeds, as of many; but as of one, And to thy seed, which is Christ" (Gal. 3 : 16).

Genesis 49 : 10. "The sceptre shall not depart from Judah, nor a lawgiver from between his feet, until Shiloh come; and unto him shall the gathering of the people be." This passage has been applied by Jews as well as Christians to the Messiah. Up to the time of the birth of Christ the sceptre did remain with Judah, until the death of Herod the Great, but seventy years after his birth, at the destruction of Jerusalem, the power, polity, and records of the Jewish people ceased to exist.

Isaiah 7 : 14. The passage particularises the birth of the Saviour as being born of a virgin. Much ingenuity has been resorted to in order to deprive this passage of its peculiar force, but the keenest investigative criticism on the other side allows the traditional meaning of the passage. To attempt to weaken the force of this passage in the light of the approbation with which it is quoted in the first Gospel (Matt. 1 : 23) must arise from wilful ignorance or a rooted desire to impugn the power and wisdom of God.

Isaiah 9 : 6 undoubtedly refers to Christ, and Isaiah 52 and 53 though written centuries before the incarnation are as accurate and specific in their description of the sufferings of Christ as if written by an eyewitness. Dan. 9 : 24-27 specifies the **time** Christ would appear and the **work** he would perform. Much paper has been spoiled in discussing the recondite meanings of these passages. So far as dates are concerned, the various opinions do not differ more than ten years or so. If we accept the common usage of prophetical chronology, we may presume that Daniel prophesies that forty-nine years from the end of the captivity the city, Jerusalem, would be rebuilt and that four hundred and thirty years after the rebuilding of the city, the Messiah would appear; and that during the period of one week of years he would confirm the covenant and in the middle of that week be cut off. In order to fit in this prophecy with the advent of Christ, there is no need to juggle with figures, and this some of the Jews well knew, for they were so perplexed by this prophecy that they refused to discuss it, and they pronounced a curse on any who presumed to calculate the weeks of Daniel. Mal. 3 : 1 refers to Christ as the Messenger of the covenant, who was expected and who would soon appear. This is confirmed by Matt. 11 : 10, Mark 1 : 2, and Luke 7 : 27.

From these and other proofs it has been demonstrated that Christ is the Person referred to in the prophecies and that he came in the time predicted. Herod was the last king of the Jews, and before the end of the century Jerusalem was destroyed and the Jews were scattered over the face of the earth, thus losing their identity as a nation though not as a people. The sceptre with its pomp and accompaniments had departed. Jerusalem was no more, and it would be impossible after that time to work out the lineage of the Messiah, since the genealogical records of the chosen people had disappeared. All the prophecies relating to Christ in their essentials and circumstances have been accurately fulfilled. He was born of the tribe of Judah of the family of David. He was preceded by a forerunner and born of a virgin. All these prophecies have been fulfilled in Christ and can never be fulfilled in another.

III. THE PERSON OF CHRIST

The gravest errors in Christology have arisen in connection with the constitution of the Person of our Lord. The teaching of Scripture on this important doctrine has been mis-represented by individuals and sections of the Christian Church. This has necessitated creedal statements by the Christian Church against those who professed to accept the Scriptures but who rejected what is called the orthodox interpretation. It is quite a common experience to meet with those who profess to believe Scripture, are quite ready to quote it, and are prepared to charge others with repudiating the Bible because others do not accept their views of Scripture teaching. The Fathers of the Church in the early Christian centuries had to contend with such persons, and they found it necessary to declare the true doctrine in such a specific phraseology as would confute the heresies of so-called believers in Scripture. Arius, for example, would acknowledge that Christ was God and yet assert that he was merely a creature. The classic deliverance on this subject is to be found in what have been called the **five points.**

1st. Jesus of Nazareth is very God, possessing the divine nature and all its essential properties, 2nd. He is also true man, his human nature derived by generation from the stock of Adam. 3rd. These natures continue united in his Person, yet ever remain true divinity, and true humanity, unmixed and as to essence unchanged. So that Christ possesses at once in the unity of his Person two spirits with all their essential attributes, a human consciousness, mind, heart, and will, and a divine consciousness, mind, feeling and will . . . 4th. Nevertheless they constitute as thus united one single Person, and the attributes of both natures belong to the one Person. 5th. The Personality is not a new one constituted by the union of the two natures in the womb of the Virgin, but it is the eternal and immutable Person of the **Logos,** which in time assumed unto itself a nascent human nature with the divine in the Personality which eternally belongs to the latter.[42]

"The only Redeemer of God's elect is the Lord Jesus Christ, who, being the eternal Son of God, became man, and so was, and continueth to be, God and man in two distinct natures, and one person, for ever."[43]

42. Dr A. A. Hodge. **Outlines,** page 380.
43. **Shorter Catechism,** 21.

IV. THE HUMAN NATURE OF CHRIST

In order to simplify discussion we may note that the main errors combated are: (1) the denial of Christ's absolute Deity, (2) the denial of his real humanity, (3) the assertion that he possesses only one nature, (4) the assertion that he possesses two persons, (5) the assertion that the two natures interpenetrate, and (6) the assertion that the human nature was sinful. Christ, the Second Person of the Trinity as distinguished from the other two Persons, assumed unto himself a human nature with all the infirmities thereof, sin excepted. The human nature he assumed, that is a true body and a reasonable soul, was impersonal. A nature has been defined by the terms **substance** or **essence**. A person is an intelligent, individual subsistence. Personality is a nature with individuality added. A true body and a reasonable soul must be thought of as including a person when there is a union of these two. It is therefore difficult, if not impossible except in an abstract way, to think of a true body and a reasonable soul without a personality. The human nature of Christ was never without a personality although **per se** we may think of it as impersonal. Neither will it do to say that the human nature of Christ was incomplete because not personalised, since, at the moment in which the human nature was brought into being, it was taken into the Person of Christ. Whether we follow the drift of these terms or not, the purpose in stating them is to guard against the idea that Christ possessed two persons. The human nature assumed by Christ does not therefore lack any of its essential qualities and was never for a moment impersonal. It should be noted that a human soul or a human body or both of them together do not constitute a person. The person is so constituted when both are united together mysteriously by God. It will, of course, be replied that a soul separated from the body possesses personality. But in dealing with this abstruse subject, it should be considered that the person **was** in the body and that the body **belongs** to the person, even if they are now separated. Even in this case, however, the soul does not possess a complete personality.

Scripture specifically states that Christ was man. He was conceived in the womb of the Virgin Mary by the Holy

Ghost. He was nurtured by his mother as other children were, and he increased in wisdom and stature and in favour with God and man. We must, therefore, believe that as man his mind was infantile, that he grew in intelligence and wisdom, and that he learned by reflection, observation, and experience. It has been said that the consciousness that he was the Son of God dawned upon him at the age of twelve when he was in his Father's house. The mystery of the workings of his human consciousness may not correspond with this pious thought, but we do know that he suffered and obeyed as man, was crucified and rose from the dead. He was subject to natural infirmities such as hunger and thirst, physical weariness and pain; and he endured sorrow, temptation, persecution, and unspeakable bitterness of soul. But as to moral infirmities he had none, and he had no experience of penitence or remorse. How these frames and feelings co-existed with the possession of the Divine nature, we cannot fathom; but as a truth distinct and fully proved, we have abundant evidence in the Gospels.

In the statement that the "Word was made flesh" it is denied that God was changed into a man or that he divested himself of his Divine attributes, since the Divine nature remained what it was before. The meaning is that the Son of God possessed a human nature in addition to the Divine nature. The human nature of Christ was no different in its essence from the nature of any other human being, in any state; that is, whether in a state of innocence, of guilt, in a state of grace, or glory. And if we accept the dictum that holiness and sin are not properties or entities, we can readily understand that the nature of Christ and the nature of Adam were the same. Adam in innocence had no natural infirmities; the Saviour had. According to theological phraseology, Christ was unlike Adam in the sense that he was not able to sin, **non posse peccare;** whereas Adam was able not to sin, **posse non peccare.** How the non posse peccare can be applied to Christ in view of his natural infirmities and the temptations with which he was beset is a problem which theologians have not been able to solve. But when it is said that Christ "was made in the likeness of sinful flesh," it is intimated to us that he united himself so closely to sinful man as was possible without partaking of his sinful nature.

As to the expressions in the Messianic Psalms and his life-experiences which appear to give the impression that he was conscious of sin, these are to be explained in the light of the truth that he not only bore the sufferings and penalty of sin, but that he made sin his own when he suffered in our room and stead.

It has been stated that Christ possessed two distinct natures but only one personality, two centres of consciousness but only one centre of self-consciousness; for though the Saviour spoke in terms of his human nature, he never spoke in terms of his human self because there was only one Self, the Person of Christ. An attempt has been made to distinguish between the two consciousnesses, but it is not likely that a proper explanation can be given. The difference between consciousness and self-consciousness may be partly explained as follows. A human being is sometimes conscious of self. Here the object of thought and the subject are the same; that is, he is thinking of the self that thinks. One may also be thinking of something outwith his very self. The first is self-consciousness and the second, consciousness. The Self of Christ is the Person of Christ, and in terms of his human nature he was conscious of his human frame and feelings in a manner analogous to a person who is conscious of a physical pain in his arm. But in terms of his Person he was self-conscious; that is, he was conscious of himself as the Son in relation to his Father.

It has been pointed out that right views of the Person of Christ will take into account that the Person is the controlling factor in all the activities of the God-man. The two natures are distinct, one being infinite and the other finite, and so what is true of one nature cannot be ascribed to the other in respect of these categories. If we ascribe human activities to the Divine nature, we limit the unlimited. On the other hand, if we ascribe Divine attributes to the human nature, we destroy its integrity. At the same time we hold to the truth that what is true of **both** natures is ascribed to the Person. He is Prophet, Priest, and King in both natures. And what is true of the **human nature** is ascribed to the Person. He was crucified, he died, he rose again. What is true of the **Divine nature** is also ascribed to the Person. "I and the Father are one" (John 10 : 30). "Before Abraham was, I am" (John 8 : 58). The attempt has been made by individuals and sects to ascribe Divinity to the human nature of Christ. It is said that on the human side he knew all, was everywhere, was able to do anything without restraint and without difficulty. To apply some of these expressions to the Saviour in respect of his human nature is a grave error, since it makes it Divine. In opposition to such views Scripture tells us that Christ suffered and obeyed. Neither suffering nor obedience can be ascribed to the Divine nature, but it can be ascribed to the Person who is God and as God suffered and died in the human nature. Such a view of the Saviour's Person gives us a better appreciation of the reality of his manhood and the humiliation and sorrows he underwent in order to effect our salvation.

V. THE DIVINE NATURE

In seeking to overthrow the absolute Deity of Christ, heretics prove that he was man, which they labour to do. This being admitted and a great concession being granted, they attempt to prove, or rather infer from this, that he was a mere man. Then they prove that God is one. This again being admitted, all they require to do is to deny the true force of passages which refer to Christ's Deity and his Personality as the Son of God. We are told that the word **Trinity** is not used in the Bible; neither is the word **unity.** But we are clearly taught in Scripture that there is a distinction as to Persons. Christ speaks of himself, and he speaks of his Father as a different self and of the Holy Spirit as a different self. This cannot be denied and if men were satisfied with these explanations, it would not be necessary for theologians to make such distinctions in respect of person, essence, property, and accident, which evidently must be done in order to meet the objectors on their own ground. It is true that the word **person** does not convey precisely the same meaning as it does in human relations; but when Christ speaks of himself and his Father, he is not speaking of one Person but of two.

The production of proofs from Scripture that the Second Person is God must begin by an examination of the various passages and references in Scripture which point to that proof. The method sometimes used by divines is to bring the doctrine to the proof by stating the evidence under four or five heads; namely, the **pre-existence, titles, attributes, works,** and **worship** which are ascribed to Christ in the same sense as they are applied to the Father. Any **one** of these five proofs being established, the argument is conclusive. But theologians have succeeded without much difficulty in proving Christ's Deity under all those headings. Where the **pre-existence** of Christ is admitted, as by Arians and Semi-Arians, it must also be proved that Christ was not a creature but God Himself.

Under the heading of the **works of Christ,** we find abundant proof in Scripture of his Deity. The following are quoted as examples, which may be multiplied. **Creation:** "All things were made by him" (John 1 : 3). "My Father worketh hitherto, and I work" (John 5 : 17). "For by him were all things created" (Col. 1 : 16). "By him all things consist" (Col. 1 : 17). **Miracles:** "For as the Father raiseth up the dead, and quickeneth them; even so the Son quickeneth whom he will" (John 5 : 21). **Judgment:** "For the Father judgeth no man, but hath committed all judgment unto the Son" (John 5 : 22). "When the Son of man shall come in his glory, and all the holy angels with him, then shall he sit upon the throne of his glory: and before him shall be gathered all nations: and he shall separate them one from another, as a shepherd divideth his sheep from the goats; and he shall set the sheep on his right hand, but the goats on the left" (Matt. 25 : 31-33). The evidence of these few Scriptures alone are sufficient to attest the truth that Christ possesses absolute Deity. The creation of all things, the performance of miracles of Divine power, and the right to judge the eternal destinies of all men imply the Divine attributes of omnipotence, omniscience, and omnipresence.

VI. THE CONSUBSTANTIALITY OF THE SON

The doctrine of the consubstantiality of the Son with the Father was treated in the Fourth Chapter in the discussion of the Trinity. There is some repetition in its treatment here. This doctrine was formulated in 325 A.D., and is incorporated in the Nicene Creed. It was directed against

Arians and Semi-Arians and settled once and for all the Confession of the true Church on this subject.

By **consubstantiality** is meant that Christ is not a creature and that he is of the same essence as the Father, possessing the whole Divine nature and attributes. The term used to express this relation was **homo-ousios.** The word was used by the fathers to indicate that Christ not only possessed the same nature as the Father but was of one and the same substance, or the same numerical essence. This is in accordance with the teachings of Scripture which assert that the three are one in nature though distinguished by personal properties. The word **homo-ousios** was directed against Arians who used the word **heter-ousios** to indicate that he was of a different substance from the Father, and against the Semi-Arians who used the word **homoi-ousios** to denote that he was of a like substance with the Father. It seems remarkable that the omission of one letter in a word should make such a difference as between the true doctrine of the Son and heresy, but the difference consisted in the fact that one party in the Church refused to acknowledge that Christ was truly God though they admitted that he was like God. A moment's thought will convince any reasonable person that similarity is far different from identity. There are counterfeit coins, counterfeit gold and silver, etc. They are like but are not the genuine. Those who preferred the word **homo-ousios** maintained the absolute Deity of the Son possessing the same numerical nature as the Father, while those who preferred the term **homoi-ousios** would only acknowledge that Christ was like God. It is but fair to say, however, that there were persons in the Fourth Century engaged in this bitter controversy who, though they objected to the term **homo-ousios,** still held to the orthodox doctrine.

CHAPTER XII

THE OFFICES OF CHRIST

I. THE MEDIATORIAL OFFICE

The general office or function which the Redeemer assumed is that of Mediator between God and men. This office, committed to him by the Father, was not only that of a messenger or advocate, but that of an efficient peace-maker to whom was entrusted the administration of salvation and reconciliation by the sacrifice of himself. "There is one God, and one mediator between God and men, the man Christ Jesus" (1 Tim. 2 : 5). The word **man** is used in the last phrase to denote the incarnate Son. The great design of the mediatorial office of Christ was to make efficient reconciliation between God and men. In the execution of this work he administers the whole economy of salvation as Prophet, Priest, and King, both in the estate of humiliation and exaltation.

Some have denied that Christ could be Mediator between God and men since he himself is God. For the explanation of this seeming contradiction it is expedient to distinguish between the ontological and economic Trinity. As explained earlier, the former constitutes the intrinsic relations subsisting within the Trinity. These relations are ontological in the sense that they refer to the internal relations of the Trinity. The economic relations, however, have to do with matters outside the Trinity, such as the salvation of men. In these economic relations the Father was the offended party while the Son was the mediating party or Mediator. These distinctions are to be found in Scripture. "I and my Father are one" (John 10 : 30). "Before Abraham was, I am" (John 8 : 58). These passages refer to the ontological Trinity or the original constitution of the Trinity. But when Christ speaks of the economic Trinity or his relation to God as Mediator, he speaks of an office which was not original but assumed. "My Father is greater than I" (John 14 : 28). "I have finished the work which thou gavest me to do" (John 17 : 4). "I came down from heaven, not to do mine own will, but the will of him that sent me" (John 6 : 38).

It has also been disputed whether Christ as Mediator acted in one or both natures. The Romanists say that Christ was Mediator in his human nature only, since it was impossible that God could mediate between man and himself. This has been referred to in the previous paragraph. The true doctrine is that the single Person of the God-man performed all actions involving the use of Divine attributes in virtue of the Divine nature, and all actions involving the use of human attributes in virtue of the human nature. But all the acts of the Mediator are attributed not to the natures but to the Person or Agent performing them. An imperfect analogy is that the actions of a human person whether mental as thinking or material as eating are attributed to the person or agent and not to the material or immaterial part of his being.

It has been proved from Scripture that Christ possesses two natures and that this was necessary to constitute him a perfect Saviour. It was necessary that Christ be very God: that he might represent God, that he might adequately reveal God to man, that he might be able to endure the curse due to us for sin, that his sacrifice might possess an infinite value, and that he might be competent to administer effectually to all the redeemed the fruits of his Passion. It was also necessary that he be man: that he might represent man, that he might be passable and so suffer, that he might suffer in the nature that sinned, that he might leave us a perfect human example, that he might sympathetically enter into the trials of his Church, and that he might bring redeemed humanity into the very bosom of God.

The distinction between the three offices of Christ, as Prophet, Priest, and King, is one of the common doctrines of theology. This distinction has been criticised but it is not difficult to prove from Scripture that Christ was a Prophet, Priest, and King. We are, however, to remember that the three offices or functions are united in one Person and we must not sharply discriminate since no single work can be limited to any of these offices. When Christ teaches, he is a royal and priestly Teacher; when he rules, he is a prophetic and priestly King; and when he intercedes, he is a prophetic and kingly Priest. If the question be asked which is the most important function or office of the Redeemer, it should be answered that all three are necessary to complete his mediatoral work. At the same time, it should be understood that the prophetic and kingly offices are based upon his Priesthood.

A Mediator was not required in the state of innocence, for notwithstanding the infinite distance between the Creator and the creature there was no obstacle to the union and communion of the latter with God. His relationship to him as a moral being consisted in his innocency and perfection. But when man rebelled against his Creator, he lost his moral excellency and became ignorant, guilty, and polluted. And if he were to be restored a Mediator was required. Hence, Christ is represented in Scripture as such a Mediator, being a Prophet, Priest, and King. The prophetic office respects our ignorance, which Christ as the Light of the world has come to remove; the priestly function respects our guilt, which the Saviour has removed by the sacrifice of himself; and the kingly office has respect to our depravity or pollution, which Christ removes by the sanctification of our nature so that in the language of Scripture, he "is made unto us wisdom, and righteousness, and sanctification, and redemption" (1 Cor. 1 : 30). The last word in this passage has been taken to mean that Christ as the Mediator is made unto us, in view of these three functions of the Mediatorial office, a complete redemption from ignorance, guilt, and pollution.

In dealing with this subject divines refer to the office sustained by the Holy Ghost in relation to the mediatorial office of Christ such as, the formation and replenishing of his human nature and the acting for him and leading to him in the quickening and sanctifying of his people. It has also been pointed out that while Christ makes intercession for his people in heaven, the Spirit makes intercession **within** them by exciting and leading them in prayer and praise. And according to the Scriptural formula we have an introduction **to** the Father, **through** the Son, **by** the Spirit (Eph. 2 : 18).

Christ continues to exercise his mediatorial office in heaven by making effectual his own sacrifice for sin to all his people, by undertaking their protection, and by interceding for them before the throne. How long Christ will continue to exercise this mediatorial office in heaven has been a matter of dispute. It has been said that the office is eternal, and this is partly based on such proof texts as Luke 1 : 33, Heb. 6 : 20, Heb. 7 : 17, and other passages. It has also been argued that the office will cease after its design has been accomplished. Scripture has been cited in favour of this view where it is said, "Then cometh the end, when we shall have delivered up the kingdom to God, even the Father; when he shall have put down all rule and all authority and power" (1 Cor. 15 : 24-28).

II. THE PROPHETIC OFFICE

There are three different words in the Old Testament for prophet and one in the New, and it is presumed that the general meaning of all these is that a prophet denotes one who receives revelations from God and one who speaks in his name. Dr Berkhof lays emphasis on this distinction, for he says that Abimelech, Pharaoh, and Nebuchadnezzar all received revelations but were no prophets. The prophetic function is therefore passive and active, passive to receive and active to give. The former, says the above writer, is more important because it controls the active element. It should also be noted that a prophet is not one who merely speaks of the future but one who speaks out, though the future may and does often occur in his prophecy. A prophet is one who is so by Divine calling, receiving Divine communications, which he reveals to others. A prophet is therefore a spokesman on behalf of God revealing truth to man.

Theologians point out that Christ's exercise of the prophetic office began before the incarnation, was continued while he was on earth, and will continue throughout eternity. The office is exercised externally through his Word and Spirit, and internally by the illumination of the heart. Christ exercises this office mediately through his messengers, his Word, and his Spirit; and immediately, while he was on earth, and since then, before the throne. The Scripture proofs for the prophetic office are scattered throughout Scripture. The following are commonly cited: Deut. 18 : 15; Isa. 11 : 2-5; Matt. 7 : 29; Matt. 21 : 11, 46; Luke 7 : 16; John 1 : 9; John 3 : 2; John 7 : 16.

The prophetic office has not been disputed much in any age, but when the emphasis has been laid exclusively on his prophetic office, it has been retorted that Christ did not come to teach but to do. It is proper to say that he came to do both. According to Old Testament prophecy he is called "a witness to the people" (Isa. 55 : 4). Christ himself refers to his prophetic office: "The Spirit of the Lord is upon me, because he has anointed me to preach the gospel to the poor; he hath sent me to heal the broken-hearted, to preach deliverance to the captives, and recovering of sight to the blind, to set at liberty them that are bruised, to preach the acceptable year of the Lord" (Luke 4 : 18-19). There is a clear reference here to his prophetic office. In his conversation with Pilate he says that he has come to bear witness to the truth (John 18 : 37).

It hardly needs to be said that Christ was no ordinary prophet, for he is source to all others who prophesied. This is brought out in a striking way in Scripture itself. "God, who at sundry times and in divers manners spake in time past unto the fathers by the prophets, hath in these last days spoken unto us by his Son" (Heb. 1 : 1, 2). The prophets were mere instruments who here and there shed light upon the doctrines of the truth according to the measure in which they reecived it from God, but the Son who was the source of all this light gave it forth will fulness, authority, and ease. The fact that the Son of God himself came to earth and took our nature in order to reveal to us all that it was necessary for us to know should fill us with astonishment and gratitude. As a prophet he not only reveals to us the whole truth, but He himself is Truth. The prophetic office as exercised by Christ is based upon the fact that we are not able to discover the character and will of God until he reveals it to us.

III. THE PRIESTILY OFFICE

The Shorter Catechism, Q. 25, says: "Christ executeth the office of a priest, in his once offering up of himself a sacrifice to satisfy divine justice, and reconcile us to God; and in making continual intercession for us." In the Scriptures we are told: "For every high priest taken from among men is ordained for men in things pertaining to God, that he may offer both gifts and sacrifices for sins" (Heb. 5 : 1). The general idea of the priestly function is that of mediatorship, and includes the offering of sacrifice and intercession. And in conceiving of the priestly function of Christ, we are to think of him as offering himself a sacrifice for sin. This Priest was taken from among men (Heb. 5 : 1), was chosen by God (Heb. 5 : 4), was morally perfect (Heb. 7 : 26), offered sacrifice for sins (Heb. 5 : 1), and offered sacrifice once (Heb. 10 : 14). It is expressly declared and emphasised that Christ was a Priest, a real Priest, consecrated by the oath of God, and possessing all priestly qualifications. The sacrifices and services of the Mosaic dispensation could not take away sin (Heb. 10 : 4), but they were all typical; that is, they pointed to the only and real sacrifice which could and did take away sin. The Epistle to the Hebrews sets forth at large and in detail the superiority of the priesthood of Christ in its nature, efficacy, and perfection.

The following passages show clearly the nature, design, and efficacy of Christ's priestly functions. "Christ was once offered to bear the sins of many" (Heb. 9 : 28). "A merciful and faithful high priest in things pertaining to God, to make reconciliation for the sins of the people" (Heb. 2 : 17). Christ . . . suffered . . . , the just for the unjust" (1 Pet. 3 : 18). "He is the propitation for our sins" (1 John 2 : 2). "Christ also both loved us, and hath given himself for us as an offering and a sacrifice to God for a sweetsmelling savour" (Eph. 5 : 2). "Who his own self bare our sins in his own body on the tree, that we, being dead to sins, should live unto righteousness: by whose stripes ye were healed" (1 Pet. 2 : 24).

1. The Order of Melchisedec

The subject of Melchisedec has given rise to much discussion. Christ as a Priest had as much in common with Aaron as with Melchisedec, so we presume that the likenesses are found in certain aspects of Melchisedec's office which Aaron lacked. As a **person** Melchisedec was born and died as other men, but as to his **office** he was a royal priest, possessing an exclusive and perpetual priesthood and dispensing blessings to Abraham and the whole Levitical priesthood and their posterity. The priesthood of Aaron, however, lacked regal authority, was interrupted by death, and consequently was exercised by many priests. The priesthood of Christ is a royal priesthood, without predecessor or successor, concentrated in one Person and not subject to interruption by death. **His** priesthood, therefore, is **royal, underived, perpetual,** and **exclusive. None** of these features are to be found in the Aaronic priesthood and they are **all** found in Christ.

The only reference to Melchisedec in the Old Testament is in Genesis 14 : 18-20 and Psa. 110. The New Testament references are: Hebrews 5 : 6, 10, 11; 6 : 20; 7 : 1-21. The Genesis reference does not say that Melchisedec offered sacrifices at the altar on behalf of Abraham, but we may presume that he did. He blessed Abraham and refreshed him with bread and wine. And Abraham as the father of the faithful offered him homage and gave him tithes of all. Between the pivots of Heb. 5 : 6 and Heb. 5 : 10, the priesthood of Christ after the order of Melchisedec is stated to be based upon the offering, obedience, and perfection of the Son of God. This perfection makes him competent to become the Author of salvation to his people. In Heb. 6 : 20 Jesus is represented as having entered Heaven itself, a Priest after the order of Melchisedec; and in Heb. 7 : 24, 25 it is shown that he has an unchangeable priesthood and that he is able to save to the uttermost; that is, he is able as the perpetual and exalted Priest to bless sinners and to receive their homage and service. It is possible, therefore, that the priesthood of Christ is not only represented as royal, underived, exclusive, and perpetual; but that it is also exercised in the state of exaltation. And if the royal priesthood of Christ does not lay emphasis upon his priesthood in Heaven as dispensing salvation and receiving the homage of his people, it certainly does not exclude this feature of his priesthood. The priesthood of Aaron ended at his death, but the priesthood of Christ in respect of the blessings which were the fruit of the same had their fullest exercise and eternal revenue after he entered into that within the veil, made an high priest for ever after the order of Melchisedec.[44]

IV. THE KINGLY OFFICE

"Christ executeth the office of a king, in subduing us to himself, in ruling and defending us, and in restraining and conquering all his and our enemies."[45] The regal office of Christ is distinguished from his universal dominion as the Son of God and refers to the kingdom he rules as the God-man and the Mediator of his Church. This is conferred upon him as the Saviour of the Church. As the Mediator the whole universe is his imperium, which is ordered in all things according to his will for his own glory and the well-being of his people. To this end he overrules the movements and destinies of nations to subserve the interests of his redeemed people. Christ was formally invested with his regal authority as the reward of his labours when he was exalted to the right hand of God (Ps. 2 : 8, 9; Phil. 2 : 9-11).

Christ as the Mediator exercises his dominion over the Church by calling sinners into the kingdom, administering all its affairs, and restraining and conquering all the enemies of his people. He is Head of the Church in virtue of his union with the people of his choice, and King in virtue of his absolute authority. These functions he exercises as the God-man. The Headship of the Church, in the opinion of Berkhof, is subservient to the Kingship. This view is not contrary to the logical order of the Westminster Confession on this subject.

In further considering this subject a distinction is made between the invisible and the visible Church. The visible members are those, together with their children, who make

---

44. Bruce. **Humiliation of Christ,** pages 281-283.
45. **Shorter Catechism,** 26.

a profession of faith and obedience to Christ. The invisible members are those who are truly his people in heart as well as in life. Those visible members who are only so in profession, subserve the designs of Christ's kingdom through the exercise of his restraining grace. Much controversy has been provoked as to who are true spiritual members, and this has largely expended itself in the discussion of non-essentials. Christ has plainly told us who they are; and even if we are unable to judge our own state and condition, the marks of those people are described from various aspects in the Word of God. These blessed people are described by Christ himself as being poor in spirit, mourning, meek, hungering and thirsting after righteousness, merciful, pure, and peaceable; and enduring persecution for righteousness' sake (Matt. 5 : 3-12).

Modern teaching has made a distinction between the **Kingdom of God** and the **Kingdom of Heaven.** The former, it is said, is the universal kingdom of God; the latter, the future mediatorial kingdom of Christ. This view has been partly abandoned because the distinction has not been proved to be valid and because it serves no useful purpose. It is truly remarkable how much paper and ink is wasted in discussions of fine points which serve no practical purpose whatever. The terms referred to are evidently interchangeable as used by Matthew and Luke, who quote the same statements of Christ, one referring them to the kingdom of God and the other to the kingdom of heaven (Matt. 13 : 11 with Mark 4 : 11; Matt. 13 : 31 with Mark 4 : 30; see also Luke 8 : 10). The kingdom of Christ is both present and future, but in its essential features — whether past, present, or future — it consists of those who are subject to the Kingship of our Lord.

"Christ as the Mediator received this appointment as Mediatorial King in the depths of eternity, and began to function as such immediately after the fall (Prov. 8 : 23, Psa. 2 : 6). During the Old dispensation he carried on the work as King partly through the judges of Israel, and partly through typical kings. But though he was appointed to rule as Mediator even before the incarnation, he did not publicly and formally assume his throne and inaugurate his spiritual kingdom until the time of his ascension and elevation at the right hand of God (Acts 2 : 29-36; Phil. 2 : 5-11)."[46]

The question has been agitated as to the duration of the Kingdom of Christ. The above writer has summed up this subject as follows. Christ's kingship over the universe was the promised reward of his work so that the God-man in his human nature was now made to share in the glory of his royal dominion. This dominion will last until the victory over his enemies is complete and the kingdom will then be returned to the Father (1 Cor. 15 : 24-28). Some say Christ did not become King until his ascension; others, that he will not sit upon the throne as Mediator until the second advent. But he was appointed King from eternity though he was not inaugurated until his ascension. Some think, as Dick and Kuyper, that this kingship will cease when the work of redemption is completed, but Berkhof maintains that Scripture teaches it will endure forever.

46. Dr Berkhof. **In loc.**

CHAPTER XIII

THE STATES OF CHRIST

I. THE HUMILIATION OF CHRIST
    1. The Incarnation (1) The doctrine of the Kenosis
    2. The Virgin Birth
II. THE SUFFERINGS OF CHRIST
III. THE DEATH OF CHRIST
IV. THE DESCENT INTO THE GRAVE
V. THE EXALTATION OF CHRIST
    1. The Resurrection (1) The Importance, (2) Its Proof, (3) The Nature of the Resurrection, (4) Denials of the Resurrection
    2. The Ascension
    3. The Session at the Right Hand of God
    4. The Physical Return of Christ

"Christ, as our Redeemer, executeth the offices of a prophet, of a priest, and of a king, both in his estate of humiliation and exaltation."[47] The estate of humiliation has been said to extend from his conception to his burial, and the state of exaltation from his resurrection to the second advent and forever.

I. THE HUMILIATION OF CHRIST

A brief survey of the humiliation of the Mediator, that is the God-man, may be given under the following headings; namely, his incarnation, his sufferings, his death, and his descent into the grave. These states follow one another in a descending scale. The doctrine is built upon such passages as Acts 2 : 23; 2 Cor. 8 : 9; Gal. 3 : 13; Phil. 2 : 6-8; 1 Pet. 2 : 23, 24; Rev. 1 : 5.

1. The Incarnation

(1) **The Doctrine of the Kenosis.** Some theologians have supposed that the assumption of our nature was rather a condescension than a humiliation, since every mediatorial

47. **Shorter Catechism,** 23.

act supposes the constitution of his Person as the God-man and since he retains this nature in his state of exaltation. This has been said to be a distinction without a difference. Reformed theology distinguishes two elements in the humiliation of Christ; namely, the **kenosis,** or emptying, consisting in the veiling of the Divine glory; and the **tapeiriosis,** or the assumption of man's natural infirmities and his subjection to the demands and curse of the law issuing in his shameful death. The classic passage which is made the subject of the **kenosis** is Phil. 2 : 7, 8. The interpretation of this passage has given rise to various opinions, and there has been a difference of opinion even among the strictly orthodox. The best interpretation of the passage is probably given by Dr Gifford. According to this learned writer the subject spoken of is the Second Person of the Godhead, the **form of God** referring to the whole nature and essence of Deity. If this is the case the Son of God could not divest himself of this form without ceasing to be God. The **equality** with God mentioned in the text is the condition of glory and majesty which was the manifestation of his Divine nature and which he resigned for a time by taking the form of a servant.[48]

Christ, therefore, emptied himself by taking the form of a servant; that is, he became man. We have thus in the incarnation the mention of two natures, the Divine nature as the form of God and the human nature as the form of a servant. Hence, the Second Person, while he did not cease to be God, laid aside the equality of conditions which he possessed in his pre-incarnate state by taking the form of a servant, that is by becoming man. The view of the kenosis as elaborated by Bishop Gifford disposes of all the items which hint at any depotentation or limitation of the Divine nature, while at the same time it establishes the view that Christ assumed a real human nature, sin excepted.

2. The Virgin Birth

The orthodox doctrine that the human nature of Christ was conceived by the Holy Ghost in the womb of the Virgin Mary is based on such passages as Isa. 7 : 14; Matt. 1 : 18-

48. Sifford. **The Incarnation** (London, 1897).

20; Luke 1 : 27, 31, 34, 35; and Gal. 4 : 4. This doctrine has always been a part of the Church's creed from the earliest times and is held by the Roman as well as the Protestant communions. Its denial in modern times is a matter of concern to true believers.

Several arguments have been advanced to suggest that it is a doubtful doctrine and at best unimportant. Besides the supposed proof of its impossibility, it has been stated the Apostles do not insist upon it as they do on other doctrines, such as the Passion of Christ and the Resurrection. The short answer to this is that the virgin birth pre-supposes all the important doctrines of salvation, such as the Saviour's exclusion from the covenant of works and the guilt of sin, and his consequent fitness as the God-man to undertake the redemption and salvation of a countless multitude whom no man can number.

To those who may be enamoured of the new doctrine, it should be shown that the objections made against the virgin birth do not derive their force from the lack of Scriptural evidence but from the efforts made to dispose of that evidence in order to dispense with the miraculous features connected with the conception and birth of the Saviour. And, indeed, if there were not special circumstances connected with the glory of God and the good of man, it would be inconceivable that the Second Person of the Trinity would assume human nature according to the mode in which the Scriptures define it. The attempts made within recent years to modify the force of Isa. 7 : 14 and the proof text in Matt. 1 : 23 shows the scant respect paid by the destructive critics to the sacred text, and it would be needless to comment upon how little respect we should pay to their expositions of other texts in the Word of God.

II. THE SUFFERINGS OF CHRIST

The Lord's sufferings were twofold, ordinary and extra-ordinary. His ordinary sufferings were all those he endured in virtue of his being born of a woman, made under the law, and undergoing the sufferings, trials, and temptations which are to be found in a sinful world. These sufferings followed him during the whole course of his life so that it could be truly said of him that he was a man of sorrows and acquainted with grief. He suffered in soul and in body; and although some have emphasised his bodily sufferings and others his sufferings of soul, we must remember that since human nature includes both, Christ suffered in soul and body. Our Lord, while he was in this world, endured suffering from all points. His afflictions came from his own people and especially from the leaders of the Jewish Church, who sought to destroy him. He endured the greatest indignities from the state represented by the Roman power, but the greater guilt lay with the former power of its representatives (John 19 : 11). Christ also suffered at the hands of some of his disciples who failed to understand the purpose of his mission. They all forsook him, and one of them betrayed him to his enemies. Furthermore, the mysterious assaults of Satan added to his trials; and finally, the hiding of his Father's face filled to the brim the cup of his sufferings. In the midst of all this suffering we are to remember that while he was "holy, harmless, undefiled, separate from sinners" (Heb. 7 : 26), yet he was publicly and vehemently accused of treason, the highest crime against the state, and blasphemy, the highest crime against God. These sufferings, moreover, were not encountered by Jesus merely in the path of duty and obedience but by One cherishing the deepest love to God and man. Indeed, he not only suffered because he came to save, but he suffered from those whom he came to save. In discoursing on the sufferings of Christ, we are liable to forget that he not only suffered but obeyed. According to the theological formula, we are to remember that his **active** obedience embraces his entire life viewed as vicarious obedience, and his **passive** obedience embraces his entire life, and especially his sacrificial death, viewed as vicarious suffering. Having said that some of these sufferings were ordinary we should add that more than this there was a unique element in all these sufferings because he was a unique person.

The extraordinary sufferings of Christ were brought about by a positive act and infliction on the part of God. "Yet it pleased the Lord to bruise him; he hath put him to grief" (Isa. 53 : 10). God "spared not his own Son" (Rom. 8 : 32). There is no doubt that the assaults of Satan and his being forsaken by God exceeded the force of the trials and sufferings endured by ordinary men. The Saviour's experience in the Garden of Gethsemane, including his prayers, his mental sufferings and tears; his cry to God on the cross, his death on the cross before the expected time, and the effect of the spear wound in his side cannot be explained by the operation of natural principles but must be accounted for by the fact that he was no ordinary sufferer but One whose specific purpose in coming into the world was to suffer "the just for the unjust, that he might bring us to God" (1 Pet. 3 : 18). "For he hath made him to be sin for us, who knew no sin; that we might be made the righteousness of God in him" (2 Cor. 5 : 21).

There are, however, two episodes in the Lord's life in which his sufferings are given the greatest prominence. Not to mention his temptation in the wilderness, his experience in Gethsemane and the expression used on the cross in terms of his desertion by the Father are deserving of special consideration. The two latter experiences of the Saviour give us an indication of the unfathomable depths of his passion. The former incident seems to be referred to by the writer to the Hebrews (Heb. 5 : 7). According to some theologians the emphasis here is on his inward and mental sufferings in his conflict with sin, which he finally overcame by the strength and perseverance of his faith. Godet's statement here is pertinent. He says: "At Gethsemane Jesus did not drink the cup he consented to drink it"

By his successful issue from this conflict he was strengthened to endure his further trials and the cursed death of the cross. The cry on the cross in which he expresses himself as being forsaken of God has been variously interpreted. Some are of the opinion that he was not actually forsaken but that he felt as forsaken as if he had been. Others try to avoid the dilemma by saying that he was forsaken in some sense. If a solution of the mystery could be found, we might obtain it, not from general considerations, but from ascertaining the meaning of being forsaken in this context. The following gives an account which we think is agreeable to Scripture.

49. Dr Godet on **Luke 22.**

It cannot strictly be said that Christ suffered absolute despair for it could not be hid from him that the union between the human and divine nature could not be dissolved. Yet he bore to the full the penal desertion due to us for us, and he experienced to the full the lack of the comforting influences of his union with God. The divine nature in the Second Person did not forsake the human. Neither did the divine nature in the Third Person forsake the human: but the desertion was in terms of all influence of comfort and all evidence of love from God. Despair signifies (1) a total want of the evidence of faith as to acceptance with God and (2) a resolution to seek no further after such acceptance. In the first way Christ did despair, that is **penal** only, in the second, he did not. That is sinful also. There is a total intercepting of all evidence of love from God, but not a ceasing in him to wait upon God for the manifestation of that love in his appointed time. Remember Christ was thus forsaken that his people might never be forsaken.[50]

III. THE DEATH OF CHRIST

The death of our Lord sets before us the consequences of sin. While physical death is the separation of soul and body, Scripture regards it as one of the results of sin. Spiritual death, however, is separation from God, which may be temporal or eternal. Union with God is life, while separation is spiritual death with all its malignant effects upon the soul. Spiritual and physical death are not merely the inevitable consequences of sin but an inexorable infliction of punishment, "For the wages of sin is death" (Rom. 6 : 23). "The soul that sinneth, it shall die" (Ezek. 18 · 4, 20) The death of the cross, attended with all its manifold terrors, was inflicted upon the Mediator as the punishment of sin. And lest we attach to penalty the commercial ideas of satisfaction and ruthless severity upon the part of God, we are to remember that while it is true that "Christ also loved the church and gave himself for it" (Eph. 5 : 25), it is also true that "God **so loved** the world, that he gave his only begotten Son" (John 3 : 16). Christ endured the full punish-

50. John Owen. **Sacramental Viscourses.** (Edin. 1851), Vol. IX, pages 533, 587.

ment of sin: death temporal, death spiritual, and death eternal. This eternal punishment due to the Church for sin he bore intensively, but not extensively, and this was possible because of the dignity of his Person as the God-man. This part of the subject has occasioned much controversy. Principal Cunningham in dealing with this subject says that "His suffering though temporary in duration, being, because of the infinite dignity of His person, properly infinite in weight or value as a penal infliction, and this substantially identical, in the eye of justice and law, with the eternal punishment which sinners had deserved."[51]

Although the death of Christ effected a separation between soul and body, there was no separation between the Person and the soul or between the Person and the body. According to Zachary Ursinus, 1612, "the Logos coheres with His flesh more closely than the soul with the body, so that even when His soul was separated from His body by death, He was not separated from either." The Word of God, however, seeks to impress upon us the truth that the Person of Christ in his human nature experienced the pains of a cruel and shameful death.

IV. THE DESCENT INTO THE GRAVE

The burial of the Saviour was the last stage in his humiliation. In that hour his enemies were satisfied that they had accomplished his destruction, and his friends had lost hope in their Saviour. And even when the resurrection was reported "their words seemed to them as idle tales, and they believed them not" (Luke 24 : 11). Satan had now obtained a master victory the second time. Having conquered the first covenant head, he had now vanquished the second, and the seed of the woman had failed to deliver his people. Though the righteous shall flourish as a palm tree, and prosperity and the attendant blessings of happiness and honour are promised to the faithful, yet Jesus coming into the world as a Deliverer of his people encountered opposition from the beginning, which increased throughout his ministry ending in his betrayal and death by his own people, the Jews. Judging

51. Cunningham. **Historical Theology.** Edin. 1870, Vol. 2, page 307.

by human standards, the work of his life as a teacher, preacher, and Divine healer was a comparative failure. Others having toiled diligently and with great success had received their merited rewards in the acclaim and honours bestowed upon them by their beneficiaries, but the Saviour of lost men ended his honourable course in infamy and death.

Our Saviour stooped low indeed when he assumed our nature, but lower still when he submitted to be laid in the grave. This is the last degree of humiliation. All the glory of man is extinguished in the tomb. If we viewed his prosperity with an eye of indifference, we now pity him; if his splendour excited our envy, the feeling dies away and hostility relents when he, who like a flourishing tree spread his branches around, now lies prostrate in the dust. Who is this that occupies the sepulchre of Joseph? Is it a prophet or a king? No, it is one greater than all prophets and kings, the Son of the living God, the Lord of heaven and earth; but now there is nothing to distinguish him from the meanest of the human race; the tongue which charmed thousands with its eloquence is mute, and the hand which controlled the powers of the visible and invisible world is unnerved. The shades of death have enveloped him, and silence reigns in his lonely abode.[52]

In the Apostle's Creed it is said that Christ "descended into hell". According to Berkhof, who combines Calvin's interpretation with the usual Reformed position, this means "that Christ suffered the pangs of hell before his death, in Gethsemane and on the Cross, and that He entered the deepest humiliation of the state of death."[53] The reference in 1 Pet. 3 : 18, 19 to Christ preaching "unto the spirits in prison" has been taken to mean that the Spirit of Christ preached through Noah to the antediluvians before the flood came.

Some have curiously inquired as to the state and condition of Christ's soul and body between his death and resurrection. The common opinion is that the body of Christ rested in the grave until the resurrection and that his soul went immediately to Heaven. We are to remember, however, that the soul and body were both united to the

52. Dr Dick. **Lectures on Theology,** Vol. 3, pages 167, 168.
53. Berkhof. **Systematic Theology,** pages 342, 343.

Person. This disposes of the idea that he was passive during that period and rather indicates that the Person continued active as the Mediator of the Church. According to the view of some, he, at the moment of death, sprinkled the blood in the Most Holy Place after the manner of the High Priest; that is, he entered Heaven itself to appear in the presence of God for us. In any case, the death of Christ did not interrupt the exercise of his Priesthood. "And they truly were many priests, because they were not suffered to continue by reason of death: But this man, because he continueth ever, hath an unchangeable priesthood" (Heb. 7 : 23, 24).

At his death the human soul of Jesus went into the presence of the Father. This is borne out by two of his sayings on the cross, one to the Father and the other to the penitent thief (Luke 23 : 43, 46). The truth that Christ died and descended into the grave serves to deprive death of its sting and terror when his people are assured that this path to Heaven has been prepared and consecrated by the Forerunner himself.

V. THE EXALTATION OF CHRIST

The main ideas dealt with under this heading are: the resurrection, the ascension, the session at the right hand of God in Heaven, and the physical return of Christ. It is hardly necessary to mention here that the exaltation of Christ as to his Godhead was impossible, and his exaltation must therefore refer to the God-man, who in the state of humiliation through the union of his Person with a human nature had his glory veiled. It is evident, however, that even in his state of humiliation, when he "made himself of no reputation" by taking upon him the form of a servant, the glory of his Person could not be altogether hid. Visitors from Heaven celebrated his birth and signs from Heaven confirmed his mission, while his doctrines and miracles impressed many; and some were constrained to acknowledge that they had seen his glory, that of the only begotten of the Father. Even at the scene of his death, Heaven revealed its interest in the Divine sufferer. Profound darkness reigned for a time over the scene of the crucifixion. The veil that concealed the Most Holy Place in the Temple was rent from top to bottom by invisible hands; an earthquake opened the graves, and some of the dead saints arose **after the resurrection;** and although the life of Jesus was clouded by trial and sorrow, his burial was not without honour, his body being wrapped in fine linen and precious spices and deposited in the magnificent sepulchre of a rich man.

The exaltation of Christ consisted essentially in the unparalleled glory and dignity bestowed upon him as the Mediator, a reward for his voluntary self-humiliation and the complete success of his mission. The veiled glory of the Messiah was now revealed while his human soul and body were inconceivably exalted.

1. The Resurrection

(1) **Its Importance.** If Christ be risen from the death, then all the prophecies are fulfilled in him and he is the true Messiah and the eternal Son of God. The resurrection is a public declaration by God of his approbation of the finished work of Christ. The resurrection is also a pledge that we have Christ as an Advocate in Heaven and have the assurance of a risen and glorified life beyond the grave.

(2) **Its Proof.** The sources of proof of the resurrection are Scripture passages such as Psa. 16 : 10 and Acts 2 : 24-31. Further, we have his own predictions such as Matt. 20 : 19 and John 10 : 17, 18; the testimony of honest and faithful witnesses who were competent to attest the event; the miracles of the Apostles after the resurrection, which confirmed the truth of their testimony; and finally, the change of the Sabbath from the last to the first day of the week as a standing monument to the belief of the Christian Church in the resurrection of our Lord.

(3) **The Nature of the Resurrection.** It is said that Christ raised himself from the dead (John 2 : 19-21; John 10 : 18; John 11 : 25). The resurrection is also attributed to the Father (Rom. 6 : 4; Gal. 1 : 1; 1 Pet. 1 : 3) and to the Holy Spirit (Rom. 1 : 4; Eph. 1 : 17-20; 1 Pet. 3 : 18). The reason for this is that all the economical works are works of the Trinity. At the same time it must be maintained with sufficient emphasis that Jesus Christ rose from the grave by his own Divine power. We may credit that the

Jews believed that God could raise up Jesus if he would. They did not, however, believe that Jesus was the Son of God, and therefore proof must be shown by the personal act of resurrecting himself from the dead. This was given by Jesus himself in **word** (John 2 : 19, 21; John 10 : 18; John 11 : 25) and in **deed** (Matt. 27 : 63; 28 : 6, 7; Mark 16 : 6, 9; Luke 24 : 6, 34, 46). It is written that "In him dwelleth all the fulness of the Godhead bodily" (Col. 2 : 9). This cannot mean less than that the whole nature of God is in Christ and that really, essentially, substantially, and also personally, by the nearest union, as the soul dwells in the body. This union was not disrupted at the death of the Saviour and consequently the resurrection was an exercise of personal power that took place within the tomb, for the Person of Christ truly dwelt in the body in the tomb as he dwelt in that body before his death. Christ, thus, through the eternal Spirit quickened his own body and raised it from the dead, spoiling "principalities and powers, he made a shew of them openly" (Col. 2 : 15). Nevertheless, we are not to suppose that the work of the resurrection is to be exclusively attributed to Christ, since all economical works are works of the triune God. John Owen says, "the resurrection is ascribed to the Father on account of his authority and declaration therein of Christ's perfect accomplishment of the work committed unto him (Acts 2 : 24), and when the law was fully satisfied the Lord Christ was acquitted from its whole charge by the act of God the Father as Judge. Yet the Son also took his life again by an act of the love, care, and power of his Divine nature, his living again being **an act of his Person** [bold ours] although the human nature only died. But the peculiar efficiency in the reuniting of his most holy soul and body was an effect of the power of the Holy Spirit."[54] "Although the resurrection of Christ be frequently ascribed to the **Father,** as in Eph. 1 : 20, yet, in opposition to the Socinians, and other enemies of the Deity of Christ it is to be maintained, that he also rose by **his own divine power** as is evident from Rom. 1 : 4. He expressly affirms that he would **raise up the temple of his body** on

<hr />

54. Owen. **The Work of the Holy Spirit.** (Edin, 1852), pages 181, 182.

the **third** day, John 2 : 19, and that he had power to **lay down** his life and to **take it again,** Chapter X : 18."[55] The foregoing remarks dispose of the Socinian idea that the Father put life into his dead body and united it to the soul, and that he afterwards lifted himself out of the grave. According to this method of reasoning, Lazarus resurrected himself, and indeed the whole world at the last day will resurrect themselves when God has put life into their dead bodies.

Various opinions have been broached in regard to the changes that took place in the human nature of Christ in the interval between the resurrection and the ascension. After the resurrection the body of Christ was material as before, endowed with the same senses and exercised in the same manner, yet in greater degree, though not subject to mortality or the other natural infirmities of this life. We are not to think, however, that it was clothed with the glory which he possessed after his ascension, since in that case men could not bear his unveiled presence. But we should remember that Christ could accommodate his person to his disciples. It is evident from the Scripture narrative of the after-resurrection life that Christ's appearance was not different since when he revealed himself, there was no doubt in the minds of the disciples and others who knew that he was the same Person. The Roman Catholics and the Lutherans are not the only persons who seem to err on this subject, since they have attributed omnipotence and ubiquity to the human nature. We must, therefore, maintain the truth that neither the soul nor body suffered any essential change. It has been replied to this that Christ after his resurrection performed miracles which evidenced a profound change, but he also performed miracles before the resurrection. To maintain that he passed through material stone and doors during his post-resurrection days is to assert what the Word of God does not reveal. In the same way it has been maintained either, that Christ's body is in, with, and under the elements (the bread and wine), or that the elements are changed into the body of Christ. Consubstantiation and transubstantiation are not favoured by

55. **Fishers' Catechism.** (Edin. 1805), pages 153, 154.

orthodox circles and a leaning toward them should not be encouraged when dealing with this subject.

(4) **Denials of the Resurrection.** Jews and infidels have denied the resurrection of Christ. It has been asserted that the disciples were deceivers, that Jesus merely swooned, that the disciples **thought** they saw him, and that the resurrection is a revived version of heathen mythology. That the versions of some of the witnesses differ is brought forth as a proof of their unreliability, but experienced jurists inform us that sameness of evidence among a number of witnesses is considered suspicious, while differences are bound to arise if witnesses give their own independent versions. For example, Matthew refers to a scarlet robe (Matt. 27 : 28), while Mark points to the same robe as being purple (Mark 15 : 17). Without discussing the specific meaning of these words or the theories of colour, we may conclude that one saw more of the purple in the robe, or rather more of the blue, and the other saw more of the red; and so they referred to the robe as it appeared in their eyes.

Some of the objections to Christ's resurrection made by infidels in ancient and modern times had been anticipated by the enemies of Christ, who after the event circulated a report that the disciples had stolen his body. This method of disputing the resurrection (Matt. 28 : 11-15) refutes itself; for if the soldiers were asleep, how could they know that the disciples removed the body? The refusal to credit the miraculous is a reflection upon the power of God. Besides all this, it was obviously necessary for the fulfilment of Scripture and the purposes of redemption that the proofs of the resurrection should be sufficient and attested to by a considerable number of competent witnesses.

2. The Ascension

The ascension is described as the visible ascent of the Mediator from earth to Heaven. The ascension itself was an added proof of the resurrection and a visible evidence that Christ's work on earth was fully completed. We are told that before his departure he remained forty days upon earth instructing the Apostles in the things pertaining to the Kingdom of God (Acts 1 : 3). His ascension took place from the Mount of Olives near Bethany in the presence of

the eleven Apostles and other disciples. John Owen thinks
that the season of Christ's entrance into Heaven at his
ascension affords us the greatest instance of created glory
that ever was or ever will be. He also adds that the saints
who entered into a blessed rest in the presence of God, were
now admitted into the fulness of glory at the ascension of
our Lord.

3. The Session at the Right Hand of God

Christ's sitting on the Throne must signify his state of rest
after his labours and his official capacity as Sovereign and
Judge. His standing may indicate his active work of intercession or the posture of one who rises to receive his friends
(Acts 7 : 55). The right hand must bring to our minds the
notion of infinite power and endless happiness, while from
the throne of grace is exercised all the mercy and compassion of the Saviour to his militant Church.

4. The Physical Return of Christ

Some divines are of the opinion that the physical return of
Christ should not be omitted from the stages of his exaltation,
since the highest point will not be reached until the Saviour
who suffered at the hands of men returns to judge the
world. The purpose of Christ's physical return will be to
judge the world and perfect the salvation of his people.
Much controversy has arisen with regard to the second
coming of Christ, which would have been needless if men
were prepared to accept what the Word of God has to
say and to study that Word so as not to be misled by the
opinions of men or to be persuaded to accept speculations
and conclusions about this event which are not warranted
by Scripture. To us the following verses would settle the
controversy, and they give far more information on this
subject than some of the volumes with which we have been
burdened, written by men who go elsewhere than to the
Word of God for their teaching on this subject. "This same
Jesus, which is taken up from you into heaven, shall so
come in like manner as ye have seen him go into heaven"
(Acts 1 : 11). "For as often as ye eat this bread, and drink
this cup, ye do shew the Lord's death till he come" (1 Cor.
11 : 26). "So Christ was once offered to bear the sins of

many; and unto them that look for him shall he appear the second time without sin unto salvation" (Heb. 9 : 28). "For the Lord himself shall descend from heaven with a shout, with the voice of the archangel, and with the trump of God: and the dead in Christ shall rise first: then we which are alive and remain shall be caught up together with them in the clouds, to meet the Lord in the air: and so shall we ever be with the Lord" (1 Thess. 4 : 16, 17). The section in the Gospel according to Matthew in chapter twenty-five from verse thirty-one to the end should be carefully read without partiality, as we have here from the mouth of Christ himself the scene of his coming and the last judgment: "When the Son of man shall come in his glory, and all the holy angels with him, then shall he sit upon the throne of his glory: and before him shall be gathered all nations: and he shall separate them one from another, as a shepherd divideth his sheep from the goats . . . Then shall the King say unto them on his right hand, Come, ye blessed of my Father, inherit the kingdom prepared for you from the foundation of the world: . . . Then shall he say also unto them on the left hand, Depart from me, ye cursed, into everlasting fire, prepared for the devil and his angels . . . And these shall go away into everlasting punishment: but the righteous into life eternal" (Matt. 25 : 31-41).

CHAPTER XIV

THE ATONEMENT

I. THE SOURCE OF ATONEMENT

The atonement, that is the obedience unto death of our Saviour, has been called the heart of the Gospel; and this it must be since it is the procuring cause of the salvation of sinners. "For the wages of sin is death; but the gift of God is eternal life through Jesus Christ our Lord" (Rom. 6 : 23). Yet it must be stressed that the atonement is the effect and not the cause of God's love. A modern conception of the Gospel plan is that the **penal** doctrine of the atonement presents God as a ruthless Judge, who is determined to inflict punishment upon heedless sinners. Christ, however, offered himself as their Saviour and by his sacrifice he has produced a change in the Divine mind so that he has now become what he was not before, a loving and forgiving God. Such a one-sided conception appears to give the greater honour to Christ, the Peace-maker. The atonement in reality effected no change in the Divine mind, and if we believe that God loved sinners and gifted Christ to be their Saviour, it follows that it was this very love in God which provided the atonement to satisfy the righteous principles of God's moral government by removing the obstacles that lay in the way of a full manifestation of the Divine goodness. The atonement comes under the larger category of the covenant of grace and must be referred, not to one Person, but to the Trinity. The Baptismal Formula and the Apostolic Benediction make the source of salvation to proceed from the Father, Son and Holy Ghost, the Triune God (Matt. 28 : 19; 2 Cor. 13 : 14).

II. THE NATURE OF THE ATONEMENT

In the Old Testament, the word **atonement** means to cover, that is to cover sin from the eye of God by a sacrificial victim offered on God's altar. The picture we have here is the deliverance of the sinner, that is, the putting away of his sin. We are to remember, however, that the sacrifice was offered to God to placate or appease Him. That is why it has been deemed better to use the word **satisfaction** since it expresses two truths. First, the satisfaction of God in the obedience to death of Christ, and, secondly, the putting away of sin through that obedience. The sacrifice when slain was put in the place of the offerer who deserved death. The blood of the sacrifice was offered on the altar to placate God. The theological word **expiation** means that man's sin was put away by the death of Christ. Here the sinner was delivered. **Propitiation** means the satisfying of God for sin, and results in the acceptance of the sinner in God's sight. According to the strict terms of justice, the sinner must suffer for his disobedience, but God, as the Supreme Sovereign, was pleased to appoint Christ as the **substitute** to undertake the sinner's obligation. In the discharge of his office, Christ suffered and obeyed in the room and place of sinners, so that his sufferings were **vicarious,** that is, in the stead of others. It is often said that Christ endured the same sufferings as sinners would endure. It all depends upon what this statement means. In any case, we must consider that Christ had no sin in him, that he had no experience of remorse or penitence, and that his sufferings were temporal.

In illustrating this point of doctrine, three modes of statement have been adopted. Some believe that Christ suffered the same identical sufferings that sinners would suffer; others, that he suffered the full equivalent, or what the law demanded. The third theory is that Christ suffered what was a substitute for the full payment demanded, or a nominal payment. The Latin terms used were **idem,** or the very same sufferings; **tantadem,** or a full equivalent, and **acceptilatio** or a nominal equivalent. Those who maintained the first view did so, partly to guard against the danger of detracting from the value and efficacy of the atonement by toning down the idea of equivalency to something less than the full satisfaction rendered by Christ. The sufferings he did endure were the adequate sufferings demanded by the law for transgression according to the divine and inexorable formula that "the wages of sin is death". Therefore the strict sentence of justice was executed, but the Sovereign Will appointed that the penalty be transferred to a substitute appointed by Himself. The second view, therefore, is to be preferred. "The Scripture doctrine of the substitution and satisfaction of Christ seems to be fully brought out if His death be represented as a **full** equivalent or an adequate compensation for the sins of men." (Principal Cunningham, Historical Theology, Vol. 2, Edin. 1864, page 307).

A consideration of the **merits** of Christ's work brings to the fore the distinction made between his **active** and **passive** obedience. Although this distinction has been criticised, it serves a useful purpose in directing our minds both to the sufferings and obedience of our Lord. His passive obedience consisted in paying the penalty of sin and thus releasing his people from the obligation to suffer. His active obedience expresses all that he did as the condition of meriting eternal life for his church. While we distinguish between his active and passive obedience, we must not separate them, as the two accompanied each other during the whole course of the Saviour's life. It was part of his active obedience that he submitted himself voluntarily to suffering and death; it was also part of his passive obedience that he lived in subjection to God's Law, and that he acted in the form of a servant.

The atonement brings before us the difficult subject of imputation. Sin is said to be transgression, a moral quality, or a legal obligation to punishment. It is in the last sense only that sin can be borne by another. The sins of his people were put to the account of Christ and he suffered for them, but they were not personally his own. Of the three who suffered on the cross, the impenitent thief had sin **in** him and **on** him; that is, sin was put to his account and he was a sinful man. The penitent thief had sin **in** him but no sin **on** him because, though sinful in himself, his sin was not put to his account because he was forgiven. The Divine Sufferer had sin **on** him but no sin **in** him, that is, he was suffering for the sins of others but he had no sin in himself.

III. THE NECESSITY OF THE ATONEMENT

It has been affirmed that the atonement was not absolutely necessary if men were to be saved, and men have used this argument as a proof against its truth or reality. Some orthodox divines have therefore undertaken to prove that the atonement **was** absolutely necessary. Scripture does not give us any direct information on this subject; yet there are general considerations set down which seem to favour an absolute necessity. Since men have taken upon themselves to prove its non-necessity, the advocates of an absolute necessity have endeavoured to disprove the argument for a non-necessity or a hypothetical necessity.

It seems foolhardy to assert that God could not pardon sinners without this atonement, but there are peculiar circumstances touching the character of God, the nature of sin, and the nature of the atonement which seem to afford evidence for its absolute necessity. It has been stated against the objection of an atonement being not necessary that, in fact, atonement **was made.** It has also been argued that the **placability** of God, or the truth that God is essentially merciful, does not of itself prove the non-necessity of an atonement; and it has been denied by the advocates of the atonement that God would forgive sinners on the ground of repentance, though they have asserted that in the economy of grace there is an invariable connection between true repentance and forgiveness. Indeed, this repentance and this forgiveness is based upon the atonement Christ made for sinners and upon nothing else. It has also been pointed out that the incarnation, sufferings, and death of the Eternal Son of God; his humiliation and the terrible indignities he suffered; the pain and shame of a cruel, degraded, and cursed death cannot be explained except on the view that this plan for saving sinners was appointed by God because there was no other way by which the salvation of sinners could be effected. We are also told that there are some things that God cannot do. He cannot lie, and he cannot deny himself. This implies no want of power or wisdom but is explained by the thought that these acts are contrary to his infinitely perfect nature. We could also say that he cannot obey or that he cannot suffer because these exercises are incompatible with the Divine nature. The moral attributes of God would come into conflict if he were to pardon a sinner without adequate satisfaction; and if the sentence of the law against sinners were not carried out, it would seem that God had set aside his own law and revoked his threats, which is inconceivable. Indeed, if we consider the importance and efficacy of the satisfaction of Christ, we shall reflect that nothing less than the best takes away everything else; and gives us a proper conception of the power and wisdom of God.

According to some theorists the atonement was not necessary since the plan of salvation could be decided by the arbitrary will of God. The thrust behind this view of the non-necessity of the atonement is a denial that there is such justice in God as requires the satisfaction of God. Past and present schools of thought became wedded to this opinion. It has been said that both Calvin and Luther, as well as Twisse and Rutherford, maintained a hypothetical but not an absolute necessity.[56] I hardly think that the words of Calvin taken in their context should lead us to think that he was an advocate of the hypothetical view, but it should teach us that excessive dogmatism on questions like these should be avoided.

The following remarks by Principal Cunningham, and indeed his whole treatment of the subject, are worthy of consideration.

The incarnation of the eternal Son of God, the assump-

56. Calvin. **Institutes,** II : XII : 7.

tion of human nature by one who was at the same time possessor of the divine nature, the fact that this being, who is God and man in one person, spent a life on earth of obscurity and humiliation, that he endured many sufferings and indignities and was at last subjected to a cruel and ignominious death; all this, if it be true, if it be an actual reality, as Scripture requires us to believe, is so peculiar and extraordinary in its whole character and aspects that whenever we are led to realise it, we feel ourselves at once irresistibly constrained to say that this would not have taken place if it had been possible that the result to which it was directed — namely the forgiveness and salvation of sinners could have been effected in any other way or by any other means.[57]

IV. THE EXTENT OF THE ATONEMENT

In popular theology the discussion of this subject has been reduced to the precise question as to whether Christ died to procure salvation for all men or for the elect. Some believe he died for all men and that all will ultimately be saved. Others affirm that he died for all men but that all will not be saved. The defenders of a definite atonement maintain that he died for a definite number of men and that they will be saved and no others. The Arminian believes that Christ died for all men without exception, but only those will be saved who avail themselves of the salvation procured for them. According to the formula of the strict Calvinist, Christ died, not to make the salvation of all men **possible,** but to make the salvation of a definite number **certain.** Principal Cunningham says that the **nature** of the satisfaction of Christ decides the **extent** of the atonement. In other words, if we have matter in Scripture for proving that Christ died in the room and stead of a definite number of sinners, we shall have no difficulty in proving that these sinners will be saved and no others.

In order that the state of the question may not be misunderstood, the defenders of a definite atonement affirm: that the satisfaction of Christ is sufficient for all men, that he died for all men without distinction, namely for all classes

57. Cunningham. **Historical Theology,** Vol. 11, page 254.

of men; and that through the satisfaction of Christ various benefits accrue to unbelievers in this life. The doctrine they hold is that those for whom Christ suffered and died are saved and no others. The most common arguments used to defend this view are the other doctrines of Calvinism, such as predestination and effectual calling; the investigation of the precise nature of the atonement as a priestly work; the purpose of the God's redemptive work; and the nature and effects of the sufferings and obedience of our Lord.

The defenders of a definite view are on safe ground in maintaining that "To all those for whom Christ hath purchased redemption, he doth certainly and effectually apply and communicate the same."[58] This they contend for and need not contend for more. The Calvinistic universalists, maintaining as they do that Christ died for all while they deny that all are saved, are bound to maintain and to prove that Christ has purchased redemption, that is, pardon and reconciliation for many to whom that salvation is not administered. The Calvinistic universalists have made a distinction between a **general** and **special** reference of the atonement. By this they mean that Christ died in a general way for some and in a special way for others. If by this is meant that Christ's death has brought general blessings to those who will not be saved and salvation to others, then no fault can be found with the distinction. But, unhappily, this theory of a general and special reference is too vague to serve any useful purpose since the general reference does not specify what Christ did for those for whom he died. The doctrine of a special reference only, that is that Christ died with the intention of saving those for whom he died, is more consistent with the declarations of Scripture and more in harmony with the declared purpose of God.

The most plausible argument used by the Calvinistic universalists is that there are several specific passages of Scripture which plainly state that Christ died for all men without exception; and, of course, if they can prove this, they believe they can ignore all the other difficulties, such as the declared purpose of God and the specific nature of the atonement. On this aspect of the controversy they have

58. Westminster **Confession of Faith,** VIII : VIII.

spent much of their strength, and by keeping out of view the other stronger points of Calvinism, they have succeeded' in convincing others of the rightness of their view that Christ's atonement is universal.

In order to deal with this objection it seems necessary to point out that the strict Calvinist agrees with the Calvinistic universalist that Christ's sacrifice is infinite and therefore sufficient to save all men and that all men do derive various blessings in this life from the satisfaction of Christ. He has also repeatedly asserted that he is in full agreement with all the Scriptural truths that Christ died for all, even for the whole world in the sense that he died for all classes of men in all ages. "And hast redeemed us to God by thy blood out of every kindred, and tongue, and people, and nation" (Rev. 5 : 9). But if all the texts which refer to Christ's dying for all men be examined in their context, it will be found that the universalists will have the greatest difficulty in proving from any of these texts, without straining the meaning, that Christ died equally for all men without exception.

The word **world** has a variety of meanings, and if it means, as they say, every individual in the human nature, how are they to explain such passages as these: "The Lamb of God, which **taketh away** the sin of the world" (John 1 : 29). If the sin of every individual is **taken away,** how then can any individual fail to enjoy this life? "By the righteousness of one the free gift came upon all men unto **justification of life**" (Rom. 5 : 18). With these statements the Calvinistic universalist is placed in a difficult predicament, for according to his use of them it would follow that these would mean that every individual will be saved, which the Calvinistic universalist will not admit; therefore, these passages must not mean all without exception and so with other passages of the same import. It seems reasonable to presume that the word **world** used in this connection means either all nations of men or sinners of mankind as such, or sinners out of the world of mankind (Matt. 26 : 13; John 3 : 16; 1 Cor. 1 : 21; 2 Cor. 5 : 19; 1 John 2 : 2; John 6 : 32, 33; Rom. 4 : 13; Rom. 11 : 12, 15). There are several passages often quoted as having a universal application, such as those following. "As in Adam all die, even so in Christ shall all be made alive" (1 Cor. 15 : 22). The reference here is not to re-demption but to the resurrection of believers, and therefore cannot be quoted as favouring a universalistic interpretation. "That he by the grace of God should taste death for every man" (Heb. 2 : 9). The word **man** is not used in the original and is to be literally translated **everyone, everything,** or **every.** This **every** is further referred to in the context as **many sons, sanctified, brethren,** and the **children of God.** The word **every** must therefore be applied to believers and to believers only. This shows the necessity of a cautious investigation of Scripture passages that we may be acquainted with the point of reference. "And he is the propitiation for our sins: and not for our's only, but also for the sins of the whole world" (1 John 2 : 2). It is presumed that the universalists admit that Christ propitiated the sins of all men without exception, and if so, we fail to see why the law would demand satisfaction twice over. In any case, we believe that the **whole world** means all men without dis-tinction; and this phrase is sufficiently extensive so as to apply not only to those to whom the letter was written but to multitudes, whether Jews or Gentiles, of all ages. The Apostle, it seems to us, stresses here the infinite and ever-lasting efficacy of the atonement.

The advocates of a universal atonement must also take into account that their theory conflicts with certain Scriptural principles, such as the engagement and fulfilment of a con-vention between the Persons of the Trinity. According to this covenant Christ was to be rewarded by the blood-bought gift of a countless multitude. The universalist views this reward as at best a possibility dependent in some way upon the desire and power of sinners to avail themselves of the blessings of the Gospel. This would defeat the purpose of the Trinity and reduce the covenant of grace to a provisional arrangement which could be nullified at the option of the would-be beneficiaries.

The doctrine of the satisfaction of Christ affords abundant proof of a definite atonement. Christ's sacrifice was made to put away sin and to make reconciliation between God and sinners. This could not in reality be called an atonement if satisfaction were made in a general way for an indefinite number of people, some of whom do not avail themselves of it and will not avail themselves of it unless provision is made to administer it to them in terms of a definite transaction. This satisfaction for sin **did** reconcile men to God, not in respect of procuring his love for sinners, but in removing certain obstacles in the outflow of his love. These obstacles were the sins of men which required to be put away as a satisfaction to the divine law which had been violated. It appears reasonable to conclude that the universal principles of justice recognised by all reasonable men would lead men to accept the view that if Christ died in the room and stead of sinners, then these persons, whoever they were, would be put in possession of the fruits of his suffering and obedience. Such may be inferred from the teaching of the Old Testament sacrifices and this is in accordance with the rest of sacred writings.

Witsius says that no man can honestly believe that Christ died for all men without exception until he has explained away the real nature of the substitution of Christ. Principal Cunningham points out that the doctrine of a limited or definite atonement has been called the weak point of the Calvinistic system and that the Arminian view that Christ died for all men without exception has some appearance of Scriptural evidence. On account of this fact the strict Calvinists have used some of the other stronger points of Calvinism to disprove this universalism. This Principal Cunningham refrains from doing because he believes that these stronger points need not be brought forward, since it can be easily proved that the Scriptural view of the nature, purpose, and effects of the atonement provide an unassailable argument against its universality.

The same author says that the question regarding the extent of the atonement is commonly referred to as amounting in substance to this: whether Christ died for all men or only for the elect, for those who ultimately believe and are saved. But he says that this state of the question does not bring out the true nature of the point in dispute with sufficient fulness, accuracy, and precision; and he shows that the Confession of Faith and the Synod of Dort do not give any deliverance on the question **as stated in this way** although Arminians are fond of so stating the matter; that is, whether or not Christ died for all men. The precise position with regard to the extent of the atonement as held by the strict Calvinists was simply: that those for whom Christ died, whoever they are, have not only been redeemed by Christ but that pardon and reconciliation have also been procured for them. Principal Cunningham further points out that the advocates of a universal atonement are bound to produce evidence that atonement was made for those to whom the fruits of that atonement, pardon and reconciliation, are not administered.[59] The substance of the Calvinistic position is therefore summed up in the aforementioned Confessional deliverance: "To all those for whom Christ hath purchased redemption, he doth certainly and effectually apply and communicate the same."[60] If this statement is correct, it completely shuts out Calvinistic universalism.

V. THE ATONEMENT AND THE GOSPEL OFFER

Calvinistic universalists as well as Arminians point out that a definite atonement is inconsistent with what they call the Gospel offer. The main thrust in this objection is that if the atonement benefits a certain number only, it should not be offered to all and sundry, but to the elect. Now it is true that Christ in the Gospel invites all and sundry to come to him for salvation: "Him that cometh to me I will in no wise cast out" (John 6 : 37); "And whosoever will, let him take the water of life freely" (Rev. 22 : 17). The inference made is that the only reason why salvation is offered to all is that it was made for all. But this proves too much, since there may be other reasons why the Gospel is offered to all, though indeed the truth is that some never did hear the Gospel. The defenders of a definite atonement sometimes reply to the above by saying that the atonement is sufficient for all and adapted to all and that the non-elect may have it if they will. Even if we admit all this to be true, we feel that the defenders of a definite atonement do not gain any ground by these reasons. The truth is that the Gospel is to be preached to all because God has commanded this to be done, and no other reason need be given. It would,

59. Cunningham. **Op. sit,** page 326.
60. **Confession of Faith,** VIII : VIII.

of course, be impossible to preach the Gospel to the elect only since we know not who they are. The objection that it would be insincere for God to invite sinners in general to repent and believe is a reflection on the goodness as well as the wisdom of God. If it is right for God to command all men to love and obey him, surely it must be right for God to command them to repent and believe the Gospel. We believe that those who are appointed to preach the Gospel should proclaim a full and free Gospel to sinners even if they do not know all the reasons God may have for appointing this ordinance. And we think that their opinions bearing upon the extent of the atonement or the actual condition of lost sinners should not modify their instructions in preaching the Gospel to every creature. They preach not because they understand all the reasons but because they are commanded to do so, and of course because they know, as they must know, that it is an ordinance commanded and appointed to bring men into a state of salvation.

The **Gospel offer** must not be thought of merely as certain blessings made available to sinners. The blessings of salvation are treasured up in Christ, they are received from Christ, and they are received only because sinners receive Christ himself as their Lord and Saviour and in him and with him the blessings they need. A practical illustration made on this point may shed light on the question at issue. A teacher offered a beautiful watch to any in his class who would raise his hand. There were many in the class but only one watch. There was one boy in the class who, being impressed by the sincerity of the teacher's offer and observing that no other made an attempt to claim the watch, put up his hand and claimed the prize. The unbelievers in the class were then convinced that though there was only one watch, the offer was sincere. The Gospel of Christ is preached to sinners as such, and they are not only invited but commanded to come to Christ that they may be saved. Many to whom this Gospel has been made available have not concerned themselves overmuch with the secret purposes and manifold works of God. Having understood the mercy of Christ, the adaptability of the Gospel to themselves, and their pressing need of it, they acknowledged the record as being true, and they embraced Christ in the promise and were not disappointed. "Incline your ear, and come unto me: hear, and your soul shall live; and I will make an everlasting covenant with you, even the sure mercies of David" (Isa. 55 : 3).

In preaching the Gospel it is necessary to make known to men their need of such a salvation, and the means and ways God has appointed to make it effectual to sinners. Men are invited — yea, even commanded — to come to Christ in the way of his appointing, even by faith in the Son of God. It is neither Scriptural nor profitable to tell sinners that Christ loved them and died for them in particular; and indeed this we cannot do if we believe in a definite atonement, since we have no information on this point other than that Christ died for sinners without distinction. But it **is** necessary to tell them the great and precious truth that Christ died for sinners and that whosoever believeth in him hath everlasting life.

We are told that it would not be proper to preach a free Gospel unless we had assurance that Christ died for all sinners without exception. This is just an attempt to reason from abstract speculation apart from the declarations of Scripture and savours very much of an impeachment of God's plan of salvation, even though it is impossible for the objector to know the manifold purposes of God. These two truths, a definite atonement and an indiscriminate offer of the Gospel, may appear inconsistent with our modes of thinking, but if they are plainly stated in Scripture, as we are sure they are, we must believe them both to be true even if we cannot see their consistency. They are, as someone said, like two parallel lines which as far as man can see never come together, but they do meet in God's eternal purpose.

VI. THEORIES OF THE ATONEMENT

All theories as to the nature of the atonement whether ancient or modern, may be brought under three classes. First, the atonement is no true satisfaction for sin. Secondly, the atonement is **some** satisfaction. Thirdly, the atonement is a **full** satisfaction. The first class comprises such theories as the example theory, the moral influence theory, the mystical theory, and the vicarious repentance theory.

1. No Satisfaction Theories

(1) **The Example Theory.** This view is a product of the Socinians and affirms that there is no such justice in God as requires that sin be punished, since he can dispense forgiveness without any penal satisfaction. The atonement was no satisfaction nor does it move God to pardon sin. Christ indeed saves men by revealing to them the way of life and through his life and death giving them an **example** of true obedience. The only sense in which it is admitted that Christ died for our sins is that as a reward for his obedience unto death he receives power to bestow eternal life.

(2) **The Moral Influence Theory.** This theory, which is practically identical with the above and was first elaborated by Abelard in 1142, asserts that there is no justice in God which requires him to punish sin. Therefore the death of Christ was no expiation. The atonement is, however, a manifestation of the benevolence of God suffering in and with his creatures and so leading them to repentance.

(3) **The Mystical Theory.** The theory here is that Christ at the incarnation entered like leaven into the life of humanity and gradually purified the human nature. The amiable Edward Irving, one of the exponents of this view, believed that Christ's human nature was virtually sinful though the Holy Ghost kept him from actual corruption. By his life and death Christ destroyed this inborn corruption and brought human nature to a state of perfection and reunited it to God.

(4) **The Vicarious Repentance Theory.** Here the idea, attributed to Macleod Campbell, is brought forward that a **perfect** repentance is all that is necessary as the ground of forgiveness. This, however, man is unable to exercise, and so Christ offered God a **vicarious** repentance and by his suffering and death he entered sympathetically into the Father's condemnation of sin. This condemnation of sin tends to produce in man the holiness which God demands of the sinner.

It is possible that some of the above theories by the

extensive elaboration of their arguments were not properly understood and that the theorists would deny some of the inferences drawn from their arguments. It is also possible that those who read those arguments were unable to comprehend them. But however much truth they contain — and they do bring out truths which are, however, incidental to the nature of the atonement — they deny expressly or by inference the simple and Scriptural doctrine that Christ died in the room and stead of sinners, that his sufferings and death was a propitiation for the sins of men, and that he procured for them the forgiveness of sin and restoration to God's favour.

2. Some Satisfaction Theory

(1) **The Governmental Theory.** The second class of theories is that Christ made **some** satisfaction to the justice of God. The governmental theory was elaborated in the monumental work of Hugo Grotius in 1645 under the title of **The Satisfaction of Christ.** Grotius set out to combat the Socinians who held the first view. His work is professedly a defence of the atonement. The author, however, gave up the cause he sought to defend by adopting a middle theory of satisfaction. Grotius admitted that the attribute of justice in God demanded satisfaction. But this justice is derived from the divine **will** and not the divine **nature,** and hence God can pardon sin without satisfaction if he will. But pardon without satisfaction will not reveal the heinousness of sin and would be a reflection on the moral administration of God. And so, in order to display his abhorrence of sin and maintain the provisions of the Divine Law, God determined that Christ should suffer. These sufferings were not a full satisfaction for sin, but they served to display the Divine anger against sin and his determination to punish it.

A similar theory had been previously broached by Duns Scotus, who advocated a nominal satisfaction which God accepted not because of its intrinsic value, since Scotus denied it to be infinite, but because he was pleased to do so. This is called the theory of **acceptilatio,** an acquittance from the creditor by word of mouth, or an imaginary payment. Grotius denied that he held the acceptilatio theory. The Grotius theory, however, is not so much **satisfaction** to

justice as a **display** of God's justice; consequently it must
be classed as essentially a theory of a partial or nominal
payment for sin.

There are several objections to this theory. Dr Berkhof
concludes some of his objections by stating that

A real execution of the penalty might make a profound
impression on the sinner, and might act as a real
deterrent, if man's sinning or not were, even in his
natural state, merely contingent on the human will,
which it is not; but such an impression would hardly
be made by a mere sham exhibition of justice designed
to show God's high regard for the law.[61]

3. The True Satisfaction Theory

The satisfaction doctrine of the atonement embraces the
ideas contained in the divergent theories referred to, since
the satisfaction of Christ produces all the results pleaded
for in these theories. The precise point to be determined in
this matter is the true and objective nature of the atonement.
The theory of proper satisfaction will be found embedded
in the statements of the church. It was held by the Apostolic
Fathers in opposition to the Ebionite and Gnostic heresies
though without any attempt at formulating doctrinal statements. Such men as Ignatius, Barnabas, and Clement of
Rome defended the doctrine by Scriptural quotations. Subsequent to the Apostolic Fathers, some attempts at scientific
treatment were made, but these were marred by statements
that the satisfaction of Christ was a ransom to Satan.

Anselm in 1109 in his work **Cur Deus Homo,** Why a
God-man, sets forth in a masterly way the doctrine of
satisfaction. Anselm strongly holds to the necessity and
vicariousness of the satisfaction of the Eternal Son of God.
Man is a debtor to God and cannot pay; therefore he must
suffer. None but God, however, can make infinite satisfaction
for sin. The solution of the problem, therefore, is to be
found in the work of the God-man, whose obedience procured the reward of everlasting life for sinners. The substance
of the Anselmic view is thoroughly Biblical and consistent,
though in point of accuracy and completeness it does not
come up to the Reformed view. The view of Anselm has

61. Berkhof. **Systematic Theology**, page 389.

been attacked by the orthodox and unorthodox schools of theologians, but there is a sufficiency of evidence that the main thesis of the **Cur Deus Homo** is the same as that of the Reformers.

The blemishes in the work are no doubt due to the circumstances of the time and to the fact that the critical study of the Word of God was not freed from Popish influence until after the Reformation when the doctrine of justification by faith was more fully examined by the Reformers. The Reformers studied the atonement in its subjective aspect and brought out its appropriation in the experience of the sinner. Some statements in the work itself such as the following may be cited as an evidence that Anselm understood substantially the true nature of the atonement:

> "The **compassion** of God, which appeared to be lost entirely when we were considering the justice of God and the sin of man, we have now found to be so great and so consistent with justice, that nothing greater or more just can be conceived of. For what compassion can equal the words of God the Father addressed to the sinner condemned to eternal punishment, and having no means of redeeming himself: 'Take my only-begotten Son, and make an offering for thyself', or the words of the Son: 'Take me and ransom thy soul'?[62] For this is what both say. They invite and draw us to faith in the gospel." There are incidental views and positions in this tract with which theologians would not wholly agree; but certainly as far as the general theory of vicarious satisfaction is concerned this little treasure contains the substance of the Reformed doctrine.

The defenders of the Reformed view of the nature of the atonement protest against the charges made against it, such as that the atonement as held by the Calvinistic school is a mere penal or commercial theory, which abstracts from the benevolence of God and charges him with ruthlessly sacrificing his Son in order to satisfy his vindictive nature. These imputations can be met in the gross by pointing out that Scripture declares death to be the **penalty** of sin and that Christ died to satisfy the claims of a broken law and to

---

62. **Cur Dens Homo**, 2 : 20, quoted from Dr Shedd. **History of Christian Doctrine**, Vol. 2, pages 284, 285.

render a full obedience on behalf of the sinner. The illustrations used by divines on this subject which possess a commercial point of view are drawn from the representations of Scripture which refer to sin under various aspects such as "Forgive us our debts" (Matt. 6 : 12). Neither can it be forgotten by the devout reader of Scripture that the atonement made no change in the nature of God who loved his people from everlasting. And we therefore read that "God so loved the world, that he gave his only begotten Son" (John 3 : 16). It must also be remembered that Christ came to finish the work which his Father gave him to do and that "Christ also loved the church, and gave himself for it" (Eph. 5 : 25).

IV THE WORKS OF GRACE (RAISE HEADING))

CHAPTER XV

THE DOCTRINE OF SALVATION

Introduction

Soteriology, or the doctrine of salvation in a wide sense includes the doctrine of the Person and Work of Christ, but in a narrow sense it brings before us the application of the blessings of the gospel through the agency of the Holy Spirit. It has been pointed out that the Atonement refers to the work done **for** the church by Christ, whereas, the application of the gospel through the Spirit refers to the work done by Christ's Spirit **in** the church. According to some theologians the nearest approach to the order of salvation in this work of the Spirit is set forth in the following words: "Moreover whom he did predestinate, them he also called: and whom he called them he also justified, and whom he justified, them he also glorified" (Rom. 8 : 29, 30).

According to the order of salvation set down here predestination is prior to calling, calling to justification, and justification to glorification. In regard, however, to priorities in calling, regeneration, justification, faith, repentance, etc., there have been some differences among theologians. These differences relate mainly to orders such as, the **causal** order of salvation, the **logical** order, and the **chronological** order. For example: regeneration is **causally** prior to faith as the root of faith. There is also a **logical** or natural priority since we always think of faith as following regeneration. As to the question of time or temporal priority we may suppose conversion to follow conviction of sin. Yet, although regeneration is causally and logically prior to faith we cannot say that chronologically there is a difference since we cannot think of the existence of regeneration without the existence of saving faith. There are also two **natural** orders, one natural in respect to the subjects themselves and another in regard to us, or as they appear to our minds. We must not, therefore, perplex our own minds and the minds of others by refined speculations.

Most of the important topics dealt with under Soteriology, or the application to the sinner of the benefits of redemption, may conveniently be dealt with in the following order:— Effectual Calling, Union with Christ, Regeneration, Justification, Faith, Repentance, Sanctification and Adoption. The headings referred to here are considered by some as traditional but it is a useful exercise to consider them in themselves, for they are all dealt with in the sacred text. We shall first, however, begin with the topic of common grace since this will serve as an introduction to the application of redemption.

I. COMMON GRACE

A distinction has been made between the natural and moral benefits bestowed upon man generally, and the saving graces enjoyed by the Lord's people. The former has been called **common grace** and the latter special or **saving grace.** The subject of common grace is extremely complicated and mysterious and indeed it is not surprising that no adequate Scriptural exposition of this subject, in all its bearings, has yet been given to the church. Any discussion of the subject here must be introductory and general.

There is a sense in which all men are subjects of common grace otherwise we could not account for the temporal benefits enjoyed by a totally depraved world under condemnation. Some of the heathen enjoyed a good measure of common grace if we are to accept the written accounts of their high standards of morality; while a considerable number of individuals within the visible church have benefited greatly through the influences of the gospel: and if we attend to the declarations of Scripture we shall find that men in various circumstances have been enriched by God's benefits. Such passages as Gen. 17 : 20; Gen. 39 : 5; Psa. 145 : 15; Matt. 5 : 45; Acts 14 : 17; and 1 Tim. 4 : 10; clearly evidence that God blesses the wicked as well as the good. We have also some cases on record in which the wicked have benefited on account of their association with God's people (Gen. 39 : 5).

Objection has been made to calling these benefits graces since it is assumed that there is only one grace and that is saving grace. But since all benefits come to men, through the graciousness of God it would be foolish to deny that these common benefits issue from the grace of God. Some who acknowledge the existence of common grace deny that these benefits are communicated to men by the Holy Spirit since they can be accounted for by the providence of God and the natural gifts and powers bestowed by God indiscriminately on sinful men. Those who reason thus usually confine the ministration of the Spirit to those who are the subjects of saving grace. It is questionable, however, if the agency of the Holy Spirit can be excluded in the communication of any natural or moral benefits whatever, since he is the author of all the blessings and graces enjoyed by his creatures; and it is hazardous to maintain that man can use any of the benefits of common providence without the aid of the Holy Spirit. What these persons probably mean is that God has endowed men with reasonable and natural powers which they can exercise without any special influences of the Spirit of God. A sufficient account of the whole matter is that "he giveth to all life and breath and all things"; "for in him we live and move and have our being" (Acts 17 : 25, 28). Yet when we speak of common grace we have in mind these communications of the Holy Spirit in which he exercises such a moral influence upon sinners, without renewing their hearts, that sin is restrained, order is maintained in civil life, God's laws are respected, and the interests of Christ's kingdom are promoted in the world. Common grace includes such blessings as health and strength, shelter and provision, and the comfort and happiness which God is pleased to bestow upon unregenerate men. "Yet let us not forget that these are most excellent gifts of the Divine Spirit, which for the common benefit of mankind he dispenses to whomsoever he pleases . . . . for when the Spirit of God is said to dwell only in the faithful, that is to be understood of the Spirit of sanctification, by whom we are consecrated as temples to God himself. Yet it is equally by the energy of the same Spirit that God replenishes, activates and quickens all creatures, and that according to the property of each species which he has given it by the law of creation."[62a]

Our special interest in this subject is the common grace enjoyed by means of gospel ordinances. Under this benevolent economy we may observe three classes of persons. (1) Those whose conduct seems to evidence that they derive little or no benefits from gospel ordinances. (2) Those who are evidently impressed by God's message of salvation, and (3) Those who are truly converted. It may be replied to this that there are only two classes, the saved and the unsaved; yet, the representations of Scripture and especially the parables of the Saviour such as that of the **Sower** and the parable of the **Virgins** make a distinction between those who possess a degree of knowledge, conviction, and morality which is above the ordinary, and yet comes short of saving grace; and those who are truly the children of God. The former are referred to as those "who may be called by the ministry of the word and may have some common operation of the Spirit yet they never truly come unto Christ". We are also to take into account the Spirit's dealings with men before they are saved producing in them a knowledge of their lost state, conviction of sin, and a great change in their outward conduct; and sometimes it is impossible for the subjects concerned to know whether they are the subjects of common or saving grace until they attain to some measure of spiritual maturity and growth. The general view held with regard to this subject is that the communication by the Holy Spirit of common grace is **mediate** through general and special revelation and moral persuasion, while saving grace is **immediate** and supernatural and wrought in the soul directly by the Holy Spirit.

62a. Calvin. **Institutes**, 2 : 2 : 16.

Some theologians believe that common grace is not connected with the Atonement since the purpose of Christ's saving work is to redeem his people. Common grace on this view issues from the goodness and mercy of God in general. At the same time there is a feeling among Reformed theologians that other purposes are served by the Atonement which subserve the interests of his own church in the world. Though Principal Cunningham objects to the notion of a **general and special reference** in connection with the Atonement of Christ, he allows that many blessings flow to mankind at large from the death of Christ; and Dr A. Hodge says that any plan designed to secure the salvation of the elect cannot do so without affecting for better or worse the rest of mankind. These positions can be proved not only from general consideration but from positive statements of Scripture.

There are no doubt several difficult problems in this doctrine of common grace but it seems plain enough from Scripture that others besides believers enjoy many benefits, and especially those within the visible church. Nor does it seem reasonable to deny that these gifts and benefits are communicated to men, as saving benefits are, through the ministrations of the Holy Ghost and not through the workings of common providence. It should be common knowledge to readers of Scripture that creation, preservation, government, miracles, the government of the church, and the various natural and moral gifts bestowed upon men are attributed to the Holy Ghost. (Gen. 1 : 2; Psa. 33 : 6; Psa. 104 : 30; Matt. 12 : 28; Acts 13 : 2; Gen. 6 : 3; Ex. 31 : 3; Num. 24 : 27; 1 Sam. 10 : 10; John 16 : 8).

II. EFFECTUAL CALLING

1. The Gospel Call

It does not require to be proved that Christ commanded the gospel to be preached to every creature, and that those preached to are invited to believe that they may be saved (Matt. 16 : 15, 16). The Old Testament commission in this respect is as liberal as the New. "Unto you, O men, I call; and my voice is to the sons of man" (Prov. 8 : 4). "Look unto me and be ye saved all the ends of the earth; for I am God and there is none else" (Isa. 45 : 22). "Ho, every one that thirsteth, come ye to the waters and he that hath no money come ye, buy, and eat; yea, come, buy wine and milk without money and without price" (Isa. 55 : 1). "Have I any pleasure at all that the wicked should die? saith the Lord God; and not that he should return from his ways, and live?" (Ezek. 18 : 23).

The New Testament terms are to the same effect, "go ye into all the world and preach the gospel to every creature" (Mark 16 : 15). The parables of the Marriage Feast and the Great Supper are couched in terms of the gospel invitation (Matt. 22 : 1-14; Luke 14 : 16-24). "In the last day, that great day of the feast, Jesus stood and cried saying, If any man thirst, let him come unto me and drink" (John 7 : 37). "The same Lord over all is rich unto all that call upon him. For whosoever shall call upon the name of the Lord shall be saved" (Rom. 10 : 12, 13). "Whosoever, will, let him take the water of life freely" (Rev. 22 : 17). There are also other passages which virtually set forth the gracious character of the gospel and the grave consequences of refusing to comply with its terms. "And he that believeth not the Son of God shall not see life" (John 3 : 36). "In flaming fire taking vengeance on them that know not God and that obey not the gospel of our Lord Jesus Christ" (2 Thess. 1 : 8).

The gospel call therefore is a declaration of the plan of salvation, with an invitation to embrace Christ the Saviour, and a promise of forgiveness to all who respond to its overtures. Did we not know any better we should conclude that such a message addressed to lost sinners promising everlasting life upon faith in Christ would be followed by a universal response. The truth is that for various reasons men will not avail themselves of those blessings; and consequently, if sinners are to be saved there must be an effectual call from God to enable them freely to choose Christ as their Saviour. "This effectual call is of God's free and special grace alone, not from anything at all forseen in man, who is altogether passive therein, until being quickened and renewed by the Holy Spirit, he is thereby enabled to answer this call and to embrace the grace offered and conveyed in it" (Confession 10 : 11).

2. Results of the Gospel Call

The common or external call of the gospel produces various effects in the world, though it has not been designed to enrich any with salvation, without the internal call. Biblical history and the various events in the annals of nations and individuals are descriptive of the beneficial results of God's call to men to submit themselves to his authority and guidance. The teachings of Scripture and the influence of God's Spirit have set their marks upon men's lives and character in restraining and curbing their evil dispositions and in constraining them to give some external obedience to the principles of righteousness.

3. The Effectual Call

The call of God to sinners is external by the gospel in which the message of salvation comes to them. There is also an internal call which accompanies the external call and it is through this internal call that sinners are enabled to exercise faith in Christ. The former is ineffectual to salvation without the latter. One way of explaining this is to say that the objective call of the gospel with all the reasons and motives attached to it is not saving without the subjective call of the Holy Spirit. In the words of Dr Warfield previously quoted, "It is the function of the word to set before the soul the object to be believed; and it is the function of the Spirit to quicken in the soul belief in this object; and neither performs the work of the other or its own work apart from the other."

It is a common opinion that sinners are called effectually through the influence of the Holy Ghost as the author of Scripture impressing the teachings of Scripture upon the human mind and heart and so persuading men to embrace its teaching. This treatment of the subject fails to take into account the total depravity of the human heart, while it further attributes to the Spirit a suasive rather than a quickening power. The internal call is not merely a powerful constraint exercised objectively upon the soul by the Spirit through the truth but a special exercise of the divine Spirit operating immediately within the human spirit communicating a new life and producing a new mode of spiritual activity, so that the sinner, "being quickened and renewed by the Holy Spirit is thereby enabled to answer this call and to embrace the grace offered and conveyed in it." The Word of God does not change. Its majesty, truth suitability and beauty are forever the same. What is required at this stage is a mind to understand and a heart to respond to the gracious message sent to sinners by the Lord: and it is the Spirit alone who enlightens the eye and purifies the heart.

It is the emphasis upon the power of the Word and the teachings of men to the exclusion of the divine agent that makes for the free and easy way and taken by some evangelists to convert men. Pains are taken to explain how simple and easy faith is, and attempts are made to constrain sinners to believe. They are informed that the Lord Jesus loves them and that Christ died for them, and that all they have to do is believe. Now it is quite true that the gospel is the power of God unto salvation to everyone that believeth, and it is also true that the gospel is to be explained, that a simple gospel is to be preached, and that men are to be constrained, to commit their hearts to Christ. It must not be omitted, however, as is too often done to declare plainly that sinners are totally depraved and totally unable to exercise saving faith; that they are without strength and cannot believe, and that the effectual power of the Holy Ghost is necessary not only to impress upon them the truths of the gospel but to work in them effectually to enable them to repent and believe. And indeed it is a lesson in Christianity to be able to say feelingly "Create in me a clean heart and renew a right spirit within me". This thesis may appear to be inconsistent and an easier way may be taken to explain the difference between the common and effectual call. But the conclusions we are constrained to infer from the representations of Scripture on this point are: that the gospel is to be preached in all its fulness and freeness to all men; that some hear it and are not converted, and that others are.

Why these are converted and not the others must be attributed to the effectual operations of the Holy Ghost that accompany the call. It is not the preached gospel which opens the heart as if nothing else were necessary but external means, there is also an operation of the Spirit required to remove prejudices and renew the heart. The picture may be clear and beautiful in itself but this will produce no impression upon the blind eye; and what is needed here is the opening of the eye which can only be effected by Him who makes old things pass away and causes all things to become new. The distinction between the preaching of the gospel and the application of it by divine power is stated in various passages of Scripture. "For our gospel came not unto you in word only, but also in power and in the Holy Ghost" (1 Thess. 1 : 5). Dr John Kennedy says that "He (the Spirit) by a work in secret, bearing directly on their passive souls, quickened them when they were dead in sin and by means of the word of the truth of the gospel applied with power elicited in the exercise of faith, the life which he imparted" (**Sermons**, Eph. 2 : 8, page 7).

4. Divergent Views of the Gospel Call

The Pelagian view is that man possesses power to respond to the gospel call and that the Holy Spirit as the author of Scripture presents moral truths and motives which in their own nature exert a moral influence upon the soul. These influences become effectual when one man makes a better use of his ability than another. If this is Pelagianism his disciples are today as active as ever. The semi-Pelagian believes that God's grace is necessary to enable a man to return to God but man must first desire to return when he may expect God's aid in carrying his desires into effect.

The Arminian of the sounder sort acknowledges man's total depravity and therefore maintains that man is unable of himself to repent. Since, however, Christ dies equally for every man sufficient grace is granted in the Gospel to all. This grace becomes effectual when it is co-operated with and improved by the sinner. In criticising the sounder Arminian we must therefore be careful to recognise that he too with the Calvinist believes in man's total inability although his plea for sufficient grace modifies his position. This modification, however, is we believe a serious error. Lutherans agree with Calvinists in denying the ability to turn or co-operate with grace in the first instance. They affirm however that Gospel becomes effective when the human will ultimately yields to the grace of God. The Pelagian says that one rejected the gospel and the other willed to believe. The semi-Pelagian says that one made no effort and that the other commenced to strive and was helped. The Arminian says that one refused to co-operate with common grace and that the other did. The Lutheran says that one persisted in resisting grace and that the other finally yielded. The Calvinist says that one was regenerated by the power of God's Spirit and the other was not (freely quoted from Dr A. A. Hodge).

These distinctions may appear to be too subtle, and to mar the simplicity of the gospel. They however serve to show us the difference between those who refuse to acknowledge the clear testimony of Scripture and those who attempt to solve the problem of God's sovereignty and man's responsibility. Some say that there is only one call which is made effectual in the one case and not in another. This is just a matter of terminology. It should however be noted that the stages of calling can only have a preparatory significance until the call becomes effectual by the power of the Holy Spirit renewing the heart and uniting the sinner to Christ.

III. UNION WITH CHRIST

Although calling precedes union with Christ yet the latter is a basic and central doctrine in the application of redemption. We should not however think of sinners being actually saved until they are effectually called by the Spirit into that union. Before sinners are united to the Saviour they are under condemnation and destitute of spiritual life but at the moment of this union their state and nature is changed and they become new creatures in Christ.

In order to guard against error divines have maintained that this union is not **essential** as that subsisting among the Persons of the Trinity, or **personal** as that union between the divine and human natures in Christ, or **political** as between a leader and his followers, or **moral** as between close friends. A comparison of the similitudes used in Scripture is of great assistance in giving us information as to its nature. It is compared to the union between a vine and its branches. The vine is Christ who diffuses life and sap through the branches (John 15 : 1-5). It is like the union between a building and its foundation, Christ as the foundation sustains the building which is cemented to him and together in one whole (Eph. 2 : 20). It is like the union between

the head and members of the body. Christ as the Head is the
source of life and energy and all the members are united
to him and to one another (Eph. 4 : 15, 16). The union
between a man and wife is in some respects the most illumin-
ating of these illustrations. The marriage union is legal,
sacred, intimate, an dindissoluble. The parties are bonded
together by a tender affection, a community of interests and
legal obligations, and through a legal marriage they become
one in the eyes of the law (Eph. 5 : 23-33). Any description
of this union must of necessity be inadequate but we may
emphasise two essential elements, namely, that our union
with Christ is both legal and spiritual. Our union with
Christ is a lawful or **legal** union in the highest sense. By
his atonement he has satisfied the law claims upon us, and
we are justified because his righteousness becomes ours.
We are one with him in the eyes of the law. We are
crucified with Christ, died with him, and rose from the
dead with him. He has met all our obligations and has
secured for us spiritual and everlasting rewards. As our
lawful husband the Lord undertakes to protect us and to
provide for us and this he does in common providence and
in grace, and by faith we may humbly crave for these
benefits since they are there for us. Our union with Christ
is also a **spiritual** union through which we are made partakers
of the spiritual influences of our Head. This includes,
regeneration, sanctification and all the other benefits procured
by the Atonement. The word **mystical** has been used in
dealing with this subject to inform us that it is a secret
union invisible to human perception and not identical with
any outward profession.

The results of this union are that the Holy Spirit enters
and dwells in the human heart bringing to the believer
vitality and power. And since provision is made to counter-
act the evils of sin, union with Christ brings with it all the
benefits of the covenant of Grace. This union also provides
for the communion of the saints who are animated by the
same Spirit, possess the same faith and love and are
dedicated to the one aim of loving and serving Christ and
serving and loving one another. There is a difference,
however, between Church fellowship and Christian fellowship, and it must be evident from the course of church

history that Church fellowship is not always possible. The modern ideas of super-church unions fail to take this into account. Church unions, where a working and cordial agreement on doctrine, worship and practice is not possible, are no real unions at all. It is far better for churches which cannot agree to remain separate and to carry on their own work and leave other churches to carry on theirs.

Various errors have been propounded in an attempt to explain this mysterious subject of union with Christ. Some have alleged that the union referred to here is Christ's union with the human spirit. Some mystics conceived of it as a partaking of the divine substance, others would reduce it to a mere union of love and sympathy as between friends. The sacramentarians seem to think that men become members of Christ's body by partaking of sealing ordinances. But Baptism and the Lord's supper are administered to **believers.** Nominal Christians think union with Christ is a belief in certain doctrines. All these fancies would exclude Christ as a personal Saviour whom we must receive by a personal faith in Himself. Union with Christ is effected by the Holy Spirit and according to Dr A. Hodge it consists of two parts. "First, the offering of Christ **externally** by the Gospel, and **internally** by the illumination of the Spirit. Secondly, the reception of Christ which on our part is both **passive** and **active.** The passive reception is that whereby a spiritual principle is ingenerated into the human will, whence issues the active reception, which is an act of faith with which repentance is always conjoined."

Q. Is Christ united to us before we are united to him?

A. The union is mutual, but it begins first on his side (1 John 4 : 19).

Q. How does it begin first on his side?

A. By unition, which is before union.

Q. What understand you by unition?

A. It is the Spirit of Christ uniting himself first to us, according to the promise, "I will put my spirit within you" (Ezek. 36 : 27).

Q. How does the Spirit of Christ unite himself first unto us?

A. By coming unto the soul, at the happy moment appointed for the spiritual marriage with Christ, and quickening it, so that it is no more morally dead, but alive, having new spiritual powers put into it (Eph. 2 : 5). Even when we were dead in sins, he hath quickened us.

Q. What is the immediate effect of quickening the dead soul by the Spirit of Christ passively received?

A. The immediate effect thereof is actual believing; Christ being come in by his Spirit, the dead soul is thereby quickened and the immediate effect thereof is, the embracing him by faith, whereby the union is completed (John 5 : 25). (Fisher's **Catechism,** Q. 30).

We should also remember the causes and basis of such a union. The Reformers, who as usual dealt with their subjects from a **theological** point of view, set forth the federal or covenant union between Christ and his people formed from eternity by which he voluntarily assumed all their obligations, and when Christ suffered and obeyed the whole Church was included in him as the head. All the blessings therefore which belong to them by divine donation are treasured up in Christ to be administered to the chosen people in due time.

And indeed they actually enter into this union when they embrace Christ by faith.

IV. REGENERATION

The term **regeneration** has been used to express various meanings and a proper understanding of the various aspects of the term is of assistance if we are to get a tolerable grasp of the subject. In the broadest sense it was used by Calvin to indicate not only regeneration but conversion and sanctification. This use of the word passed into Puritan theology so that regeneration and conversion were not generally distinguished. Regeneration was therefore understood in a less wide sense to indicate not only the communication of spiritual life but the activity of faith and repentance. It was also used to design the impartation of spiritual life with the first phase of activity in that life. In a stricter sense it is used by some theologians to denote the implantation of spiritual life as distinct from its first exercise.

According to this scheme of things, regeneration may be considered under four aspects: (1) Spiritual life and sanctification; (2) Spiritual life including faith and repentance; (3) Spiritual life with its first exercise, and (4) Spiritual life as distinct from the first act of faith which it produces. Whether or not we agree with these distinctions we should recognise that works in theology would have been better understood, and there would have been less disagreements about the term **regeneration** if more attention had been paid to these aspects of the terms. Theological writers have devoted particular headings to such subjects as Effectual Calling, Regeneration, Justification, Faith, Repentance, Conversion and Sanctification, therefore, it would be better to consider this subject by itself and to settle in our minds that regeneration strictly speaking must be taken in the third or fourth sense mentioned above.

"Regeneration (says Principal Cunningham) may be taken either in a more limited sense as including **only the first implantation of spiritual life,** by which a man dead in sins and trespasses is quickened or made alive, so that he is no longer dead; or it may be taken in a wider sense, as comprehending the whole of the process by which he is renewed, or made over again, as including the production of saving faith and union to Christ, or very much what is described in our standards under the name of effectual calling. Now it is only of regeneration as understood in the first or more limited of these senses, that the Reformers maintained that man in the process was wholly passive and not active; for they did not dispute, that before the process in the second and more enlarged sense was completed, man was spiritually active and continued so ever after during the whole process of his sanctification (Historical Theology, Vol. 1, p. 617). The same writer in dealing with this subject elsewhere says: "Man is dead in sin; the making him alive, the restoring him to life, is represented in Scripture as in every part of the process, from the commencement to the conclusion, the work of God's Spirit. The instrumentality of the truth or the word is indeed employed in the process, but in the nature of the case, and in accordance with what is clearly taught in Scripture, there must be antecedantly — at least in the order of nature, though not in time — to the truth being so brought to bear upon men's minds as to produce instrumentally any of its appropriate effects be a work of God's Spirit, whereby spiritual life is implanted, and a capacity of perceiving and submitting to the truth, which had hitherto been rejected — a capacity which indeed previously existed, so far as concerns the mere intellectual framework of man's mental constitution — the mere psychological faculties which he possesses as being still a man though fallen — but which was practically useless because of the entire bondage or servitude of his will, which required to be renewed only by the immediate agency of God's Spirit."

A proper understanding of the meaning of regeneration or the implantation of spiritual life in the soul as distinct from the progress of sanctification in the believer's life would obviate some of the gross errors in modern theology on this subject. Regeneration does not necessarily involve the consciousness of spiritual life neither is it to be confounded with the assurance of faith. When spiritual life originates in the soul it takes its rise in man's innermost being working its way into all the faculties until it transforms not only the inmost thoughts and feelings but the outward words, actions and behaviour. It is the common observation of some believers that they were born again on such a date whereas the truth is that they were assured of their salvation on the date mentioned. To assert that every believer must be immediately conscious that he is a believer is contrary to the gradual order of Christian development. Such views introduce confusion into the discussion of regeneration; and besides, they discourage weak believers when they are told that they are no believers at all unless they possess certain qualifications which belong to grown believers and not infants in the faith: and when we read such passages as Matthew 5 : 3-16 and Galatians 5 : 17-26; we are directed to the true character of believers as distinguished from the world. In these passages nothing special is said as to their personal assurance of salvation. Yet it is a common practice in public and private exhortations to direct attention to the subjective and to institute a process of investigation as to the frames and feelings of inquirers instead of calling their attention to the gospel of Christ, inviting sinners to commit themselves to him, and setting forth the character of the believer as distinguished from the world.

It has become a common practice in some quarters to distinguish regeneration from being begotten. This appears to be supported by the different English words used in the New Testament, but if we take such examples as 1 John 2 : 29; 1 John 3 : 9; and compare them with 1 John 5 : 1, and 1 John 1 : 18; we shall find that the same Greek terms are used for both, and therefore to suggest that a person may be begotten first and then born again later on is simply to depart from the New Testament meaning of the term. It is true of course in the natural order that begetting and being born refer to differents events; it is also a matter of common knowledge that attempts have been made to spiritualise the new birth by speaking of a period between being begotten and being born as in the order of natural births. Scripture, however, makes no such distinction between the meanings of these words.

The question of the regeneration of infants has been made a subject of debate, and most divines appear to conclude that infants who are regenerated possess no faith. Since, however, all who are regenerated must possess the qualifications of regeneration we must allow that even if infants do not possess conscious adult faith yet since they are translated from darkness to light we must believe that they possess faith in its rudimentary state. In the natural order there are certain exercises of a new born infant which are similar to those of a grown up and so it is in the spiritual order. And while we cannot think of an infant being regenerated in infancy and converted later we can assert that a regenerate infant grows and develops until it attains the maturity of a person regenerated after infancy. Some controversy has arisen on this subject in connection with texts which appear to teach that we are begotten by the word and not by the Holy Spirit, viz. James 1 : 17, and 1 Pet. 1 : 23. If attention had been paid to the distinction between regeneration in the narrow and broader sense, this idea would not have arisen. For example, James speaks of the result of being born again in verse 18 as if he had said you are believers through the word of truth, and in 1 Peter 1 : 23, Peter refers in the context to **obedience to**

the truth (verse 22). This obedience to the truth could not exist without the implantation of the principle of grace in the heart by the immediate operation of the Holy Spirit. Surely it must occur to us if we ponder the subject carefully that the truth will not be believed until the soul is made alive by God.

Further, if we pay attention to the statements made on this subject in John 3 : 3; 1 John 4 : 7; 1 John 5 : 1; 1 John 5 : 18; we shall see that a distinction is made between the implantation of a spiritual principle and the exercise of it. A man must first be born again before he can see or enter the kingdom of God (John 3 : 3). It is one who is born of God who loves and knows God (John 14 : 7). It is one who is born of God who believes that Jesus is the Christ (1 John 5:1) and it is one who is born of God that sinneth not and keepeth himself (1 John 5 : 18). Indeed it would appear that some who differ do so in terminology and not in the substance of the doctrine they maintain. The Word of God is true and valuable for the unregenerate as well as for the regenerate but the unregenerate man cannot understand or appreciate the Word of God because he is spiritually blind. It is not the truth that gives sight to the blind but the Holy Ghost who creates spiritual life and vision. When this takes place it is in connection with the Word of God (at least in the case of adults), which is then believed. Regeneration in the narrow sense is the origination of spiritual life; faith is the exercise of that life. Regeneration is an act of God: faith is an act of man. There is not one without the other and they are both together in the beginning of saving grace.

V. JUSTIFICATION

The term **justification** has become a stranger nowadays but the doctrine referred to is of primary importance as it sets forth the way of salvation through Christ. Persons who disparage or omit this theological term should be reminded that it is often used in Scripture and insisted upon as a central doctrine in the application of redemption. If we accept the truth that all men through sin are under condemnation and so subject to the wrath and curse of God it must be of utmost importance that they should know how they are to obtain and enjoy pardon of sin and acceptance with God. This knowledge is obtained through the teaching of justification by faith. "Justification is an act of God's free grace, wherein he pardoneth all our sins and accepteth us as righteous in his sight, only for the righteousness of Christ imputed to us, and received by faith alone." (Shorter Catechism, Q. 33). The importance of the doctrine must appear if we read carefully Romans 3 : 21-31.

The Reformers in their controversies with the Church of Rome, while not disputing generally the views held by Popish writers on such subjects as the Doctrine of the Trinity, the Divinity of Christ and his Atoning work maintained that that Church had perverted the truths of Scripture on this basic doctrine. They therefore spent much of their strength in explaining and enforcing the doctrine of justification, and they succeeded in vindicating the truth of Scripture and so overturning the views held by the church of Rome on this subject.

1. The Meaning of Justification

Justification is said to be a declarative and not an efficient act of God. By an efficient act is meant the infusing of goodness or holiness into the sinner. Justification, however, is a declarative act by which God as the righteous Judge declares a sinner to be righteous because Christ has suffered and obeyed in his room and stead. Perhaps the matter will be clearer if we remember that justification refers to what God does **for** the sinner and not what God does **in** the sinner. Justification is strictly a legal term and consists in the act of a judge who declares or reckons a person to be free from condemnation. In human courts the office of a judge is to **declare** persons innocent or guilty not to make them so: to be **not guilty** procures acquittal, to be **guilty** procures punishment. God as a righteous Judge acquits us of guilt, **and restores us to his own favour** not because we are innocent or good but because Christ has suffered and obeyed as our substitute. Justification according to Scripture means more than mere pardon as it includes acceptance with God because Christ has purchased for us the blessings of spiritual and everlasting life.

The following passages set forth the drift of this doctrine.

"They shall justify the righteous and condemn the wicked" (Deut. 25 : 1). The meaning of this must be they shall declare them to be what they are, "He that justifieth the wicked, and he that condemneth the just, even they both are abomination to the Lord" (Prov. 17 : 15). The clearest indications of the meaning of the term are seen from passages where sinners are justified without works; by the blood of Christ, that is by means of the satisfaction of another (Rom. 3 : 24, 25, 26). The words and phrases used in these passages make it evident that justification is declarative and forensic; and that sinners have their sins forgiven and are accepted with God for the sake of the righteousness or the Atoning work of Christ.

To be just is to be righteous or blameless in the sight of the law, but to be blameless must often mean to be inherently good or righteous in heart or life. It might also mean to reform or make a person good or better than he is; or it might mean the state of being good. We may, therefore, expect that in a Book dealing with moral themes these meanings would occur and this is the case here. For example there is the **stative** use of the word to describe a state of being or condition and behaviour of a person or thing. "She hath been more righteous than I" (Gen. 38 : 26). "The judgments of God are true and righteous altogether" (Psa. 19 : 9). "Shall man be more just than God" (Job 4 17). These meanings of the word set forth a **state of being**. The **causitive** use of the word as in Dan. 12 : 3, "They tha turn many to righteousness", that is causing them to turi to righteousness. There are other passages bearing thii meaning. There is also the exhibitive sense **showing o**ı demonstrating to be righteous. "And the LORD said untc me, the backsliding Israel hath justified herself more than Judah" (Jer. 3 : 11). The meaning of this is that Israel had shown herself more righteous than Judah (Professor John Murray, Lectures on Justification, 1955). It would be useless to deny that these senses of justification are brought out in Scripture; and it is possible that several others could be found which do not connote the forensic meaning which we contend for in justification. All we are concerned about is to show that in the references to the justification of a sinner justification can have no other meaning than the forensic sense of declaring a sinner to be just only for the righteousness of Christ.

Justification is not only an act of God's free grace but it is a righteous act and since God will not justify the wicked we must enquire into the reason for the justification of a sinner, for God would not justify the sinner or esteem him to be righteous unless he were so. The reason is that the righteousness of Christ is put to our account and therefore we are declared to be what we are in law, that is righteous persons. Our justification is therefore procured by the righteousness of Christ which is put to our account as our own, at the moment we believe in Christ. The question may be asked as to when this state of righteousness or justification comes to be. The answer to this is that God for Christ's sake constitutes the sinner righteous on the event of his union with Christ and declares him to be so. Indeed if we attend to the matter carefully we shall see that God does not in any way execute his power in making the sinner any better than he is in justifying him. But he does constitute him a righteous person in the eyes of the law on the event of his union with Christ. Rom. 5 : 19 declares that by one man's disobedience many were made sinners. This cannot mean that they were made sinful but it must mean that being in Adam they were constituted or brought under condemnation. The Judge pronounced them as being under condemnation because they sinned in Adam. In like manner by the obedience of Christ many were brought into justification. The Judge pronounced them justified because they were in Christ. Sinners are justified not on account of any merit of their own; and when it is said that we are justified by faith we are not to think that we are justified on account of our faith since this faith itself is merely a condition or instrument by which we receive Christ. Whatever terms we use in dealing with this part of the subject it must be evident that if Jesus Christ shed his blood for the church then there is nothing left for sinners to do: and were they able to do something to save themselves it would not be necessary since he did everything. But when we think of a sinner who seeks pardon of sin and acceptance, and when we consider that he is a personal, responsible and moral being, we are almost bound to conclude that if he is to receive these blessings it must be in a gratuitous way, and the manner in which he does receive it is by committing himself to Christ. Faith itself possesses no value as an action of the sinner, but when it is exercised in committal to Christ it puts the sinner into possession of Christ himself and the blessings of salvation.

Justification is by faith alone. This excludes any meritorious exercise such as repentance, hope, love and new obedience. All these blessings stem from union with Christ and faith in him. We should say that faith itself is excluded **as a work.** The whole purpose of the argumentation about justification is to bring home the conviction that justification is based entirely upon the righteousness of Christ which is imputed to us. The reason that faith itself is considered in our justification is because it is the vinculum or bond of union between Christ and the sinner. Scripture never says we are justified by love, repentance or hope, but always by faith, and when it is said that we are justified by works it simply means that our good works demonstrate or evidence our faith in Christ.

It is evident that the foregoing explanation of justification by faith gives no account of the **spiritual condition** of a justified person. This is because justification relates to the law and terminates upon the state of the person and not upon his nature. But faith is never alone in the justified person but is always accompanied by the graces of the Holy Spirit who bestows upon the sinner a new heart. Justification is instantaneous and complete and does not depend upon any further satisfaction for sin; sanctification or holiness in the believer is not complete and continues throughout life. If God were to justify us on account of our sanctification as believers it would appear that the judgment was not just because we are not yet completely sanctified. But in justification the judgment is just because we are believed who did not cordially accept Jesus as their Saviour accepted in him. If we say that justification is making a person righteous or holy we fail to distinguish between what is done **for** the sinner and what is done **in** him. The objective work of Christ does just what was intended to be done, namely, the procuring of the forgiveness of men's sins and their acceptance with God. Sanctification, however, as a work produces a new heart and a new life. Justification is not pardon of sins alone, for we are to remember that suffering for the sins of men is only one aspect of Christ's work. The other aspect is obedience to the law which is accounted to God's people and procures acceptance for them with God. Very few persons would say that Christ's work was of no effect yet some will maintain that something must be added to it of our own to make it complete. The design of justification however is to procure forgiveness of sins and acceptance with God by the atonement of Christ alone. It is quite evident that the Galatians were in error on this important subject and that the Apostle Paul considered it a grave heresy when we read his severe and withering rebukes to some among them, who attempted to supplement the complete righteousness of Christ by the works of the law. (Gal. 1 : 9; 3 : 1-5; 3 : 13; 4 : 5; 4 : 9; 5 : 3; 5 : 11, 12).

VI. SAVING FAITH

1. Faith in General

Faith as a mental act has been variously defined and the discussions relating to it are useful if only to prevent us from holding defective views of Scriptural Saving Faith. Faith as such is determined by a sufficiency of evidence which cannot be resisted by the subject. If the evidence is not sufficient we cannot believe it even if we would; on the other hand the evidence may be sufficient though the subject may fail to evaluate it as such. We do not believe something to be true because we wish to, or because we expect to benefit from it, but because we are convinced of its truth. If our faith consists in trust in a person it is not because we desire him to be trustworthy but because we are assured that he is so.

According to some philosophers — and they have been supported by individuals in the Christian Church — faith is weaker than knowledge. Opinion is said to rest on grounds subjectively and objectively insufficient; while faith rests on grounds subjectively sufficient but objectively insufficient; knowledge, however, rests on grounds subjectively and objectively sufficient. For example, I think

John Williams is a Chinaman and that he is very tall and fair, because some people have told me so. This is opinion. I may also believe that John Williams is a Chinaman but that he is small and dark, because I have it on the highest authority given by competent and impartial witnesses. This is faith or belief. I may know that John Williams is a Chinaman because I have seen him for myself. This is knowledge. Yet my faith may be as strong as my knowledge since I could be mistaken in my perception. In any case the reports of several competent and impartial witnesses may be as certain as my own sense perception, since a Chinaman whose mother is English may be very like an Englishman.

The difference between faith and knowledge is that faith is based upon testimony and knowledge on perception; and when we say that we know that Christ is our Saviour we are just saying that we believe Christ to be our Saviour. Indeed if our assurance is strong enough it is equivalent to knowledge. Faith in general is assent to a truth or confidence in a person; and in order that faith may exist there must be sufficient evidence to induce belief. If the truth proposed has no interest for us it is speculative; if we feel it to be of importance to us our faith is practical. Faith in God is not only an assent to his promises but a hearty reliance upon him and a coming to him for the help we need. Saving faith both in the Old Testament and in the New partakes of this element of trust. In Scripture the word faith has various meanings such as to be firm, to regard as true, to be persuaded of the rightness or wrongness of an act, to give assent, and to trust in a person. In the Old Testament it is often spoken of as trust in God. In the New Testament it is referred to, as looking to Christ, believing in him or on him, coming to him, receiving him, and knowing him. In the infancy of the Christian Church outsiders such as Jews or Gentiles were required to accept the fundamentals of the Christian profession and especially faith in Christ as the Saviour of lost men. It is evident from the history of the New Testament however that some and who were of the opinion that a speculative belief without a corresponding obedience was sufficient. The Apostle James stresses the danger of this interpretation of saving faith. Theologians have mentioned at least three kinds of faith which differ from saving faith. **Historical faith** is an assent to the doctrines of the gospel. This faith is produced by the discipline of Christianity, and when cultivated from infancy is bound to produce some impressions of the reality of Christianity; and in some cases the evidence elicits strong convictions. **The Faith of Miracles** is a persuasion that God is able to perform miracles on behalf of ourselves or others, or through us. **Temporary faith** is a belief and acceptance of the truth but it is later extinguished by the temptations or allurements of this world. Broadly speaking historical faith is intellectual, temporary faith is emotional, and the faith of miracles is volitional. This analysis must not be stressed since all these various elements are more or less present in all the exercises referred to.

"Faith in Jesus Christ is a saving grace, whereby we receive and rest upon him alone for salvation, as he is offered to us in the gospel" (Shorter Catechism 86). This exercise is said to consist of three elements, **notitia, assensus, and fiducia.** The first element is intellectual (notitia or knowledge) and is based upon a discovery of God as a Saviour and a plan of Salvation suited to man's need. It is difficult to say how little or how much this knowledge involves but in the nature of the case it is present in the act of justifying faith and in all subsequent acts of faith. The second element is assensus or assent, and consists in a belief in the truth of the gospel. This aspect of faith considered in itself is a conviction of the priceless value of the gospel for ourselves, and in the case of believers it is not only mental but also emotional. We believe and we feel that the gospel is good and good for us. The third element is fiducia or trust. It need hardly be said that this element is not just a committal of ourselves to certain doctrines but a reliance upon Christ for salvation. This is the crowning element of faith and implies a committal of ourselves to Jesus Christ by a spiritual movement of our whole being. This act of faith secures our union with Christ and brings to us Christ himself and with him all the blessings of the gospel. In regard to the psychological order of these exercises we must not attach a temporal significance to them since the act of justifying faith embraces all three, and if it is said that knowledge comes before faith this just means that an intellectual knowledge of the gospel is indispensable to our receiving of it. But such a knowledge may exist without the saving faith which contains these elements. The truth that saving faith comprises these elements may be proved from such passages as: "Believe in the Lord Jesus Christ and thou shalt be saved". The Jailer was not bidden merely to assent to certain doctrines but to receive and rest upon Christ for salvation. "He that believeth on the Son hath everlasting life" (John 3 : 36). "I know whom I have believed" (2 Tim. 1 : 12). "Justifying faith not only assenteth to the truth of the promise of the gospel but receiveth and resteth upon Christ for pardon" (Larger Catechism 72). Justifying faith therefore contains an intellectual, emotional, and volitional element. "With the heart man believeth unto righteousness" (Rom. 10 : 10).

Professor John Murray in discussing this element of trust says: "It is this confiding character of faith that precipitates the engagement of person to person, namely the person of the sinner as lost, and the person of Christ as Saviour. In this exercise there is an inner movement of the whole man in abandonment of all confidence in our own resources or any human resources, to receive and rest upon Christ alone for salvation in the conviction of his all-sufficiency, ability, and willingness to save us. It is in this aspect, element, or ingredient that the volitive character of faith appears. It is here that the distinguishing character of faith evidences itself" (Lectures Westminster Seminary, Philadelphia, 1955).

Faith itself is said in Scripture to be the gift of God and is the product of a renewed heart. At the same time we must not confuse the issue by refusing to allow that faith is the sole exercise of a sinner and that it proceeds from the heart. The Reformers in their controversies with the Romish communion in dealing with such subjects as justification and faith were careful to distinguish these acts from the exercises that accompanied or proceeded from them, such as repentance, love and new obedience. Divines also distinguished between justifying faith and saving faith. The former comprehends the first exercise of a renewed sinner which unites him to Christ; the latter constitutes the further exercises of a true believer. It has been said that faith is the instrument which receives Christ. Objections have been made to the word **instrument,** and indeed it is not a happy term for this subject; but the meaning is that faith is not the moving or meritorious cause of our salvation but the instrumental cause. The word **condition** is a much better term but unfortunately it has been so much abused that some are led to believe that sinners are justified by the exercise of their faith; and so some orthodox divines prefer to use the word instrument. The question may be asked why is faith rather than any of the other graces mentioned as the condition or instrument of our salvation. The short answer to this question is that first, we are put off from trying to save ourselves by our own efforts and exercises, and secondly, because Christ has proved to be a real Saviour by blotting out the iniquities of his people, and so we are to commit ourselves to him that we may be saved; and thirdly, union between Chirst and the sinner is formed in the only way, so far as we know, in which such a union could be formed between the Saviour and the sinner, that is, by faith through which we unite ourselves to him in a self-committal of our persons, this being the immediate effect of our being quickened by the Spirit of Christ.

2. The Assurance of Faith

"Are all true believers, at all times, assured of their being in the estate of grace, and that they shall be saved?" "Assurance of grace and salvation not being of the essence of faith true believers may wait long before they obtain it and after the enjoyment thereof, may have it weakened and intermitted through manifold distempers, sins, and desertions, yet are never left without such a presence and support of the Spirit of God as helps them from sinking into utter despair" (Larger Catechism 81). The above statement affirms that assurance is not of the essence of faith and that believers may wait long before they obtain it and that after they obtain it, they may have doubts as to whether they are true believers or not. The assurance spoken of here is not faith but the consciousness that we do possess this saving faith. It is a common opinion held by some evangelicals that if we possess saving faith we are bound to know it. This sweeping assertion is contrary to the experience of some believers whose faith has not been brought to maturity, and lays a stumbling block in the way of weak Christians, who because they are not assured of the reality of their faith are induced to conclude that they are destitute of saving faith. Some church authorities will not permit these weak believers to be partakers of their own spiritual privileges such as sealing ordinances, while others despise them or accuse them of unbelief because their knowledge and experience is not so great as their own. In setting this subject in a clear light we must distinguish between assurance of the truth of the gospel and assurance of our own interest in it. It is not denied that some believers possess both these assurances nor is it denied that all believers trust in Christ and adhere to him as Saviour. Neither is it denied that a state of doubt is not an ingredient of faith or is commendable. All that we contend for is that a believer may rely upon Christ for salvation and at the same time may not be assured of the reality of his faith (Isa. 50 : 10; 1 John 5 : 13; 2 Pet. 1 : 10).

The assurance of faith, or what some call the assurance of sense is sometimes vouchsafed to the weak believer in such a striking light that he may conclude that previously he was no believer. The only real difference between his condition today and his condition yesterday is that today he is full of happiness, strength and thankfulness, whereas yesterday he was in a state of doubt and weakness. But as to his actual inward and outward spiritual exercises they were as fervent, hearty, and loving yesterday as they are today. Yesterday he possessed the faith of adherence through which he trusted in Christ and devoted his heart and life to him. Today he possesses the faith of assurance through which he looks into himself and discovers that Christ is his own Saviour, and in view of his present condition he is happy, strong, and thankful. In the case of others the assurance of their own salvation may be in such close proximity to their faith in Christ that they find it difficult to distinguish them. In the case of some others the path to assurance may be long and dreary and may perhaps be torturous and difficult because of human frailties or temptations.

The assurance of sense or faith of assurance has been

called faith, strong faith, or a reflex act of faith. The propriety of using these terms is not too apparent. Saving faith is a movement out of self towards Christ, while assurance is a knowledge of our state by introspection. It is true we get all the reliable information we require in Scripture but the knowledge of our state is not obtained by faith or the reflex act of faith but by a discovery in ourselves that we are believers. When this discovery is given with impressive power we are able to say, This promise is for me and therefore I am saved.

VII.   REPENTANCE

"Repentance unto life is a saving grace, whereby a sinner out of a true sense of sin, and apprehension of the mercy of God in Christ, doth, with grief and hatred of his sin, turn from it unto God, with full purpose of, and endeavour after new obedience" (Westminster Catechism, 87). Repentance comprises therefore a sense of personal sinfulness, a discovery of the mercy of God in Christ, and a resolute turning from it to God and to a new life of obedience. According to Drs Berkhof and Strong repentance includes three elements: (1) An **intellectual** element which consists of a recognition of sin as involving guilt, defilement, and helplessness. The Greek words used to describe this element, such as "knowledge of sin" will be found in Rom. 3 : 20; (2) An **emotional** element which denotes sorrow for sin as being committed against a holy God. The Greek word used here, "a change of mind", will be found in 2 Cor. 7, 9, 10; (3) A **volitional** element, which consists in a change of purpose. This is the most important aspect of repentance and is indicated by the word "repentance" used in such passages as Acts 2 : 38; Rom. 2 : 4.

The distinction between **legal** and evangelical repentance is important if we consider that there may be sorrow for sin and amendment of life which falls short of repentance unto life. Such repentance is exemplified in the cases of Pharaoh, Saul, and Judas. Legal repentance views sin from a selfish motive as involving evil consequences. We are sorry because the commission of sin is an obstacle to our physical, mental, or spiritual wellbeing. Legal repentance also evidences itself by endeavours to overcome sin by personal strength or by a dependence upon God's mercy in a general way. God is merciful and therefore we may expect forgiveness. **Evangelical** repentance bases its plea on the atonement of Christ — to the exclusion of all other helps, whether external or internal — for forgiveness and purification. Evangelical repentance produces a new obedience not in the sense of making satisfaction for sin, for this has been accomplished by Christ himself, but in being influenced by the grace of God in Christ Jesus, and from motives of love and gratitude seeking to please him in all things. As to its exercise it is not extorted by fear of punishment but through the constraining love of Christ, and is spontaneous and voluntary so that penitent sinners delight in the law of God after the inward man (Psa. 119 : 159; Rom. 7 : 22). Repentance itself is a gift of God for in the striking language of Scripture we can no more cease from sin by our own efforts than the Ethiopian can change his skin or the leopard his spots. It is, of course, true that unregenerate men do depart from some sins but this is a mere outward change. True repentance is a change of heart and we are told in the language of Scripture that Christ is exalted a Prince and a Saviour for to give repentance to Israel and forgiveness of sins (Acts 5 : 31).

Neither is it true that God grants forgiveness because we repent of sin and amend our ways as men forgive injuries upon confession and amendment. The satisfaction of Christ is the procuring cause of repentance and on this only we rely when we confess our sins. The doctrine of Rome is in some respects utterly opposed to the Scriptural view of repentance; and while it must be allowed that the Roman Church teaches that forgiveness comes to us through the atonement of Christ yet she has so perverted this doctrine as to place the emphasis on the merits of the sinner rather than on the merits of Christ. The elements of repentance according to Roman theologians are mainly, **contrition, attrition, confession, satisfaction** and **absolution. Contrition** does not include sorrow for inborn sin but only for personal transgression. **Attrition** is a mental conviction that sin deserves punishment, namely the fear of eternal punishment. This latter in Protestant Theology is called legal repentance. **Confession** is made to a priest; and when we consider the circumstances connected with this rite of religion we are constrained to characterise it in some of its grilling questions as degrading and revolting, and a gross invasion of all the secrets of personal relationships. **Satisfaction** is some painful penance to satisfy justice for sins committed. The **absolution** pronounced by the priest is not declarative but judicial. But the power of forgiveness exercised by the Christian ministry is declarative only, declaring the conditions upon which God pardons sin, and admitting men to sealing ordinances.

The central thought of the sacrament of penance in the Romish Church is that such outward performances constitute a satisfaction for sin. The truth however is that repentance is not an outward performance but an inward grace and the exercise of that grace is between the sinner and his Saviour. That any outward or inward performance itself procures satisfaction for sin is contrary to the plain doctrine of Scripture for Christ "bore our sins in his own body on the tree". Confession of sin and amendment of ways are properly speaking but the fruits of repentance. The question as to the relation between repentance, faith and other graces, is easily resolved if we distinguish between the logical and chronological order. Repentance is the exercise of a believer and proceeds from union with Christ and faith in him. But in the order of time union with Christ, faith, and repentance are simultaneous. The confusion of ideas connected with this part of the subject is sometimes due to the emphasis laid on the truth that sinners are exhorted to repent and believe, to this may be added the experience of believers who laboured under conviction of sin for some time before they obtained assurance of their salvation. This distinction between legal and evangelical repentance must be taken into account here, as they both agree in some respects; and because legal repentance generally precedes evangelical repentance.

Regeneration is the act of God implanting a new nature in the sinner; conversion expresses the first exercises of that nature, while justifying faith is the first act of the new nature. Conversion and repentance differ only in their usage. The former is the more general term and is used to include the first exercises of faith and other graces such as love and hope. The latter, that is repentance, is a more specific term and designates the hatred and renunciation of sin and turning to God which is inseparable from a true Christian profession. Conversion basically comprises two elements, namely, repentance and faith. The doctrine of conversion has received much attention during recent years and the "psychology of conversion" provides much useful information. Drs Berkhof and Strong devote a special section to conversion. This section is especially interesting in view of the prevailing beliefs on the subject of conversion.

VIII. SANCTIFICATION

Sanctification has been defined as the continued operation of the Holy Ghost in the hearts of believers by which the new nature imparted to them at regeneration is maintained and strengthened. In the Old Testament the doctrine of holiness is primarily derived from the quality of holiness in God which stresses his inapproachableness by sinful creatures. Consequently in the worship of his Name persons and things must be separated from moral and ceremonial impurity. Some are of the opinion that the original meaning of the word "sanctify" is to "shine" and this would express the idea of purity. Others suppose the word means to "cut" which gives the thought of separateness. The term "sanctify" is employed in Scripture in two senses, first, to consecrate or set apart. "Whom the Father hath sanctified and sent" (John 10 : 36), and secondly, to purify. "Sanctify them through thy truth" (John 17 : 17). In discussing the doctrine of sanctification the second sense of the term is dealt with here. "Sanctification is the work of God's free grace, whereby we are renewed in the whole man after the image of God, and are enabled more and more to die unto sin and live unto righteousness" (Shorter Catechism, Q. 35).

Sanctification is an efficient work of God's Spirit within the believer's nature and affecting the whole man. How this work is carried on in the hearts of believers is a great mystery, but we do know that the Holy Ghost as an agent imparts light and energy which discovers itself by the intelligent and voluntary activity of the believer in bringing his whole being into conformity with the image of God. In this work of sanctification the Spirit of God strengthens and increases the graces of the believer such as faith, hope and love so that the exercise of any of these graces increases the holiness or sanctification of the believer. This follows, also, in the exercises of penitence and humility resulting from providential chastisements. The Holy Ghost also stirs up the graces of a believer through preaching, reading, prayer, the sacraments, and the providential trials met with in the world, Sanctification affects the whole man and this includes all the members of his body and the faculties of his soul. In one word, there is a gradual change for good effected in his mental, spiritual and physical nature. This means that according to the true doctrine of sanctification there is a universal change wrought in the whole man soul and body. This does not mean that the substance of the soul or body is changed but that new qualities or principles appear in the whole man and the members of the body become willing instruments for good through the influence of a new spirit and a new heart.

Sanctification, however, is not a completed act but a gradual work which does not come to perfection in this life and Scripture teaches that there is an opposing principle called "the old nature" or "the flesh" which necessitates a continual conflict. In the new nature there is nothing sinful and in the old nature there is nothing holy. The conflict between sin and holiness in the heart of a believer is set down at large in Romans, chapters seven and eight. It is sometimes difficult for a believer to observe his own progress and, indeed, though his desires and motives may be purified he may feel he is getting worse instead of better. At times he does not see the results of grace in himself but he sees the effects of sin. We read in the "Pilgrim's Progress" that when the room full of dust was being swept the place was choked with dust but when water was sprinkled it was swept with pleasure: and when sin is stirred up in the believer he is depressed by his condition and requires the gospel to subdue his iniquities. In the same book we read that Christian observed a fire which burned up brighter though water was being poured upon it, but when he went round to the back of the wall and saw oil being poured on to the fire he received instruction. When the sun shines into a dark room we easily discern its defects and the Holy Ghost, while maintaining and strengthening the work of grace in our hearts, shows us our continual need of being purified from sin.

In sanctification the believer co-operates with God in the work of grace and this sheds light upon the exhortations given in Scripture to persevere in the faith. There is nothing inconsistent in this aspect of sanctification, and it is easily understood if we pay attention to the fact that the intelligent and voluntary aspirations after holiness are grounded in the regenerating and sanctifying work of the Holy Spirit. "Work out your own salvation with fear and trembling for it is God which worketh in you both to do and to will of his good pleasure" (Phil. 2 : 12-13). The distinction between justification and sanctification is important. The blessings procured by Jesus Christ for his people are two-fold. We are placed in a right relationship with God by what Christ has done **for** us; so that our sins are forgiven and we are accepted as righteous in his sight. Through what he has done **in** us a new spiritual life is produced and our hearts and lives are purified. Some people confuse sanctification and justification and speak of the finished work of Christ as if our salvation were complete. The work of salvation, however, includes the sanctifying of the believer and fitting him for a life of communion with God.

In distinguishing between justification and sanctification a celebrated theologian writes thus:— "They differ in their order; justification precedes, and sanctification follows; a sinner is pardoned and restored to the favour of God, before the Spirit is given to renew him more and more after his image. They differ in their object; justification takes away the guilt of sin, or the obligation to punishment; sanctification cleanses us from its stain or pollution. They differ in their form; justification is a judicial act, by which the sinner is pronounced righteous; sanctification is a physical or moral act, or rather a series of such acts, by which a change is effected in the qualities of the soul. The one, therefore, is called an act, to signify that it is perfected at once; the other is called a work, to signify that it is progressive. Justification being an act passed in a moment, is equal in all believers; sanctification exists in different degrees of advancement in different individuals. In a word, the one changes our state, translating us from a state of condemnation into a state of acceptance; the other changes our nature, or makes those holy who are unholy. I shall add only one difference more, which relates to this matter. In justification, the righteousness of Christ is imputed to us, in sanctification, an inherent righteousness is communicated; and upon the whole it appears, that in justification we receive a title to heaven, and by sanctification we are prepared for it, or made meet to be partakers of the inheritance of the saints in light" (Vol. 3 page 405, Lectures on Theology, Dr John Dick).

The means of sanctification are internal and external. The **internal** means are faith, hope, joy, peace and the other graces of the believer; and the exercise of any of the christian graces increases the holiness of God's people. The external means are the Scriptures, Prayer, The Sacraments and providential discipline (condensed from Dr Shedd, Dogmatic Theology, Vol. 2 page 555). Sanctification is intimately related to good works and when good works are referred to in a theological sense they are these works which are the expressions of a holy nature as the principle from which they spring. These works whatever they may be are considered good not only in their own nature but in the principle which evokes them. They are the fruits of a just and honest heart, are in accordance with the revealed will of God, and spring from a principle of love to God, and their final aim is the chief end of man, which is to glorify God. There are certain works performed by men which though commanded by God and beneficial to themselves and others are not pleasing to God because they do not proceed from a good heart, are not done in a right manner, according to God's word, nor to a right end, the glory of God (Confession 16 : 7). Theologians have discussed the doctrine of perfectionism and antinomianism in relation to this question. Perfectionism as a doctrine is taught in various forms but the fundamental idea is that religious perfection is attainable in the present life. It is of course true that God commands believers to be holy and perfect and that holiness and perfection are ascribed to believers in the Word of God, but it is evident from Scripture that men such as Noah, Job, Abraham and other saints were not absolutely sinless. The Word of God states plainly that no believer is perfect in the sense of being without sin (1 Kings 8 : 46; Ecc. 7 : 20; James 3 : 2; 1 John 1 : 8). Confession of sin is required of believers and it is manifest that there is an inward conflict between sin and holiness. The perfectionist, however, attempts to evade these truths, by lowering the standard of the law and making sin to consist merely of external acts of sin. It is sufficient to reply to these ideas that the standard of the law is not to be lowered. It is holy, just and good and is summed up in love to God; and it is evident from Scripture and experience that evil thoughts are sinful even if actual sin is not committed (Matt. 5 : 28).

The antinomians claim that since Christ bore the penalty of sin and met the demands of the law the believer is therefore free from obligation to serve it. This error manifests itself in different ways. Some would have it that a saint cannot sin and therefore if he commits transgression it is no sin for him. Others maintain that the law of God is outmoded and that instead we are to obey the gospel. Paul says that the Gospel established the law. "Do we then make void the law through faith? God forbid; yea, we establish the law" (Rom. 3 : 31). Some forms of dispensationalism utterly fail to grasp the relation between the believer and the law of God contained in the Old and New Testaments and give the impression even when they do not actually express it that the Gospel has annulled God's revealed principles of righteousness; and when they are criticised for the earthliness and looseness of their Christian living they glibly quote Scripture by stating that they are not under law but under grace. But a cursory examination of the passage referred to would prove that their exegises and application of it is erroneous for the following sentence in the passage warns believers against sinning because they are not under the law. "For sin shall not have dominion over you; for you are not under the law but under grace. What then? Shall we sin, because we are not under the law, but under grace? God forbid" (Rom. 6 : 14-15). Dr Berkhof quotes with approbation the following extract from Dr Strong (Systematic Theology, page 876), "Christ frees us (1) from the law as a system of curse and penalty; this he does by bearing the curse and penalty himself . . ., (2) from the law with its claims as a method of salvation; this he does by making this obedience and merits ours . . ., (3) from the law as an outward and foreign compulsion; this he does by giving us the spirit of obedience and worship, by which the law is progressively realised within."

IX. ADOPTION

The doctrine of Adoption is based upon the various references made in Scripture to the Fatherhood of God and Sonship of believers. A collation of all the passages of Scripture dealing with this subject brings before us the Fatherhood of God in its various aspects. God is the Father of Christ in a peculiar sense. He is also the Father by creation but this is not referred to in any redemptive sense. He is called the Father of the children of Israel as they were his peculiar people. We have no Scriptural evidence that he is the Father of all men except by creation; and if we are to deal with the doctrine of adoption on the basis of Scripture we must bring it under the category of redemption. "Adoption is an act of God's free grace, whereby we are received into the number and have a right to all the privileges of the sons of God" (Shorter Catechism 34). The word itself would seem to indicate the taking of a stranger and dealing with him as a son. Adoption is therefore an act of God in which he translates a sinner from the power of darkness into the household of God.

The act of adoption though closely related to the other graces of the Spirit brings before us the highest privilege bestowed upon God's people. By becoming God's adopted sons we are brought into the closest relation with him, and the most affectionate terms are used to express this state and privilege. The Apostle John who understood the meaning of this term better than we can hope to do, was transported with the thought of it when he exclaims "Beloved, what manner of love the Father hath bestowed upon us, that we should be called the sons of God" (1 John 3 : 1). Adoption is therefore expressive of God's deepest love for his people and his purpose to bestow upon them the most precious gifts of that love, and to bring them into the closest conformity with himself. "Beloved now are we the sons of God, and it doth not yet appear what we shall be: but we know that when he shall appear we shall be like him: for we shall see him as he is" (1 John 3 : 2). The realisation that God is from everlasting to everlasting, the Creator and sustainer of all, glorious in holiness and infinitely removed from the corrupt and unworthy creatures that we are, is calculated to fill us with fear and self-loathing. The doctrine of adoption, however, teaches us that God is pleased to remove all barriers between himself and his people so that they are enabled through the Spirit of adoption to freely draw near to him as loving children to a loving Father who is more than ready to supply all their needs.

The relation between adoption and the other graces has been variously stated. Effectual calling brings sinners into union with himself, regeneration gives them a new nature, justification changes their state, and sanctification renovates their nature. Adoption brings them into the status of sons, a position for which God is pleased to fit them by the manifold operations of his grace.

The Westminster Standards set forth the logical order of privileges. We are justified, adopted, and sanctified. Over and above that of justification another status is added which logically immediately follows justification, when we are adopted and receive the status of sons. And it is on the basis of sonship that God deals with his children and from that moment onward deals with them in no other way. In this sonship they are viewed by Paul in respect to their privileges and by John in respect of their nature, and not excluding their privileges. Amesius (1633) represents adoption as a new grace in advance of justification and not an element in it; a gracious sentence of God whereby a believer, having been justified, is accepted for Christ's sake into the relation and rights of sonship. Dr A. A. Hodge thinks adoption presents the new creature who is justified and sanctified in his new relationship as belonging to the family of God.

"We have seen that in civil adoption the consent of the person to be adopted was demanded and publicly expressed. Something similar takes place in spiritual adoption. The privilege is offered to us in the Gospel, but it does not become ours until we accept of it. Although we do not, and cannot merit it, yet our consent is required, and is indispensably necessary. Now this consists in faith, which implies our cordial acceptance of the blessings which Christ purchased for us; and of which God makes a free gift to us in the Gospel. Hence, to believe in Christ, and to receive him, are used in the Scriptures as equivalent terms. 'Art thou willing,' God says, 'that I shall be thy Father?' The believing sinner answers, 'I am willing.' 'As many as received him, to them gave he power to become the sons of God, even to them that believe on his name.' " (John Dick, Vol. 3 page 394).

V. THE LAST THINGS

CHAPTER XVI.

I. THE DOCTRINE OF THE LAST THINGS

1. Death

The definition of physical death according to Scripture is that the body returns to the earth and that the spirit is translated to a separate state of existence by its Creator and Judge (Ecc. 12 : 7). According to some, death is a natural process necessitated by the innate constitution of the human body. Scripture however connects death with sin and we are justified in assuming that sin affected the body with the seeds of dissolution; for, "by one man sin entered into the world and death by sin" (Rom. 5 : 12). Before our first parents sinned they were in union with God and not subject to death, but sin disrupted this union and man's body became a prey to death, and his soul and body became subject to eternal separation from God.

Since death is the penalty of sin it would seem that believers who have been justified from sin would evade this penalty. Various answers have been given to explain this problem. It has been said that the afflictions of life and even death itself are not punishments but fatherly chastisements administered for the good of believers. The trials of life and the thoughts of death have a sobering effect upon them, fosters humility, makes them more spiritually minded, and gives energy to their faith. It has also been said that if believers had been translated without experiencing death, and if unbelievers died and were buried, the scheme of the gospel would require great modifications. It has also been shown that death is a great advantage to believers. Sin and sorrow come to an end and they are immediately translated into the presence of their Saviour. Moreover it has been pointed out that certain circumstances in the lives of believers lead them to part from the world with little regret. It has also been suggested that death is inevitable even to believers because of the present constitution of the body; but the rapture of Enoch and Elijah seems to disprove this view. Dr Dabney says that "bodily appetites are the occasions of the larger part of most men's sins; as the bodily members are the instruments of all their overt sins. How natural then that when these are removed God should finally remove sin?" (Lectures in Theology, page 821). In any case the primary reason for death even in the case of believers is the fact of sin and the existence of sin in themselves.

Although death has been appointed for all there is a great difference between the death of the righteous and the wicked. The blessedness of death for the righteous consists in the complete sanctification of the soul, and immediate entrance into heaven to be with Christ which is far better. How the souls of believers are made perfect in holiness on the event of death we are unable to comprehend. We must, however, believe that the Holy Ghost removes all the traces and effects of sin that they may be in a fit state to enter into eternal blessedness and hold communion with their Saviour face to face. In the case of the believer the sting of death is removed. This consists of the condemning sentence of the law and exclusion from the favour of God. When this is removed and the believer is strengthened in his faith he is made quite willing to depart that he may be with Christ. Death must be in itself an unspeakable terror even to the believer since human nature shrinks from physical or mental pain; and the springs of grace must be in exercise in order to meet the last enemy. There is, however, a sufficiency of grace given, when it is required, to overcome fear and inspire hope. When the pilgrims approached the river they found there was no bridge and that only two had crossed without entering the river. They asked about the depth and were told it was deeper or shallower according to their faith in the King of the Palace. At first Christian began to sink in the water but Hope supported him and brought him safely across (Pilgrim's Progress).

2. Immortality

The question of the soul's immortality has been the subject of earnest thought by pagan as well as Jewish writers. The term immortality in its absolute sense can be applied only to God himself (1 Tim. 6 : 15, 16). Immortality in another sense may be taken to mean the endless existence of all spirits including human souls. Indeed there is no single instance of the absolute annihilation of any spiritual or material substance; nevertheless, the continued existence of matter or spirit is dependent upon the will of the Creator. The immortality of the soul as a substance simply means that the soul is a monad and so incapable of dissolution. This is just saying that the soul will continue forever in a separate existence. This is the reasoning of Plato and others. Those who deny the immortality of the soul say that there is no future life but that the soul is reduced to a state of non-existence.

We are concerned, however, with the views of Scripture on this subject. The Bible teaches that the souls and bodies of believers are both predestinated to a blessed and immortal existence. We read early in the sacred text that Enoch was translated to heaven (Gen. 5 : 24), and we note that when Christ argued with the Sadducees, who denied the resurrection, he spoke of God's being the father of Abraham, Isaac and Jacob, long after their death (Luke 20 : 37, 38). There are also several passages in the Old Testament which indicate a state of existence after death such as Gen. 17 : 7; Num. 23 : 10; Job. 13 : 15; Psa. 17 : 15; Psa. 31 : 5; Dan. 12 : 2, 3, 13. The Old Testament proofs for the teaching of the doctrine of a future state have been used to combat the views of heretics and modernists who deny that the Old Testament teaches this doctrine. Indeed it has been asserted by some divines that immortality like the divine existence is assumed rather than proved throughout the Scripture.

The truth of immortality is more clearly taught in the New Testament and the texts and incidents referring to it are to be found here and there in various passages such as:— Luke 23 : 43; 2 Cor. 5 : 6, 8; and Phil. 1 : 23, 24. The statements of Jesus are pointed and clear. When He argues with the Sadducees, long after the death of Abraham, Isaac, and Jacob that "for he is not a God of the dead, but of the living" (Luke 20 : 38), he establishes the immortality of these persons. And when he says to the thief: "Verily I say unto thee today shalt thou be with me in paradise," he speaks of life in heaven for himself and the thief on the cross. The Apostle believes the same truth when he speaks of "having a desire to depart, and to be with Christ; which is far better."

The most impressive and conclusive of all proofs of immortality, is afforded by the resurrection of Jesus Christ from the dead, a work accomplished in his own power, and confirming the efficacy of his atoning blood. If Christ rose not from the dead there is no hope for us. If he did, then this carries with it the resurrection of his people. Our faith brings the existence of God and our resurrection together. If we believe the former we may be assured of the promise of the latter.

When we come to examine this subject even in the light of Scripture we come to realise how little we know about the after-life and we must be contented that Christ knows the future and we commit ourselves to Him to lead us into it. Even Paul and John did not know very much about it. Paul speaks of the contrast between the present and the future and seems to indicate that we need faith even to grasp a modicum of these truths (2 Cor. 4 : 17, 18), and John says "It doth not yet appear what we shall be: but we know that, when he shall appear, we shall be like him; for we shall see him as he is" (1 John 3 : 2).

3. The Intermediate State

The Intermediate state deals with the conditions or state of the body and soul between death and the general resurrection. "The soul of believers are at their death made perfect in holiness, and do immediately pass into glory, and their bodies, being still united to Christ, do rest in their graves till the resurrection" (Shorter Catechism 37). The substance of this statement is that the souls of believers go immediately to heaven to be with Christ and are entirely blessed, though without their bodies. This view is opposed to the patristic and popish notion of the incomplete and purgatorial existence of the disembodied soul. Both the Old Testament and the New represent the intermediate state as one of happiness for believers. Christ told the penitent thief that he would be with Himself that day in Paradise, and Paul was willing to be absent from the body and present with the Lord (Luke 23 : 43; Phil. 1 : 23).

It is admitted, of course, that any Scripture may be twisted and distorted to deduce another meaning out of it, but the truth speaks for itself to the ordinary earnest reader. The views given of the intermediate state in Scripture are brief and lack detail, as becomes the mysteriousness of the subject; but the popish interpreters give a detailed account of the state of the dead before the resurrection. Unbaptised infants go to the limbus infantum, where they neither suffer pain nor enjoy bliss. Unbaptised adults and those guilty of mortal sin go immediately to hell. Partially sanctified believers go to purgatory where they suffer more or less until their sins are atoned for. During this period they may be hastened to heaven by the prayers, masses, and labours, of their friends on earth. The Old Testament saints went into the limbus patrum where they remained without suffering and without enjoying the beatific vision, until Christ, during the time his body was in the grave, released them.

The Romanists acknowledge that these doctrines are not directly taught in Scripture but that Christ and his apostles taught them. They cite such passages as Matt. 12 : 32; 1 Cor. 3 : 15. The papists however, have a better reason than all this for propagating the doctrine of purgatory, and that is the immense gain they derive from their superstitious votaries at the expense of the complete satisfaction of Christ for the sins of his people. The surplus satisfaction of eminent saints are of great value to suffering souls in purgatory while the prayers and masses which cost huge sums of money fill up the coffers of the church. And were it not for these commercial transactions between priests and people millions of souls would still be suffering in purgatory notwithstanding the vaunted charity of the church. That such a system of delusion accompanied by crude miracles, worthless charms, and puerile visions could be imposed upon a countless multitude of people can only arise from blind superstition and ignorant subservience to religious authority.

Scripture speaks of death in its various aspects such as burial, rest in the grave, the state of death, and eternal woe. The Hebrew word **sheol** and the Greek word **hades** are used in Scripture to designate some of these aspects of death; and since death is per se evil we might presume that retributive elements would be associated with it. Attempts have been made to deprive the word of its retributive force but we are bound to notice that in a number of cases in which **sheol** is used eternal retributive suffering is implied or plainly insisted upon in passages as Job 21 : 13; Psa. 9 : 17; Prov. 7 : 27; Prov. 9 : 18; Prov. 23 : 14; also Deut. 32 : 22; Psa. 139 : 8; Job. 26 : 6; Prov. 15 : 11; and Prov. 27 : 20. It may be argued that some of these passages refer primarily to the death of the wicked as a result of sin, but we cannot exclude the ultimate sense, when we know that the death of the wicked is followed by eternal punishment. There are, however, other passages in Scripture in which **sheol** is used in referring to the death of the righteous, which, of course, cannot denote retribution (Gen. 37 : 35, 42 : 38; Psa. 16 : 10). In some cases **sheol** refers to the event of death as applicable to the righteous and the unrighteous (1 Sam. 2 : 6; Psa. 6 : 5; Ecc. 9 : 10; Psa. 89 : 48; Hosea 13 : 14). We should also recognise that in some cases the idea of proximity to death or profound affliction may be in the foreground (Psa. 23 : 4; Psa. 16 : 10). There is, however, no evidence that **sheol** in the Old Testament refers to an underworld in which the good and evil reside, either in common or in different compartments such as the Elysium or Tartarus of the pagans. The word **hades** is used in the New Testament about eleven times and in almost every case it means hell (with the exception of Acts 2 : 27, 31; and 1 Cor. 15 : 55). In such passages as Matt. 11 : 23, 16 : 18; Luke 10 : 15, 16 : 23; Rev. 1 : 18, 6 : 8, 20 : 13, 14; doubts have been expressed as to the precise meaning of **hades**. In some of these passages there can hardly be any doubt about the retributive meaning, as in Matt. 11 : 23; Luke 16 : 23; Rev. 1 : 18, 6 : 8, 20 : 13, 14. There has been much discussion about Acts 2 : 27 which is quoted from Psa 16 : 10. It seems obvious that this refers to the state of the body of Christ in the interval between his death and resurrection. The reference to Christ preaching to the spirits in prison can only refer to the Spirit of Christ preaching to the antediluvians (1 Pet. 3 : 18-20). The word paradise which is mentioned in the passage referred to here (Luke 23 : 43) is used three times in the New Testament and probably refers to heaven (2 Cor. 12 : 4; Rev. 2 : 7).

4. The Second Coming of Christ

This subject has produced much theological literature especially during the past century, but the advance made in knowledge has been very meagre indeed. There are three cardinal views which deserve some consideration, but in dealing with them broadly we must remember there is much variety in the presentation of at least two of them. The three are: Pre-millenialism, Post-millenialism and A-millenialism.

Pre-millenialism. The view of the early Christian centuries sponsored by Irenaeus and others was, that the world would continue for 6,000 years, and that towards the end of that period it would be dominated by Anti-Christ. At that time Christ would appear personally and bring about the physical resurrection of the saints when a period of bliss would continue for about a thousand years: the gospel would be preached throughout the world, the Jews converted, and Jerusalem rebuilt, afterwards there would ensue a period of affliction, at the end of which the rest of the dead would be raised and the final judgment ushered in.

The modern view of Pre-millenialism introduced by Darby and others and popularised by the Schofield Bible is extremely complicated. The comings of Christ are two: the first called the parousia (appearance) is when Christ will appear in the air and the righteous dead and the living saints will be taken up into the air. While Christ remains in the air for a period of 7 years with his saints, including the Holy Spirit, the gospel will be preached and many converted. During the latter part of this seven year period there will be great tribulation. At the end of this time Christ will come not for but with his saints. The Millenial kingdom will then be established on earth and Christ's throne will be set up in Jerusalem and sacrifices will again be offered as in Old Testament times. After a period of unusual spiritual prosperity there will be a revival of Satanic energy which will be crushed; then the rest of the dead will be raised and the final judgment will take place.

One must realise that there are modifications of this scheme, and indeed some of its exponents will not be bound by any definite view. The main thrust of their teaching is the doctrine of two separate resurrections based on Rev. 20 : 4, 5; and their insistence that Christ will reign personally on the earth for a long period before the final judgment. A study of their works shows:— that they lay too much stress on a worldly kingdom administered by Christ in person; that their interpretation of Scripture is often too literal when dealing with figurative passages; and, that they are guilty of making some passages of Scripture contradict one another. For example, it is significant that they support the view held by many in Christ's own days on earth, that the Messiah was to be a powerful king who would exalt the Jewish nation and reign over the earth; whereas Christ said that his kingdom was spiritual and not worldly. Furthermore, it is beyond comprehension how the glorified Christ and his glorified saints could be expected to reign on earth until the curse of sin was removed. Besides, the idea that the throne of Christ will be set up in Jerusalem and that sacrifices will be offered seems to us to be a total misunderstanding of the efficacy of of the atonement after which there remains no other sacrifice for sin. The doctrine of two resurrections based upon Rev. 20 : 1-10, is nowhere else taught in the Word of God and the figurative setting of these passages must have reference to a spiritual and not a physical resurrection.

Post-millenialism. Orthodox Post-millenialism, or what may be called the traditional view on this subject, is, that through the preaching of the gospel accompanied by the power of the Holy Spirit the gospel will gradually extend its way throughout the world and usher in a long period of spiritual prosperity. As to the nature of this golden age of blessedness it is not claimed that Christianity will obtain a temporal sovereignty over the kingdoms of the world but that it will leaven the whole world with its influence.

There was a great spiritual revival in Jerusalem at Pentecost in the days of the Apostles, but in this case the revival will not be confined to Jerusalem but will extend over the whole earth. This is different from saying that Christ will reign personally on the earth, that every individual will be converted, or that Christian rulers will act as civil and ecclesiastical sovereigns over the kingdoms of the world; but it does mean that the gospel of Christ will obtain a spiritual sovereignty over the world which it has not hitherto enjoyed, and which will continue for a long period of time. During this imperium of blessedness the gospel, as we know it, will be proclaimed through the whole world, the Jews will be converted, and men of all classes, like the inhabitants of Nineveh, will submit to the sovereignty of Jesus Christ. This is not impossible nor contrary to the declarations of Scripture. At the end of this golden age there will be a brief period of apostacy and a terrible conflict between the enemies and friends of Christ. At this stage Christ will appear and there will be a general resurrection and the final judgment.

A-millenialism. Dr Berkhof says there have been, and are, large numbers who do not accept either the Pre-millenarian or Post-millenarian view-points, since they believe there is no sufficient ground for holding that a golden age of gospel blessings will be enjoyed by mankind on this earth. Instead of this, good and evil will continue in the world — much about the same as has prevailed since the age of Christianity —until the second coming of Christ at the last day. The A-millenarian view has been spoken of as a modern view, but the above writer claims that it had as many supporters in the second and third centuries as the Chiliasts or Pre-millenarianists, and that ever since it has been most widely accepted, and expressed or implied in the great historical confessions of the church, and is the prevalent view in Reformed circles. Dr Berkhof, however, admits that the gospel will spread through the whole world and will exercise a beneficent influence. On this basis the only difference between orthodox Post-millenialism and A-millenialism is that the latter allows for a **little** Post-millenialism and the former for a **greater** Post-millenialism.

Those who follow in the train of the Reformed thought of the past will have to choose between the last two views mentioned, and indeed the safe course is not to be too dogmatic on either side. It is quite true as Dr Berkhof points out that there are large numbers in favour of his own view if we take into account the number of eminent theologians, and the Reformed confessions, who in their writings **have not dealt** with this aspect of the subject which bears upon a golden age of Christianity; or to put it in another way they have not accepted either view and the subject being not too clear they have left it out of their theological treatises and confessions.

There are several general considerations which have been set forth to support the Post-millenarian view of a golden age in the history of Christianity:

1. The progress of the gospel hitherto does not seem to fulfil the promises of Scripture with regard to its success if we take into account such passages as the following:— "Ask of me and I shall give thee the heathen for thy inheritance and the uttermost parts of the earth for thy possession" (Psa. 2 : 8). "All the ends of the world shall remember and turn into the LORD, and all the kindreds of the nations shall worship before thee" (Psa. 22 : 27). "Yea, all kings shall fall down before him: all nations shall serve him" (Psa. 72 : 11). "They shall not hurt or destroy in all my holy mountain, for the earth shall be full of the knowledge of the LORD, as the waters cover the sea" (Isa. 11 : 9). "And his dominion shall be from sea even to sea, and from the river even to the ends of the earth" (Zech. 9 : 10). "The kingdom of heaven is like to a grain of mustard seed, which a man took, and sowed in his field: which indeed is the least of all seeds: but when it is grown, it is the greatest among herbs, and becometh a tree, so that the birds of the air come and lodge in the branches thereof" (Matt. 13 : 31, 32).

In the light of these passages and others, surely we are to look for a universal and extraordinary visitation of the Holy Ghost and the conversion of untold multitudes.

2. According to the pious calculations of some eminent divines untold multitudes will be converted before the end of the world. This glorious work will be done not at the final judgment but before the end of the world by the Holy Spirit upon the earth. Christ finished the work which his Father gave him to do and it is then in a much higher sense that he will see of the travail of his soul and be satisfied.

3. There is a clear account of the conversion of the Jews to Christianity (Rom. 11 : 26; 2 Cor. 3 : 15, 16). This event has not yet taken place and there is no evidence that it is

taking place on a large scale though individual Jews here and there are being converted.

4. We are also to take into consideration the terms of the prayer Christ taught his disciples. "Thy kingdom come. Thy will be done in earth as it is in heaven" (Matt. 6 : 10). Believers are to pray for this and to bring it to pass through their efforts and the preaching of the gospel, and they are to believe in the fulfilment of this petition. The fact that Dr Charles Hodge, Dr Warfield, Dr Strong and others maintained the doctrine of Post-millenialism yields some support to the view.

The correct interpretation of Matt. 24 and 25 has given rise to much discussion. One view is that the events mentioned here refer to the destruction of Jerusalem, another is that the passages refer both to the destruction of Jerusalem, the coming of Christ and the exit of the world. It would seem from Matt. 24 : 3, that answers are given by Christ to three questions:— the destruction of Jerusalem, the sign of his own coming, and the end of the world. Matt. 24 : 34, is taken by some to mean that within the space of a generation all these things **would begin to be fulfilled.** The prophesy as a whole must refer to the three events mentioned in Matt. 24 : 3, but it is not always easy to make the proper application. Indeed we must come to the conclusion that parts of the prophesy are obscure to us. We are not, however, to confine ourselves to these chapters since there are other passages in the New Testament bearing upon the subject.

Conclusion. If we are to choose between these several views we are to remember that eminent divines of all ages have been partial to one or other of these, others consider the subject too difficult to interpret. The modern Pre-millenarian view — apart from the fact that it teaches that Christ is to reign personally with his saints on the earth for a thousand years before his coming at the end of the world — is open to various objections; and a continued study of Scripture has already modified some of the reckless statements made by some Pre-millenarians.

The difference between Post and A-millenarianism is not of serious import although the latter has made considerable ground in Reformed circles of late; and it may appear to some that the onus probandis holds against the Post-millenarian view so far as the Reformed confessions are taken into view. The answer to this however is that the point at issue was not sufficiently clear to be included in brief confessional statements and the solution would seem to be that some of the confessions teach it by implication and that there is sufficient Biblical teaching in Scripture to warrant the doctrine of a golden age of Christianity in the future before the final consummation of all things. The main difference among the three schools is that Pre-millenarianism teaches a thousand years of Spiritual prosperity after the physical coming of Christ. Post-millenarianism holds that this period will occur before his physical and second coming; and A-millenarianism says there will be no period of unprecedented spiritual prosperity of the church in the future.

There are several passages in the Old Testament which refer to this first coming such as Psa. 22 : 1-22, and Isa. 53. These prophesies and others bearing on this subject are now fulfilled. There are other passages which deal with this second coming such as Dan. 7 : 13-14, and Mal. 4 : 1-3. The passages in the New Testament referring to the second Advent are numerous but the time, manner and results have been variously interpreted. Such passages as Acts 1 : 11; Titus 2 : 13; Matt. 25 : 31; 2 Thess. 1 : 7-10, made it clear that his coming will be personal and visible, while such passages as Matt. 24 : 36, 42, 44 make it certain that the time of His coming will be unknown to men. There are, however, certain indications of the signs of his coming and events which precede his coming in Matt. 24, but the interpretation of these evidences and events constitute a most difficult problem of exegesis. Again Matt. 25 makes it quite clear that the second coming of Christ is at the end of the world but of course Pre-millenarians will not yield assent to this point since they assure us there is a previous coming of the Lord.

Cautious divines who are not dogmatic about any one of these views will tell us that the subject defies exegesis at the present stage of our history; and they point out that great emphasis is laid by the Saviour on adequate preparation for his second coming rather than a curious prying into the details of such a mysterious and solemn subject (Matt. 24 : 42-44). The expectation of believers in the Old Testament was directed to the first coming of the Messiah to take away sin while the expectation of believers in the New Testament is directed to his second advent. "So Christ was once offered to bear the sins of many; and unto them that look for him shall he appear the second time without sin unto salvation."

5. The Resurrection

Though a number of the ancient philosophers believed in the immortality of the soul few of them admitted the resurrection of the body. Indeed they looked upon the body as a corrupt vessel and believed that the soul could function better without it. It should hardly need to be said that the resurrection is not a transmigration of souls to other bodies or substances, but the raising of the same body which perished at death. The idea held by some that the resurrection body will be a different body is a denial of a real resurrection. The objections made that such a resurrection is impossible is a grave reflection upon the power of God as the God of creation and providence. Dr Shedd says, "That it is no more strange that the human body should exist the second time than that it existed the first time. That a full-formed human body should be produced from a microscopic cell, is as difficult to believe upon the face of it, as that a spiritual resurrection body should be produced out of the natural earthly body. The marvels of embryology are, a priori, as incredible as those of the resurrection" (Dogmatic Theology, page 649).

It is said that the Jews did not believe in the resurrection of the body and that the Old Testament does not teach the doctrine. It is true that some Jews did not believe it and that the Sadducees and some professed believers and pagans denied it (Matt. 22 : 23-33; Acts 17 : 32; 2 Tim. 2 : 18), but the doctrine is taught in the Old Testament and it needs not to be proved from the New Testament as it is clearly taught there. The translation of Enoch and Elijah favour the doctrine. Abraham and his descendants such as Isaac, Jacob and Joseph believed it, and Christ proves it from the Old Testament (Matt. 22 : 32). It is taught in Isaiah 26 : 19; Job. 19 : 25-27; and Daniel 12 : 2. And it was evidently believed in the time of Christ (John 11 : 24). It is also taught in the Apocrypha (2 Maccabees 7 : 9, 23).

It was also common knowledge among some of the Jews

that the date of the resurrection is the last day (John 11 : 24),
when Christ will descend from heaven accompanied by angels
and raise the bodies of all the dead (Matt. 25 : 31, 32; John
5 : 28, 29; Acts 24 : 15; 1 Thess. 4 : 16). It has been often
said that those who are alive at the resurrection will undergo
a change equivalent to death. This may seem to be in accord
with Scripture but it is a moot question. What are we to say
of Enoch and Elijah? Did they undergo such a change, or
what is meant by it?

Scripture makes a distinction between a natural and a
spiritual body. A natural or animal body is an organism
adapted to the mode of life on earth, and a spiritual body
is a body adapted to a mode of existence in a spiritual world.
A natural body would seem to indicate a body marked by
physical qualities and passions and subject to natural infirmities. A spiritual body adapted to a spiritual existence
will be marked by the absence of these qualities and infirmities. Nevertheless the spiritual body will be material and not
spiritual like the soul. The disembodied soul possesses no
body but the embodied soul will possess its own body. If we
accept the idea that Christ after the resurrection possessed
a spiritual body we shall have some conception of what a
spiritual body is. But perhaps it will not be safe to make a
precise comparison because we are inclined to believe that
Christ's glorified body is not precisely what his post resurrection body was. It is not only a spiritual body but a glorified body. When Moses and Elijah appeared on the Mount
of Transfiguration they evidently possessed spiritual and
glorified bodies but they were recognised and were seen as
men. Their appearance and shape was evidently the same as
when they were on earth. They possessed form and extension
and therefore were not pure spirits. After Christ arose from
the dead he was recognised by his disciples as the same Jesus.
Evidently his voice and manner were the same. It is said
that there was a great outward change because he appeared
in another form and was not recognised by some; that he
passed through the stone laid at the grave, and that he passed
through closed doors. These are gratuitous assumptions
which are not warranted by the text or what we know of the
properties of material bodies. Christ himself mentioned that
he was no spirit but possessed of flesh and bones. It is, how-

ever, idle and perhaps foolish to speculate on such a mysterious subject.

The goal of the believers' faith is the resurrection of the body since the body is part of the person and the person is incomplete without the body. But to suggest that believers who have died are not perfectly blessed as to their souls and with Christ contradicts not only the general consideration arrived at by good men, but Scripture itself. Doubtless, however, there must be a difference between the condition of the embodied soul and the disembodied soul. In the case of the Old Testament believers they could not have seen the God-man until after his resurrection. But believers who died after the resurrection must have held communion with Christ face to face. We also presume that the penitent thief held communion with Christ while his own body and that of Christ's were in the grave.

II. THE FINAL STATE

Introduction

The greatest minds have exercised themselves with the solemn consideration of their state after death. Some have concluded that all living entities on this earth including man will be reduced to a condition of total annihilation. After death the soul as well as the body will cease to exist. Even the unassisted reason however, or rather the light of reason handicapped by the lack of a supernatural revelation has been impressed with the conviction that man will continue to exist after death in a state of eternal sorrow or eternal bliss.

The profound and arresting speculations of such men as Plato, Socrates and Cicero, is the last word on this subject as uttered by pagan philosophers. Even they admitted that the highest level of their knowledge was speculation and since none after them improved upon their ideas of the nature of the eternal state it is evident that nothing further could be added unless the Lord himself were pleased to give some light on this solemn theme. This is provided in Scripture with a certainty and sufficiency which gives ground for a firm faith, and which should inspire sinful men with a wholesome fear that they may flee for refuge to the Hope set before them in the gospel.

1. The State of the Wicked. The Old Testament references to the state of the wicked after death come into conflict with the denial of the resurrection according to the view of ancient and modern Sadducees, who maintain that the Old Testament teachings are not in favour of a resurrection of the just and the unjust. The translation of Enoch and the references in Genesis such as Gen. 16 : 7, 19 : 1, 22 : 11, 28 : 12, and Exodus 23 : 20, taken in connection with Christ's argument with the Pharisees (Matt. 22 : 29-32) should dispose of this question. The quotation in Daniel must also be expunged in order to disprove the doctrine of rewards and punishments. "And many of them that sleep in the dust shall awake, some to everlasting life, and some to shame and everlasting contempt. And they that be wise shall shine as the brightness in the firmament and they that turn away to righteousness as the stars for ever and ever" (Dan. 12 : 2, 3).

The truth of eternal punishment is unspeakably solemn and the references made to it by God's people are always, we hope, in order to warn men to flee from the wrath to come. The truth that God who is good and does good, decrees to permit such an evil in the universe is beyond our comprehension. Indeed it is a mystery why he permits such evils in the world today as heathenism, idolatry, murder, drunkenness, prostitution, the evils of narcotics and opium, and the other gross and flagrant evils which degrade and destroy men. These evils and sins we can give some account of and we have no doubt their proximate cause is the corrupt state and nature of humanity. Notwithstanding, the utterly depressing and overwhelming thought of these and other evils cannot change the teaching of Scripture, that it grieves God to contemplate this situation, and to banish the lost from His presence, because of their sins. Christ's weeping over Jerusalem should remind us of the yearning thoughts of God towards lost sinners of our race.

Max Muller the distinguished Oxford philologist says that this world would be miserable without eternal punishment. "Every act good and evil must carry its consequences, and the fact that our punishment will go on for ever seems to me a proof of the everlasting love of God. For an evil deed to go unpunished would be to destroy the moral order of the universe." It is surprising that such an argument should be used but it shows us that others are thinking as well as the universalists. When Dr Shedd and Dr Beecher were asked to contribute to the American review on this subject, one on either side, the proofs of Dr Shedd's writings being sent to Beecher he refused to contribute his article saying "Shedd is too much for me. I half believe in eternal punishment now myself" (Dr Strong, Systematic Theology, pages 1052, 1054).

A belief in the Scripture truth of eternal punishment might be followed by a refusal to treat of the subject by Christian men and preachers. This would seem to indicate abnormal cruelty since there are various motives set down in Scripture which can be used to warn men to flee from destruction. It would be an enemy indeed who would observe a fellow creature hastening to perdition without making some attempt to rescue him. As to the relative importance of this solemn doctrine it should be remembered that it should not be insisted on as if there were no other way to win men to Christ but by fear of punishment; nonetheless rebellious sinners must be roused lest they apprehend that there is no real danger even if they continue in impenitence. It has been asserted that the fear of punishment has a tendency to drive sinners to despair, but those referred to here are so far from such a feeling that they abuse the tender mercies of God.

"If the heart be broken and contrite and is apt to meditate little else but terror; such subjects as are as encouraging are to be insisted on. Thus when the prophet Jeremiah had been reproving the people for their abominations and threatening many sore judgments which God would execute upon them he applies healing medicines. 'Is there no balm in Gilead, is there no physician there? Why then is not the health of the daughter of my people recovered?' (Jer. 8 : 22). Elsewhere also, when he had been reprehending them for their idolatry, and putting them in mind of those judgments they had exposed themselves to he encourages them to cry unto God. 'My Father thou art the guide of my youth will he reserve anger for ever? will he keep it to the end' (Jer. 3 : 4, 5). God in his usual method of dealing with sinners, first exalts their fear by charging sin on the conscience and putting them in mind of the dreadful consequences of it, in which respect, as the Apostle expresses it 'The Law entered that the offence might abound', and then he shows that the soul may take encouragement when humbled under a sense of its own guilt, that 'when sin hath abounded grace hath much more abounded' (Rom. 5 : 20). The gospel is designed to administer comfort to those who are distressed under a dread of the wrath of God. Hence there are promises as well as threatenings; and each is to be applied as the occasion requires, so that the happiness of heaven is to be set in opposition to the punishment of sin in hell" (Dr Ridgeley, Body of Divinity, New York 1855, page 285).

The learned and genial Dr A. A. Hodge makes the following remarks which should be heeded by every preacher: "Unquestionably every Christian who understands his own heart will recognise the fact that he sympathises profoundly with the failing of his brethren who from a mistaken philanthropy seek relief from the plain teachings of Scripture as to the fearful doom of the finally impenitent. To human view the conception of never-ending hopelessness and misery is absolutely overwhelming. If we could realise its tremendous meaning it would paralyse our minds and hearts. We think and speak of it so calmly because it is so far off and so vague that it fails to impress us as an actual reality. There is nothing on earth more outrageously vulgar and profane than the coarse and careless shouting out of threats of damnation against heedless sinners by an orthodox ranter. When we declare the terrible judgments of our Lord against our fellow sinners, of our own flesh and blood who by nature are no worse than we are, we should do it tremblingly and with fear. We should remember that in all respects we deserve the same fate ourselves, and that it is only infinite, undeserved grace which has made us to differ. We should seek to treat all impenitent sinners with the yearning tenderness with which our blessed Lord wept over Jerusalem with outstretched arms and heaving breast — 'If thou hadst known even then, at best in this thy day, the things which belong unto thy place; but now they are hid from thine eyes'." (Evangelical Theology, London 1890, page 389).

2. The State of the Righteous

It has been observed that Scripture speaks much more of the righteous and their temporal and eternal blessings than of the wicked and their sufferings here and hereafter. This should lead us to recognise that the Bible is a herald of salvation and that "God sent his Son into the world not to condemn the world but that the world through him might be saved" (John 3 : 17). Truth and soberness constrain us to acknowledge that the details of the state and condition of eternal blessedness is above the level of our comprehension and that our faith must content itself with the assurance that the Saviour will be there, that his people will be like him, and that they will share in his glory. A consideration of this subject should warn us of two extremes, first that we compare heaven too much with the present life, of thought, feeling and activity; and secondly, that we imagine it has no real connection with the present life; for we are to remember that the Redeemed in heaven will possess the same identical souls and bodies as they possessed in this life.

Various theories have been advanced regarding the location and state of blessedness, the degrees of glory, the relative number of the inhabitants, and their manner of intercourse with one another and with angels; but it is best to adopt no dogmatic conclusions on the basis of general considerations, and isolated passages of Scripture. At the same time discussions on these and kindred topics are not out of place when conducted with a reverence becoming such a subject. A number of theologians are of the opinion that the location of the state of bliss will be on this earth which will be purified and restored in a manner analogous to the change taking place in the souls and bodies of those who will inhabit it. This should not mean that the heavenly host will be confined to this sphere since the infinite universe is their domain.

Some would have it that the Redeemed will occupy no particular location, but this would not hold good even in the case of the Redeemer unless we are prepared to apply some of the Romish and Lutheran conceptions of the Lord's Supper. As Turretin says both bodies and spirits possess an **ubi** though we must not apply this to God himself. It has been said that there will be degrees of glory in heaven and this I suppose would infer degreees in rank. On this, as in subjects of a like nature, we must be content with opinion.

As to whether the Lord's people in heaven will know one another and communicate with their former friends we have no reason for doubting, and this from the one consideration that their knowledge will not be less but greater. It has also been the opinion of some eminent divines that the number of heaven's host will be infinitely greater than the number of the lost; and if such be the case it will be a factor in favour of orthodox post-millenialism. Some of those theologians and others say that all infants dying in infancy will be saved. A common opinion held by some theologians is that hope and faith will cease in heaven but that love will continue. The arguments for this opinion are very strong but not conclusive.

The essential exercise of faith is trust and surely this will continue; besides, there will be scope for faith and hope in view of further discoveries of the glory of Christ. We should also recollect that the disciples had faith in Christ even when he was present with them on earth. As to the occupation of the saints in a state of blessedness we may infer from the truth that they possess bodies and souls that the intellectual, emotional and volitional powers of the soul will be exercised in the services of their Lord and King; and we may well believe that their powers, which in the present state are impeded by sin, will not only be superior in their nature but also in their exercise.

The two main considerations governing the blessedness of heaven is that believers will be for ever freed from all the effects and traces of sin and that they will be perfectly blessed through all eternity; and since the author of all these blessings is Christ, we may be assured that the central focus of interest for the believer is not the wonderful descriptions given of heaven and the glory of its inhabitants but Christ himself, the Lamb who was slain from the foundation of the world and who now occupies the throne of the Eternal. Heaven without Christ would be a mansion without the tenant or a jewel case without the jewel. Reason would indulge in speculation as to what the feelings of the Old Testament saints might be when they entered heaven before the resurrection since Christ in his human nature was not then present, but afterwards they would see Christ in his glorified body and converse with him personally. Someone said that heaven was a state of rest and peace and that there would be no strife there, but if there were, it would be about **who should get nearest to Jesus.**

We are told that when believers get to heaven that they will see Christ, that they will be like him, and that they will share in his glory (1 John 3 : 2; John 17 : 22). At this stage we cannot say what we shall be, but we know that to see Christ and to know him better is the desire of all believers and to be like him and to share in his glory is to enjoy happiness at the highest level and beyond the highest reaches of a creaturely conception. That such a state of happiness is possible and certain for a countless multitude of hell-deserving sinners is guaranteed by the love that provided it and the infinite sacrifice of everlasting efficacy that procured it; and it is in virtue of the blood of the everlasting covenant shed on Calvary that the countless host of the Redeemed will be able to sing with one voice "Unto him that loved us, and washed us from our sins in his own blood, and hath made us king and priests unto God and his Father; to him be glory and dominion for ever and ever, Amen" (Rev. 1 : 5, 6).

VI. THE CHURCH

CHAPTER XVII

Introduction

The word **church** has been understood in various senses. The root meaning is to call or to call out, and was applied to the congregation of Israel when it met to worship God. The word **eklesia** was used by our Lord to describe the company who gathered around him and submitted themselves to his teaching (Matt. 16 : 18). Dr Berkhof says the term church is derived from the word **kuriake** which means belonging to the Lord. The kuriake designated the place where the church assembled but did not manifest itself until the church gathered to worship[63] See also Dr Strong.[64] The Westminster Confession states that "The catholic or universal church which is invisible, consists of the whole number of the elect that have been, are, or shall be gathered into one, under Christ the head thereof, and is the spouse, the body, the fulness of him that filleth all in all". "The visible church," says the same confession, "which is also catholic or universal under the gospel (not confined to one nation, as under the law), consists of all throughout the world that profess the true religion together with their children; and is the kingdom of the Lord Jesus Christ, the house and family of God, and out of which there is no ordinary possibility of salvation."[65] Protestants and Romanists differ as to their understanding of the essential nature of the church. The Romish church consists of the Roman hierarchy which is called the **teaching** church headed by the Pope and the general council. The common people are called the **hearing** church. The Reformers included the whole body of believers in the church, in accordance with the distribution they made between the invisible and visible church.

63. Dr Berkhof, **Systematic Theology**, p. 537.
64. Dr Strong, **Systematic Theology**, p. 891.
65. **Westminster Confession**, 25 : 1.

1. The Invisible and the Visible Church

The Invisible Church consists of those who are true believers, and it is called invisible because of its spiritual nature, since union with Christ, regeneration, and faith are not the objects of sense-perception. "This church is said to be invisible because it cannot be discovered by the eye. It is not separated from the world in respect of place but of state. It lies hidden in the visible church from which it cannot certainly be distinguished. The qualifications of its members are internal; their faith and love are not the objects of sense. Towards our fellow men we can exercise only the judgment of charity, founded upon probable grounds but we are liable to err, and from various causes may suppose saints to be hypocrites and hypocrites to be saints. It is unseen by every eye but that "which searches the heart and tries the reins of the children of men".[66] The true church, however, becomes visible in her profession and practice so that in this sense the invisible and the visible church are identical The visible church is so called because it is visible to our senses. Its members exist as a sacred society on earth and we may see them and observe their overt exercises as worshippers of God. It is not necessary to prove from Scripture that this visible church is a mixed multitude consisting of formal professors as well as true believers. This does not mean that unbelievers and wicked persons are to be looked upon as members of the visible church until they profess their faith in Christ and obedience to him; but it does mean that church officers are not warranted to exact from professed believers positive marks of regeneration and to require of them a detailed account of their religious experiences in order to their forming a judgment upon their spiritual state. The grounds of admission to the fellowship and privileges of the visible church are a competent knowledge of the gospel, a profession of faith in Christ, and an external walk corresponding to that profession. Of this alone church officers are capable of adjudging, but to proceed upon a judgment of their spiritual state in the sight of God would be to assume a knowledge of the state of their heart. The visible church is the true church of Christ as it is in

66. Dr John Dick, **Theology**, Vol. 4, p. 303.

the sight of the Lord. There are not two churches. The church is one viewed from two aspects, one visible and the other invisible. It is possible to be a member of the visible church and to be partaker of all the outward privileges enjoyed by believers and not be a member of the true church; and conversely, a person may be a true believer and placed in such circumstances as to be deprived of the privileges of church fellowship.

2. The Church in Scripture

In the age of the Patriarchs, that is, before the Mosaic dispensation, the church was to be found in individual families, while the fathers served as priests in their own households. There seems grounds for believing that besides this there was some corporate form of worship among God's people from the statement that men began to call upon the name of the Lord (Gen. 4 : 26). At the time of the flood the church of God was confined to the family of Noah, and afterwards God separated to himself the family of Abraham. We are not to think, however, that there were no worshippers of the true God outwith this family and their dependents. We read that Melchisedic, King of Salem, was a priest of the most High God. In the Mosaic period the church was extended from the family to the nation of Israel who were brought into covenant with God as his people. As worshippers of God they were separated to Himself and brought under a spiritual economy. Besides the law of God, and the ceremonial rites of worship they were also organised as a state. Consequently the church and state were one institution with separate ecclesiastical and civil functions, and in a special way governed by God as their King. After Pentecost the church obtained an independent existence as a spiritual corporation, no longer confined to one nation, as was Israel, but possessed of a universal character with no political or civil aims, but commissioned by Christ as a missionary church to carry the gospel to all the nations of the world.

3. The Christian Church

In the Apostolic and Patristic periods the church was looked upon as a body of people who had been called out of their

Jewish and heathen elements and gathered together in various places to worship and serve the Lord Jesus Christ. In the process of time, however, the church became an external organisation ruled by a Bishop, and in the middle ages the church as a community of Saints was relegated to the background and the church as a visible organisation was emphasised. The church and State were now seen to be two different powers instituted by God for the government of the people. The church was, however, the higher power since it provided for the salvation of its subjects while the state dealt with temporal matters only. Thus the thesis was gradually developed that the King was the head of the state, and the Bishop, who had now been exalted to the dignity of the pope, was the head of the church. With the full development of popery the pope became an absolute monarch so that all the temporal and spiritual kingdoms of the world were subject to his dominion.

The Reformers broke away from this conception of the church. They maintained that Christ was the head of the church, that His Word was their law, and that their function was to preach the Word, administer the sacraments and exercise discipline in the church.

CHURCH GOVERNMENT

Some Christian sects such as the Quakers and Darbyites reject external government as being opposed to the special promptings of the Holy Ghost. Experience has shown that this theory does not work for order in practice and so some of the Quakers and Darbyites in America have regularly ordained ministers and conduct their worship very much as other churches do. Some bodies of Christians believe that the New Testament formulates no special regulations on this subject, and that believers should organise themselves according to the mode that suits their local circumstances. Roman Catholics, Episcopalians, Congregationalists and Presbyterians profess to find in the New Testament the pattern of their own particular government.

1. The Erastian System

Erastianism is a reaction against the Romish system and

teaches that the church is subject to the civil power. The officers of the church who preach and rule have no inherent power of discipline except what they derive from the civil magistrate. The state governs the church and administers discipline and if necessary penalises those who violate the laws of the church.

2. The Congregational System

Congregationalism or Independency holds two main principles. Each local church or congregation is independent of any other. The governing power is vested in the members of the congregation so that the officers who teach and administer its affairs receive their power from the members of the congregation. In theory their church conventions are advisory and not mandatory.

3. The Popish System

The Roman Catholics affirm that the bishop of Rome is the visible head of the church who exercises absolute dominion over the whole Christian world. Rome asserts that Christ appointed Peter to be the first pope; that Peter was the first Bishop of Rome, and that all his successors in office are to take his place. Neither history nor Scripture gives any countenance to this fancy, but church history does give an explanation of the origin and full development of the popish system. The claim of Rome that Peter was appointed by Christ to be the head Bishop of the church and that there has been an unbroken line of succession from the time of Peter down to the present day is contradicted both by history and by Scripture. The doctrine of the infallibility of the pope and the reliance of that church on tradition is directly opposed to Christ the Infallible Head of the church and his Word as the supreme standard of faith and morals.

4. The Episcopalian System

The Episcopalian theory of church government is a modified form of popery. In Episcopacy the power is vested in the bishops rather than in the pope. At the Reformation in England the spiritual power was transferred from the pope to the King of England who along with his successors exercised power in all cases civil and ecclesiastical. According to the 37th Article in the constitution the Queen's Majesty has the chief power over all causes whether civil or ecclesiastical. Attempts have been made to explain away this part of Episcopal government, but since the appointment of Bishops and convocation requires the permission of the reigning sovereign we must believe that he or she is the visible head of the church. Were this theory to be followed out in practice it would make the church a creature of the state without any authority to perform rites or to exercise discipline but in accordance with the wishes of the reigning Monarch. Moderate Episcopalians would deny this inference and say that their constitution was unfettered and that the Sovereign simply gave formal sanction to the proceedings as the protector of their religious liberties. The Episcopalians profess to derive their form of church government from Scripture and tradition and they point to the Jewish church constitution with its high priest, priests and levites as favouring their theory. Presbyterians, however, assert that the Old Testament ceremonial system was abolished at the death of Christ, and this the Episcopalians cannot deny. Episcopacy also claims that Christ himself instituted a gradation of ranks in the church such as apostles, evangelists and disciples. It has, however, been affirmed that the followers of Christ were under no distinctive government during his lifetime so nothing can be gained from this mode of reasoning.

The essential points of Episcopacy are the vesting of church power exclusively in the clergy and a gradation of ranks in church government. According to this view the people have no voice in the government of the church and, therefore, no appeal against the abuse of church power. In setting forth their spiritual jurisdiction they maintain that there is a three-fold order of authority. The deacon who is of the lowest order assists his superiors as required in preaching and administration of the sacraments. The priest who is above the deacon preaches, administers the sacraments, and gives absolution to penitents. The bishop ordains priests and deacons, confirms those who have been baptised, and rules over the diocese. In the government of the church neither priests nor deacons have any share since authority is vested solely in the bishops. The bishops preach if they please but this is not essential to their office.

In searching for evidence in the Word of God and in early ecclesiastical history for the doctrine of Episcopacy we find scanty support for their form of government. An exegesis of the New Testament evinces that there is no gradation of ranks in the ministry, for bishops and presbyters are one order. Episcopacy in England is a mixture of Prelacy and Erastianism. Some churchmen in that communion while teaching that there was originally a threefold order in the ministry and that there should be so now, do not consider this form of church organisation to be essential.

PRESBYTERIANISM

Presbyterians claim that their distinctive principles are to be found in the Word of God. Some also maintain that in its fundamental principles their special form of government is the only one sanctioned in the New Testament. These main principles have been stated by theologians in various ways. The following positions in their system may be adverted to here:— The Headship of Christ; The Independent power of the church; The Parity of their Ministers; The Right of the people to share in the government of the church; and the due Subordination of judicatories.

1. The Headship of Christ

Christ is the supreme and exclusive Head of the church. He appoints his own officers who receive authority and power from him to administer the affairs of his house in accordance with his own laws. In the words of Walker, "They (the Scottish theologians) meant that Christ is the real King and Head of the church, as a visible organisation, ruling it by his statutes, and ordinances and officers and forces, as truly and literally as David or Solomon ruled the covenant people of old".[67] The church of Rome attaches the greatest importance to the idea that the pope is the head of the church and as they claim infallibility for that individual, they deprive Christ of the absolute and exclusive authority and power to exact total submission from the members of

67. Walker, **Scottish Theology and Theologians.**

the church. The Reformers maintained and successfully defended the scriptural truth that Christ is the Head of the church. The Reformed and Presbyterian churches were constrained in a later period to declare the same truth in opposition to the state. The conflict was fought in the Netherlands and particularly in Scotland, and indeed a number of Presbyterians at the time of the Disruption in 1843 were forced to separate from the state church because that church with the help of the state had arrogated to itself the power to coerce the consciences of ministers and members, and so compelled them to separate from the church of their Fathers and to sacrifice the temporal benefits which belonged to them as their rightful heritage. In doing so they followed the teaching of the church of their Fathers though they separated from the external organisation.

2. The Independent Power of the Church
Various attempts have been made to deprive the true church of her spiritual power to teach and rule. Her leaders stated their position by saying that in temporal matters they acknowledged the supremacy of the state but in spiritual matters they possessed an independent power to administer their own affairs without state interference. They indeed acknowledged that individuals, whether lay or clerical, were subject to the civil authority in temporal matters, but to the church authority in ecclesiastical matters.

3. The Parity of Ministers
Rome and Canterbury have a gradation of ranks in their communions. The pope has spiritual officers under him in a gradation of ranks from the Cardinal to the lowest rank in the priestly order. Episcopacy, with its Archbishops, bishops, priests and deacons, maintains a subordination of ranks in church officers. Presbyterianism maintains that all ministers are of one order and of equal rank. It is true of course that leaders are to be found in all churches, and that sometimes they are tempted to take advantage of their position and influence; but neither age nor seniority militates against the equality of all ministers in teaching and ruling. The current trend of theology which directs attention to eminent church leaders whose voice is listened to as the

voice of the church, is reminiscent of the perpetual moderators in Scottish history and is calculated in actual practice to lead to a modified form of Episcopacy.

4. The Rights of the People

According to Roman Catholicism and Prelacy, church government is vested in the pope or in the clergy, and the people have no voice in the government of the church. Congregationalism on the other hand vests the ruling power directly in the hands of the people. Presbyterianism adopts the middle view, and so some have said that Presbyterianism is both an aristocracy and a democracy. While Presbyterians do assert that their office-bearers are appointed and qualified by Christ to discharge effectively the functions of their office in teaching and ruling, they still grant the people a substantial power of government. Church officers are chosen by the people to represent them in the government of the church; and indeed it should be remembered that the Disruption in 1843 in Scotland was occasioned by the intrusion of pastors into congregations without the consent of the people. The substance of this principle is "First, that congregations have a right to choose their own office-bearers; and, secondly, that they ought to be consulted in regard to the more important acts of ecclesiastical discipline by which they are affected; and that their consent and concurrence in them should be laboured for in the exercise of all appropriate means, and should, if possible, be obtained" (Principal Cunningham).

5. The Subordination of Judicatories

Presbyterians do acknowledge that the ruling power resides primarily in the local church or congregation but this power is not absolute for the local congregation is just a part of the whole church. There is therefore a gradation of church courts in the Presbyterian order of government consisting of Sessions (Consistories), Presbyteries (Classis), Synods and Assemblies. The higher courts do not represent a higher power but a larger measure of it so that problems met with in the local congregation can, if necessary, be passed on to the higher courts. The decisions of these higher courts are not merely advisory but authoritative and binding unless it can be shown that they are contrary to the Word of God and the constitution of the church. Presbyterians find their theory of the subordination of courts in the Word of God. In the case of the Council of Jerusalem (Acts 15) a reference was made from an inferior to a superior court and decided authoritatively with the consent of the whole church (Acts 15 : 22). We have, therefore, an apostolic example for courts of review, which clearly recognises the transference of a cause from a lower to a higher court of the church.

6. The Principle of Establishment

The principle of church Establishment has been largely ignored due to the current trend in church government. This trend is partly due to the tendency on the part of the civil authority to encroach upon the jurisdiction of the church; and partly, we think, because this principle is not properly understood. The principle of establishment is to the effect that it is the duty of the civil power to protect the true religion and to advance its prosperity. As to the measures to be used to effect this good work there have been various differences among theologians. Those holding the "voluntary" principle do not deny that individuals should protect and support the church but they do deny that this is the duty of the civil magistrate. The holding of the principle of establishment makes no provision for the jurisdiction of the civil authority within the courts of the church, which is Erastianism; or for the infliction of pains and penalties by the state upon those holding different views on religion, which is Popery. The principle of church Establishment is still maintained by the Free Church of Scotland. Presbyterianism in Scotland before 1843 was a national religion and its liberties were ratified as such by the state. Presbyterianism in Scotland was therefore fostered and supported by the civil authority. The Free Church of Scotland people, however, were compelled to sever their connection with the state church not because they objected to their state connection but because of state interference with the courts of the church. By separating from the state church they lost the good interest of the civil magistrate and they sacrificed the enjoyment of state temporalities but they asserted that they would return to a pure establishment if their ecclesiastical independence were fully secured.

Those who advocated separation between the church and the state doubtless have had grave reasons for embracing this principle, since connection with the state has almost always brought with it a limitation of ecclesiastical freedom of action; notwithstanding, the eminent leaders of the Free Church of Scotland in 1843, though they were compelled to separate from the state church, held, and some of their successors do hold tenaciously, the view that they have scriptural grounds for maintaining this principle. Dr Cunningham in his discussion of the Erastian controversy says "We have merely to advert to the unanimous and decided testimony of the Reformers in support of the general doctrine, as a portion of Scriptural truth — that the civil magistrate is bound, in the exercise of his legitimate authority, to seek to promote, as far as he can, the welfare of true religion, and the prosperity of the Church of Christ" (Historical Theology, Vol. 2, page 560). The existence of church government and organisation is set forth in clear terms in the New Testament. Such matters as stated meetings, elections, officers, ordinances, discipline and the qualifications of ministers, elders, deacons and members are mentioned in terms sufficiently specific to guide the congregations of the Lord in all ages and circumstances (Acts. 20 : 7; Heb. 10 : 25; Acts 20 : 17, 18; Matt. 18 : 17; 1 Cor. 5 : 4, 5, 13; 1 Cor. 16 : 1, 2; Acts 2 : 41; 1 Cor. 14 : 10; Matt. 28 : 19).

Presbyterians draw their main support for their form of government from the circumstances connected with the decision arrived at by the council of Jerusalem (Acts 15). The question to be resolved here was, whether or not circumcision was necessary to salvation (Acts 15 : 1). This question was disputed locally at Antioch and referred to the Jerusalem Assembly. This assembly disputed and resolved the question with the consent of the people. The principle of equality of office, of the gradation of courts, and the rights of the people is asserted here and embodied in the Presbyterian constitution. Popery would say the question should be decided by Peter; Episcopalians, that it should be decided by the clergy; Congregationalists would maintain it should be decided by the people. The decision in this case was formulated by the apostles and elders acting as ordinary office-bearers. The decision was made with the consent and approval of the people who were convinced of the justice of the measure. It should be of course admitted that Presbyterians do not claim infallibility though they believe their particular constitution to be founded on the Word of God. Neither do they claim that they have always maintained the body of truth committed to them; and they have often become conscious that they have allowed themselves to become subject to error, and at the best to acknowledge that they do not lay an equal emphasis on all the truth, in accordance with its relative importance. And indeed divines have often been constrained to admit that a complete knowledge of Biblical truth on this subject and a perfect administration of church government are not attainable in this life.

FREE CHURCH PRESBYTERIANISM

The Free Church of Scotland traces its distinctive position back to the Disruption of 1843. This branch of the visible church maintains its direct historic descent from the original Protestant and Presbtyerian Church of Scotland of 1560 and 1638. There is a frank acknowledgment that the Revolution Settlement of 1688 was not in all respects satisfactory since. Though the Presbyterian Church was restored as the official established church of Scotland, the National Covenant and the Solemn League and Covenant were ignored. The Reformed Presbyterian Church refused to acknowledge this settlement. That Church, however, departed from the principle of establishment (in America) and adopted a church and state separation as a matter of principle.

The Establishment Principle

The Free Church of Scotland maintains the establishment principle, that is, she holds as a matter of principle that it is the state's duty to establish the true religion as the state church and that the church has the right to be established as the national church, and at the same time the right to maintain her own jurisdiction without state interference: the latter is called the principle of independence. In 1834 the Church of Scotland came under the control of the Moderate party who had no true zeal for the Presbyterian faith. In 1843 matters came to a head and a large body of ministers and elders separated from the established Church of Scotland because state interference inside the church had become intolerable and all attempts to remedy it had failed.

VII. THE SACRAMENTS

CHAPTER XVIII

The term **means of grace** is used to describe the ordinances through which God ministers grace to his people. What these ordinances are must be ascertained from the Word of God. Some people speak of nature and common providence as a means of grace but they are only so as interpreted in the light of Scripture. It is true of course that such passages as Psa. 19 show that not only God's revealed will, but his power seen in the works of creation may be used by the Holy Ghost to sanctify the believer, but these evidences possess no sanctifying influences unless confirmed by Scripture. The believer, however, views all these phenomena of nature as related to his Saviour and consequently he is confirmed in his faith. The written Word of God is the great and uniform means of grace since in it we find the ordinances prescribed by God to save and sanctify sinful men; and we should remember that whatever benefits may appear to be communicated through the efforts of God's people through evangelistic services and revivals, they cannot be reckoned as means of grace, or be of lasting benefit, unless they are prescribed in his own Word; and the pretence of worshipping God by methods not appointed by himself in his Word is an affront to God and a despising of the Scriptural methods appointed and approved in the Word of Truth. And, therefore, if we are to speak with propriety of the means of grace we are to understand not every instrumentality which we think that God may use to convert sinners and sanctify the church, but those institutions which God has revealed and ordained in the worship of his Name.

The following are reckoned means of grace to be used by his church on earth:— the reading and preaching of his Word; the Sacraments; praise and prayer; the government and discipline of the church. The means of grace are both outward and ordinary; outward as objective parts of God's service, and distinguished from inward graces such as faith and repentance. They are ordinary means of grace since

God may also use extraordinary methods to convert sinners, as in the case of infants or imbeciles who are regenerated and sanctified without the use of these means.

The Word as a Means of Grace

Some liberal theologians regard the Word alone as being sufficient for the production of life and its subsequent renewal. Others go the opposite extreme and expect every blessing from the Holy Ghost without the Word. The true view is that the Word and Spirit are both required in the sanctification of the believer. It is true nonetheless that regeneration in the very narrow sense is produced by the immediate act of God's Spirit without the Word when he produces in the heart and mind of a sinner a capacity of spiritual life. This position has been misunderstood because it is sometimes forgotten that regeneration and faith are simultaneous and that the Word and Spirit co-operate to produce faith in Christ. "Indeed a person cannot have spiritual light without the Word but that does not argue that the Word properly causes that light. The mind cannot see the excellency of any doctrine unless that doctrine be first in the mind, but the seeing of the excellency of any doctrine must be immediately by the Spirit of God; though the conveying of any doctrine or proposition may be immediately by the Spirit of God so that the notions that are the subject-matter of this light are conveyed by the Word of God." (Jonathan Edwards' sermon on Matt. 16 : 17). "Some Lutheran divines" (and even some Calvinistic preachers) "represent the Holy Ghost as operating upon the truth, so that the truth becomes an efficient by means of this super-added quality, or power. The Reformed theologians regard the Holy Spirit as the sole efficient and the truth as only an instrument." (Dr Shedd in loc).

Church government and discipline are also means of grace insofar as they are in accordance with the Word of God. Church discipline when rightly exercised serves to glorify God, keeps the church pure, and works for the good of offenders, while it serves to protect those who walk in the commandments of God. Praise and prayer and the sacraments serve to set forth the character of God and his purposes and love toward his church, and in this way the church is enlightened, confirmed and strengthened to the faith. The Word of God is considered as a means of grace under two aspects. **As law:** The word considered as law is to point out man's duty to God, and comes in the form of a prohibition or command. The work of the law is preparatory producing conviction of sin and a realisation of our need of redemption. The purpose of the law is to produce penitence and humility. The law produces the knowledge of sin. In the words of the Westminster Confession, "It is of great use to them as well as others; in that as a rule of life, it directs and binds them to walk accordingly, discovering also the sinful pollutions of their nature, hearts, and lives; so as examining themselves thereby, they may come to the further conviction of, humiliation for, and hatred against sin; together with a sight of the need they have of Christ, and the perfection of his obedience." (Chap. 19 : 6). **As gospel:** The purpose of the gospel is to discover the fulness and sufficiency of Christ as a Saviour, and serves to encourage sinners to draw near to him. It is evident that those who have no consciousness of sin will not appreciate the gospel. Since the relation between law and gospel has been grossly misunderstood it is necessary to point out that the distinction is not the same as between the Old Testament dispensation and the New; nor must we suppose that the law requires us to perform certain duties and that the gospel requires none. There **is** a contrast between the Old Testament dispensation and the New but the Gospel is in the Old as well as in the New (Psa. 53, 54, 55; Jer. 31 : 33; Ezek. 34 etc.; Rom. 3 : 2; Gal. 3 : 8). There is also law in the New Testament. Christ taught the permanent obligations of the law (Matt. 5) and the authority of the law as a rule of life (Rom. 8 : 4, 13 : 9; James 2 : 8).

THE SACRAMENTS

If we maintain that the Word of God and the power of the Spirit is sufficient for salvation then it may appear that sacramental ordinances are not necessary. They may, therefore, be considered as auxiliaries to assist in strengthening the faith of believers. Sacraments have been instituted by God in condescension to our frailties since according to our metaphysical constitution the impression of the eye is more vivid than that of the ear; or rather, what is more to the point, the impression made by the eye serves to deepen that made by the ear. "God considering our frame hath not only appointed that we should be told of the great things of the gospel and the redemption of Christ, and be instructed in them by his Word: but also that they should be as it were **exhibited** to our view by sensible representations, the more to affect us by them" (Jonathan Edwards). We are also to remember that the Gospel is to be preached to all the world but the sacraments are to be administered only to those who profess their faith in Christ and obedience to him. The derivation of the word **sacrament** has been variously understood. It has been supposed to signify a military oath while some of the Fathers said it denoted a mystery revealed by God and understood only by believers. According to this latter definition Baptism signifies the mysterious doctrine of regeneration, and the Lord's Supper, the mysterious doctrine of the vicarious atonement of Christ. "These two sacraments exhibit and certify by sensible emblems these two mysterious facts in redemption" (Dr Shedd). It is just as evident that Baptism came in the room of circumcision. This has been disputed by the Baptists to bolster up their own position, but on too slender grounds, for it cannot be disproved that circumcision was a sign and seal of God's covenant, and that Baptism is a sign and seal of the same covenant.

The Romish doctrine of the sacraments is that they contain the grace which they signify and that they always exhibit or confer this grace in their administration where men do not place an obstacle in the way. This grace is conferred by some sort of power injected in the Sacraments apart from the state of mind of the participant. In one word Baptism does always justify and the Supper always sanctifies. The only reason why they may not so do is when men actually put an obstacle in the way. This is just as much as saying that the natural sun when it shines will always affect the complexion unless one places some obstacle in the way. The Protestant position is that the Sacraments convey no grace to the unworthy receiver, and that when grace is conveyed it is not through the internal efficacy of the Sacraments, or through him who administers the Sacraments, but through the Holy Ghost, who administers grace to the worthy receivers. It should be remembered here that the grace conveyed through the sacraments may be conveyed before or after their administration. It will serve to avoid a mystical extra-Scriptural view of this subject if we consider that the Word of God read or preached does not **ex opere operato,** or automatically, convey grace to the reader or hearer by some physical or mechanical necessity; but when this is done it is accomplished through the Holy Spirit and through the faith of the reader or hearer. In the discussion of this subject the relation between the sacraments of the Old and New Testaments has been brought under review. Some divines hold to a number of sacraments such as the tree of knowledge of good and evil, the tree of life, paradise, the Sabbath, the rainbow, etc. It is doubtful, however, if some of these are sacraments in any sense since they were not ordained by God as such, as indeed the various rites and sacrifices of the Hebrews cannot be properly so called. This is different from saying that some of these previous elements might possess what is called a sacramental effect. It is generally agreed, however, that circumcision and the passover were of basic importance since these ordinances signified the greatest blessings which could be enjoyed by sinful men; and that they were to be observed with strict regularity throughout the successive ages of the Old Testament dispensation. These two sacraments are substantially accordance with the change of dispensation. The evidence identical with those of the New Testament, signifying the for this argument may be briefly stated as follows:— The same blessings and administered in a similar manner in Covenant of Grace is the same in both dispensations providing the same benefits, namely justification and sanctification. The Israelites possessed the eqiuvalent of Baptism and the Supper "And they were baptized into Moses and in the sea, and did all eat the same spiritual meat for they drank of that spiritual rock which followed them; and that rock was Christ" (1 Cor. 10 : 2-4). The Supper itself is called by the name of Passover (1 Cor. 5 : 7, 8); and Baptism is declared to be the New Testament circumcision (Col. 2 : 11, 12). It is also plain that the Supper came in the place of the Passover, for immediately after the celebration of the Passover by Christ himself, the Lord's Supper was instituted to indicate that the latter was to take the place of the former in the New Testament dispensation; and as the Passover was commemorative of the redemption from Egypt so the Lord's Supper is commemorative of our redemption from sin through the atonement of Christ. Perhaps the best definition of a sacrament is given in the Shorter Catechism 92. "A sacrament is an holy ordinance instituted by Christ, wherein, by sensible signs Christ and the benefits of the new covenant are represented, sealed, and applied to believers."

In a sacrament two elements are to be considered, that is, the sign and the thing signified. The sign is the material and visible part: the thing signified is the blessing which the sign represents. The thing signified is Christ and the benefits of the New Covenant. The sacraments have been instituted or appointed by Christ himself to represent these blessings to us. There is, however, more than this implied in the definition. These blessings are sealed and applied to believers. The classic passage setting forth the sacramental use of a seal is Rom. 4 : 11. A seal confirms a promise or agreement. Judah gave his signet, bracelets and staff to Tamar as a pledge to confirm his promise (Gen. 38 : 17-18). Circumcision as a seal was an assurance on God's part that he would fulfil his promise to Abraham and his seed. The exhibition or application of the sacrament adds further to the definition, "Exhibition is a real, effectual, lively application of Christ, and all his benefits to every one that believeth for the staying, strengthening, confirming, and comforting of the soul" (George Gillespie. Aaron's Rod Blossoming). The sacraments, therefore, are more than symbols setting forth the fundamental verities of the gospel. They are also appointed to confirm our faith: and they do actually convey to worthy believers an assurance of God's love, peace of conscience, joy in the Holy Ghost, increase of grace, and perseverance therein to the end.

"The Sacrament shapes forth in symbols, just what the covenant pronounces in words. Less than the two ordinances for each could scarcely be sufficient; more than two would not be absolutely necessary. The reason is, that to the ends of every such gracious compact of

God with his creatures, two things and only two things are indispensable — one, that the covenant be entered into, the other that the covenant be fulfilled. The former of these, from its nature, requires to be performed but once; the latter is a thing of continual exercise and everlasting obligation. Accordingly, under the New Testament, baptism, which signifies and seals our first engrafting into Christ, our consequently obtaining an interest in the benefits of the covenant of grace and our having once and for ever engaged ourselves to be the Lord's; Baptism is but once administered to each individual, whereas the Lord's Supper, in which believers address their faith and love to the memory of the Lord's death to the certainty of the Lord's ascension and to the hope of his second advent, vowing perpetual service; and in which, on the other hand they are by faith made partakers of his body and blood, with all his benefits to their spiritual nourishment and growth in grace. This sacrament, as its nature dictates, is frequently partaken of by individual Christians and will unceasingly be solemnised after that manner in the church so long as the world shall last. This foundation laid, if we will but bear in mind that the washing with water of the initiatory sacraments represents the cleansing of conscience and heart by the blood and spirit of Christ, that we may be severed from our sins and united to Him; and that the bread and wine of the nourishing sacrament represent the person of Christ and all this fulness, as delivered for our offences and raised again for our justification" (Dr James MacLagan, Free Church, Aberdeen, 1853, pps. 358-359).

CHRISTIAN BAPTISM

Christian Baptism was instituted by Christ in the following terms. "Go ye therefore, and teach all nations baptizing them in the name of the Father, and of the Son, and of the Holy Ghost; teaching them to observe all things whatsoever I have commanded you; and lo, I am with you alway, even unto the end of the world, Amen" (Matt. 28 : 19, 20).

1. The Significance of Baptism

The design and purpose of this command was to instruct all people in the teachings of Christ and to formally receive them into the Christian church through the ordinance of Baptism. The rite itself which was to be administered in the name of the Triune God signified the relation of those baptised to the Lord as their God and their engagement to be his people. "Baptism is a sacrament, wherein the washing with water in the name of the Father, and of the Son, and of the Holy Ghost, doth signify and seal our ingrafting into Christ, and partaking of the benefits of the covenant of grace, and our engagement to be the Lord's" (Shorter Cate- chism 94). It is generally acknowledged that washing with water signifies our cleansing from the guilt and power of sin through the sprinkling of the blood of Christ, and the renewing grace of the Holy Ghost; but it is too often for- gotten that Baptism signifies our union with Christ which is the basis of these blessings. Baptism therefore, signifies our union with Christ through which we are purified and dedicated to him. The terms used in Col. 2 : 11-13 clearly indicate that union with Christ is the central theme dealt with by the Apostle when he says believers are "complete in him", "circumcision made without hands", "buried with him in baptism", and "risen with him". These figurative terms all teach that believers are **engrafted in Christ,** and if we accept the truth that baptism signifies union with Christ by faith we shall have no difficulty in believing that all the blessings of the covenant are included in this idea.

2. The Mode of Baptism

How the rite of baptism was to be administrated must be gathered from the various references made to it in Scripture. The general view is that baptism is rightly administered by the washing or sprinkling of water. Baptists, however, claim that the only valid mode is immersion, or placing the entire body under the water. It is easy to prove, however, from the Old Testament as well as the New that baptising was administered in other ways, but of course even if this were admitted, the Baptists would attempt to prove that the rite of baptism as it applies to believers was always by immersion. This, however, has not been proved from Scrip- ture. Indeed we might argue that **dipping** is not the same as **immersion.** For example eminent scholars tell us that the word **dip** used in Exodus 12 : 22 and Ruth 2 : 14 does not mean **immersion,** and besides the immersion of the whole body in water requires the recovery of the body out of the water, whereas, the washing or sprinkling with water seems to complete the meaning of the term. The case of Naaman which so often is quoted refers to dipping and does not necessarily mean that he was completely immersed in the water. We are informed by scholars that **bapto** occurs a number of times in the Septuagist and sometimes it means to dip and not to immerse, and the same holds with regard to Joshua 3 : 15. In the New Testament both **bapto, baptizo** and their cognates are used, and it has been proved conclusively that sometimes they do not refer to immersion (Matt. 15 : 2; Luke 11 : 38). It has also been quaintly remarked that 1 Cor. 10 : 2 gives no support for the doctrine of immersion for the Israelites were not immersed in the Red Sea though the Egyptians were. 1 Pet. 3 : 21 makes it evident that the baptism of the Noahites consisted in not being immersed. The divers baptism is Heb. 10 : 9, 23, must include rites of all kinds such as the purification of the unclean and the various sprinklings referred to in the Mosaic economy.

These baptisms will not fit into the baptistic interpretation. The baptism of the Spirit and the sprinkling of the blood of Christ referred to several times in the New Testament are far more in harmony with the ideas of affusion than that of immersion. The conclusion arrived at by some learned divines is that the precise mode of administration cannot be proved conclusively from Scripture and is not essential to its validity. At the same time the impartial conclusion arrived at by many earnest students of Scripture is that sprinkling of water is more in harmony with Scripture than the other mode; that it is simpler, and more suited to various subjects, in all conditions, and in all parts of the world. Some cannot be immersed for reasons of health; sometimes water is not always obtainable, not only in the frozen wastes of the world, but in torrid areas where water is scarce. Added to this is the fact that in many cases elaborate artificial fonts must be prepared. Another factor that must be taken into consideration is the ethical delicacy and care which must be exercised in the elaborate operations connected with the immersing of the whole body in water in the presence of a multitude of spectators. These, however, are only general considerations. The important matter to be considered is whether baptism is to be administered by affusion or immersion. The Baptists say immersion only is the mode. Many who are not Baptists say that it makes no difference which mode is used. The framers of the Confession do not commit themselves to either mode. They simply state that "Dipping of the person into the water is not necessary; but baptism is rightly administered by pouring or sprinkling water upon the person" (Westminster Confession 28 : 3).

3. Infant Baptism

The baptism of infants is not recognised by the Baptists on the Biblical grounds that there is no specific command in the New Testament to baptise infants, and because there is no clear case in the New Testament in which it is recorded that infants were baptised. These arguments are very strong and indeed perhaps there would be no disagreement between good men on this question were it not for these two points which are asserted on the other side. But we know that there are other doctrines which the Baptists and their opponents both agree upon in which we find that there is no specific precept and no clear example recorded in the New Testament. So far as we know there is no specific command to baptise females though we have two examples of females being baptised (Acts 8 : 12; 16 : 17). There are also other doctrines and truths held by the Lord's people for which they can cite no specific commands or clear examples in the New Testament but the Old Testament does lay down laws and principles which are of permanent obligation. We must also recognise that laws or principles enunciated in the Old Testament are still to be observed if there is no specific command in the New Testament to dispense with them. If we take these truths into consideration we are confident that the arguments against infant baptism fall to the ground. Indeed there is nothing specific said in the New Testament about Christ dying for infants, or that infants are capable of being justified and sanctified. These and other truths are derived, as the logicans say, from good and necessary inferences, and therefore they are as authoritative as an express command or a specific instance.

Circumcision was the seal of God's covenant with Israel and it included the infant as well as the parent and it was to be observed throughout that dispensation; and to argue that infants under the New Testament were to be deprived of the seals of these blessings would be to travel in the wrong direction and to make the New Testament dispensation inferior to the Old. If infants in the Old Testament were entitled to the seal of the covenant, are infants in the New Testament to be deprived of that seal which is Baptism? surely not ! We are to remember that the Covenant of Grace in the New Testament is just a continuation and unfolding of the Covenant in the Old. The circumcision of Abraham and his family was not confined to his own family but was to be extended to his posterity. This covenant in the New Testament was to embrace not only the chosen seed of Abraham but the whole world. So far as we can see, circumcision under the Old Testament signified precisely the same blessings as Baptism in the New. Baptism undoubtedly was administered to parents in the New to signify and seal these blessings and we would require an express command from God not to baptise infants before we would deprive them of this right.

There is, however, other corroboratory evidence that infants were baptised. Several passages in the New Testament assert expressly or by inference that infants belong to the kingdom of God; that they are to be received in Christs' name; that they are to be received into the church of God. If such be the case why should they be deprived of the seals of the New Testament covenant. The instances of household baptism in the New Testament are few and unhappily the Baptists prove too much when they assert that there were no infants among them. The truth is that very many households were baptised of which there is no record in the New Testament and the probability is that most of them comprised infants. The objections against infant baptism are various but when looked into carefully they are found to be of little force. One man, an intelligent Christian, said that he could never tolerate infant baptism after he heard it was practised by the Roman Catholics.

It is likely that he never considered that the Roman Catholics also believe in God, the Father, Son and Holy Ghost, the Atonement, the resurrection, and other fundamental doctrines.

It is said that infants are incapable of understanding the rite of baptism. The same objection holds true against circumcision and therefore does not deserve an answer. It has also been argued that we do not know whether these infants are children of God or not and, therefore, we have no right to baptise them, but neither do we know whether the grown-ups we baptise are God's children or not. Another argument based upon general considerations is, that the baptising of infants has become a mockery owing to the carelessness of the church in granting this privilege to unconverted persons; hence these children evidence in later life that their baptism was of no benefit to them. These facts may be admitted but this is really no argument against baptism any more than it is an argument about worldly church members receiving Gospel ordinances and church privileges in vain.

In conclusion it is admitted that in this controversy arguments have been used on both sides which do not really touch the crux of the subject at all. What we are meantime concerned with as students of the Bible is to ascertain what the truth is on this subject. What the effect and consequences of baptism upon adults has always been something of a mystery but there is no mystery about the rite itself. The rite of circumcision in the Old Testament was administered to all infants in the congregation to signify and seal the blessing of salvation and sanctification however much or however little it benefited these infants. And we are satisfied that the rite of baptism is to be administered to the children of the members of the visible church in the New Testament to signify and seal the blessings purchased by the blood of the everlasting covenant.

The difference between the Baptists and the Presbyterians about the mode of Baptism is a minor one since the Westminster Confession simply states that dipping is not necessary and that Baptism is rightly administered by sprinkling. The Baptists however go further by asserting that sprinkling is not the right mode and that their practise of immersion is the only Scriptural mode. With regard to the objection to Infant Baptism the debate is of more importance, and the practise adopted by some of the Baptists of officially dedicating their children to the Lord at church services somewhat modifies their disagreement on the question. And the strong and harsh arguments that are sometimes used by protagonists on both sides need not and does not prevent wise Christians on both sides from sometimes holding christian fellowship and even on occasions church fellowship with one another.

4. The Subjects of Baptism

Those who desire Baptism for **themselves** are to profess their faith in Christ and obedience to him, and the church is in duty bound to grant them this privilege if their profession is not contradicted by their outward conduct. The same standard holds for those who wish to have their children baptised. In the sight of God, however, those who profess their faith are not entitled to this privilege unless their profession corresponds to the state of their hearts, that is, unless they are true believers. The church, however, cannot determine infallibly who true believers are and therefore they must adjudge the candidates upon their outward profession. The highest ground the church can take is to instruct the candidates in the knowledge of salvation and to point out to them that only those who are true believers are entitled to this privilege; and that those who are not willing to embrace the Gospel and devote themselves heartily to the service of Christ have no right to ask for, or to receive, this privilege for themselves or for their children.[68]

Allowing all this to be true it is sometimes difficult for the officers of the church to adjudge the outward profession made; and they may either grant this privilege to all who make a mere outward profession or else restrict the privilege to a select few whom they judge to possess the necessary qualification. It would appear, therefore, that great wisdom is required and that each case must be dealt with on its merits in line with the Supreme and subordinate standards

68. **Westminster Confession**, 28 : 4; 29 : 8.
   Shorter Catechism, 95.
   Larger Catechism, 166.

of the church. The following passages and others in the
New Testament have been quoted to direct church officers
in this difficult duty: Matt. 5 : 3-12 — These verses set forth
the character of true believers who are entitled to sealing
ordinances; and the careful reader will perceive that there
is nothing said here about a personal assurance of faith in
Christ; but there is much said about the character of God's
people as to their inner experience, their conduct, and their
christian witness. Gal. 5 : 19-24 — The first part of this
section of truth from verses 19 to 21 delineates the character
of those who shall not inherit the kingdom of God and
therefore have no right to the sealing ordinances of the
church, and the second part points to the character of true
believers. Other relevant Scriptures are Acts 2 : 41; Acts
8 : 37; Acts 16 : 30-34; 1 Cor. 11 : 27-29).

The Westminster standards deal very briefly with this
aspect of the subject and speak of those who profess faith
in and obedience to Christ "and of the infants of one or
both believing parents" (Confession 28 : 4) and "infants of
parents either both or one of them professing faith in
Christ and obedience to him", and, "infants of such as are
members of the visible church". It has been debated as to
whether these were true believers or not. The answer is
that believing parents and members of the visible church
are just those who profess faith in Christ and obedience to
him. It would be unreasonable to ask the church to do
more than to state that those who profess their faith in
Christ and obedience to him are to be received as believers
without venturing to pass judgment upon the state of their
hearts.

The Church of Christ has usually dealt with this problem
by opening the door to sealing ordinances to those who
possess a competent knowledge of the way of salvation and
make a profession of their faith in Christ and promise to
obey his laws; and whose outward conduct is not contradictory to their profession. Some divines, however, make a
distinction in practise between the ordinance of Baptism
and that of the Lord's Supper in admitting candidates. They
will allow those who profess faith in Christ and subject
themselves to the regulations of their own church to claim
the privilege of Baptism, but they will not admit candidates

to the Lord's Table unless they are satisfied that these are true believers, thus requiring a much higher standard for one ordinance than for the other. This is done partly on account of the prevailing practice, and partly because of the idea that those who apply for Baptism, though they must profess their faith in Christ, are not required to profess that they are true believers, while those who apply for the other sealing ordinance must profess — and produce some positive evidence — that they are true believers. It is easy to criticise church officers because of the inconsistency of this method or procedure but the truth is that some will ask for the privilege of Baptism for their children who would not venture to approach the Lord's Table because though they may be sincere in their profession of faith and obedience they are not satisfied either that they are true believers or that they can satisfy the church authority that they possess the necessary qualifications. Notwithstanding the difficulties of this problem it could be made easier by systematic instruction over a period of time with emphasis laid upon the principle which the truth proclaims, and which the subordinate standards of the church evince, first, that those entitled to the one ordinance are entitled to the other, and secondly, that it is a profession of faith in Christ and obedience to him that is required to claim both sealing ordinances and not positive statements from the candidate as to his experience that he is in a state of grace.

Both privileges should, therefore, be granted in the same terms without an inquisitive examination into the subjective experiences and feelings of the candidate. It must however be admitted that questions leading into Christian experience may sometimes be profitable to the examiner as well as the candidate but the result of such a Christian conference should not be made the qualification for admission to sealing ordinances. It has been often stated by experienced Christians that they would generally not base their admittance of the applicant on any written or oral examination alone but rather upon a reliable report upon his outward pious conduct among his neighbours, in his family, and his consistent witness of his regard for the public and private ordinances of the Gospel. To these considerations it may be added that infancy in grace which would warrant the granting of the ordinance of Baptism to parents and their children might be inadequate in the case of the Lord's Supper, until the candidate was sufficiently instructed and had attained some maturity in knowledge and piety.

THE LORD'S SUPPER

The Lord's Supper was instituted by Christ the night before his Passion to commemorate his death; and the essential features of this ordinance are to be found in the synoptic Gospels (Matt. 26 : 26-29; Mark 14 : 22-25; Luke 22 : 19-20; 1 Cor. 11 : 23-26; and John, 13 : 2, 4, 5, 26-30). The most distinct and inclusive authority for its observance is related in the following words: "I have received of the Lord that which also I delivered unto you. That the Lord Jesus, that same night on which he was betrayed, took bread; and when he had given thanks he brake it, and said, Take, eat; this is my body which is broken for you: this do in remembrance of me. After the same manner also he took the cup when he had supped, saying, This cup is the new testament in my blood: this do ye, as oft as ye drink it, in remembrance of me. For as often as ye eat this bread, and drink this cup ye do shew the Lord's death till he come" (1 Cor. 11 : 23-26).

The Lord's Supper was instituted during the celebration of the Passover and we are, therefore, to understand that this ordinance supplied the place of the Passover in the new dispensation. The phrase, "new testament" quoted above refers to the new covenant which begins at the crucifixion of Christ. The "old covenant" or dispensation of the covenant of grace sets forth the provisions and arrangements, regulating the salvation and worship of God's people under the Old Testament economy. These rites were abrogated by the atonement of Christ. The sacraments of the old covenant were circumcision and the Passover, and the sacraments of the new covenant are Baptism and the Lord's Supper. A distinction is therefore made between the Passover feast and the celebration of the Supper which followed. According to the Greek church the bread and wine used in this ordinance was to be the ordinary leavened bread and wine. The Latin church however maintained that the bread should be unleavened since such was used in the Passover feast. We may accept the word of competent scholars that the bread used in the Passover feast was unleavened, and the ordinary wine that which was in daily use (Matt. 26 : 17; Matt. 9 : 17). The Lord's Supper however was not the Passover and it seems to us that the quality of the bread and wine is not essential to the valid observance of this ordinance.

Its Significance

"The Lord's Supper is a sacrament wherein by giving and receiving bread and wine, according to Christ's appointment his death is showed forth; and the worthy receivers are, not after a corporal and carnal manner but by faith made partakers of his body and blood, with all his benefits to their spiritual nourishment and growth in grace." (Shorter Catechism 96). The Lord's Supper shows forth the death of Christ and the benefits we receive therefrom. The sacramental acts in its distribution are, the taking, breaking and distributing of the elements to communicants, with the use of the sacramental words of thanksgiving and the Scriptural words of authority. The sacramental acts of receiving are, the taking, eating and drinking by the communicants, who receive by faith Christ and his benefits and are strengthened and consoled through his atonement as the alone ground of their salvation.

The Elements

According to all Christians the bread and wine used in this ordinance was set apart from a common to a holy use. This setting apart of the elements used in the ordinance is called by some "the consecration of the elements", the idea being that these elements undergo some transformation. The Popish doctrine is that this change takes place when the words of institution are pronounced "This is my body", and teaches that the bread and wine are changed into the body and blood of Christ. This doctrine is known as transubstantiation. The result is that when communicants eat the wafer, which is placed in their mouth by the priest, they partake of the actual body and blood of Christ and are nourished thereby. The holding of such a doctrine and the willingness of multitudes to accept it as the truth of God is sufficient to show us how the human intellect can be enslaved and degraded by the priestcraft of Rome. Romanists however insist upon following the letter of Scripture and point out the miraculous and beneficial nature of the Mass. Lutherans have hesitated to go this far in their interpretation of the consecration of the elements but they assert that the substance of Christ's body and blood, in a mysterious and miraculous manner, is in, with, and under the elements; and that the actual body and blood of Christ is literally though invisibly eaten by the communicants. This doctrine is known as consubstantiation.

The Lutheran view is objectionable for various reasons — the main one being that Christ's body is locally in heaven and therefore cannot be physically present on earth. The Reformed view is that the ordinance signifies and seals certain blessings and that these blessings are enjoyed by worthy communicants in this service. They, however, deny a physical or spiritual presence in the elements themselves. The real presence they acknowledge is the spiritual presence of Christ in the sense that where two or three are gathered together in his name he is in the midst of them. Some, however, have sought some mysterious presence in the elements different from the Lord's presence in any other of his ordinances. There is, however, a real presence of Christ when this ordinance brings before us Christ and him crucified and his benefits. This presence is to be found in the sanctified understanding and heart of the worthy communicant. "Now, a sign is very far from implying that the thing signified is present. It is rather understood to represent an absent object, and is put in its place to remind us of it, because it is removed at a distance from us. Instead of being a fair conclusion from the words of the institution, that there is a peculiar, mysterious presence of our Saviour, it might rather be inferred that he is not present at all, and that the design of the symbols is to call him to remembrance in his absence. The doctrine of his presence in the Sacred Supper, is legitimately deduced from his general promise, which relates to all his ordinances without any special respect to the Supper. "Where two or three are gathered together in my name, there I am in the midst of them" (Matt. 18 : 20).[69]

Protestant divines usually **consecrate** the elements or set them apart from a common to a holy use in their thanksgiving prayer. The consecration of the elements savours much of the ritualism of the sacramentarians, and we are sometimes in doubt as to what this means to ourselves or conveys to others of spiritual instruction or benefit. We believe of course that all our actions and services should be consecrated to God and we do believe that in this service the bread and wine used is set apart from a common to a holy use, and this is included in the thanksgiving prayer in which we follow the example of our Lord. What we actually mean is that the Lord would make effectual to us the blessing of communion with himself in this sacred ordinance.

We read in our translation that Jesus "blessed the bread" and hence it is inferred that he consecrated it, or set it apart from a common to a sacred use. The term consecration has found its way even into Protestant churches, in relation to the Sacraments; and ministers often speak of setting apart the elements from a common to a holy use. I presume that they are consecrated, or set apart, not by the actions of men, but by the institution of Christ, or become sacred by being devoted to a sacred use. "Be this as it may, the inference from the words of Scripture is groundless because the original says simply that our Saviour 'blessed' not that he blessed the bread, for the pronoun **it** is a supplement. The meaning is that he blessed God, as the substitution of the word **to give thanks,** by some of the Evangelists plainly shews (Mark 14 : 23; Luke 22 : 19). He blessed, or gave thanks, to his Father, we may presume, for his love in sending him into the world to save, by his obedience unto death. It may be questionable whether we should venture to imitate him in the consecration of the elements, the right to do which seems to be exclusively vested in him as the Head of the church, to whom it belongs to separate persons and things to the service of God; but there can be no doubt that it is our duty to imitate him in his thanksgiving." (Dr Dick, Lectures in Theology, Edin.

69. Dr John Dick, in loc.

1834, Vol. 4, p. 229). Our ministers generally "bless the portion of bread and wine to be used in this service" or words to the same effect.

The Efficacy of the Sacraments

The Lord's Supper is a means of grace dependent like other means upon the operation of the Holy Spirit. "The grace which is exhibited in or by the sacraments is not conferred by any power in them; neither doth the efficacy of a sacrament depend upon the piety or intention of him that doth administer it, but upon the work of the Spirit" (Confession 27 : 3). According to Calvin "The office of the sacraments is precisely the same as the Word of God, which is to offer and present Christ to us, and in him the treasures of heavenly grace; but they confer no advantage or profit unless they are received by faith" (Institutes, Book IV, chapter 5). Rome teaches that the Lord's Supper is not only a sacrament but possesses a propitiating value, and so the sacrament becomes effectual through its own power or value. This means that those who receive the sacrament receive the grace signified in it. They however add that this benefit may be restricted by the want of disposition or the want of intention by the priest. The Protestant view is that the sacrament does not operate by any virtue of its own or through the piety of the administrator but through the presence of Christ and the activity of faith in the believer. And those believers — who are enabled in their observance of the Lord's Supper to contemplate the suitability of their Redeemer, the sacrifice he made to free them from the condemnation and power of sin, his present love for them, and his protection of them and the invisible manner in which he has condescended to refresh their souls in this ordinance — are bound to derive a measure of assurance and comfort when they testify their love to him.

Some idea of the truths taught in the Lord's Supper is illustrated in the following part of an address given by a minister while addressing the communicants. "There are," he said, "three wonders which God sets before us in the sacrament. Firstly, the bride prepares a feast in remembrance of the death of her husband, and secondly, her husband is

not dead, but alive, and thirdly, not only is her husband
alive but he is with her at the table."

"Will ye speare at us, again, how Christ Jesus His
true bodie and blood is present? We will say, That they
are spiritually present, reallie presente, that is present
in the supper and not in the bread; we will not say that
His true flesh is presente to the hande or to the mouth
of our bodie, but we say it is spirituallie present to
thy spirit and soull, yea even als present inwardlie to
thy soul as the bread and wine are present to thy
bodie outwardlie. Will ye speare then, and if the bodie
and blood of Christ Jesus be present in the supper?
We answer in a word, They are present in the supper,
but not in the bread and wine, nor in the accidents
nor substance of bread and wine. And we make Christ
to be present in the supper, because he is present to my
soul to my spirit and faith.

"We acknowledge that the elements, by the virtue
of this word are changed, not, in their substance, nor
in their nature nor yet in their substantiall and natural
properties. But we grant that the elements are changed
in ane qualitie quhilh they had of before in sick sort
that their elements are tane fra the common use
quhereunto they served of before, and be the institution
of Christ they are applied now to ane holie use; there
is als great difference between the elements this day in
the Action and the thing that they were yesterday;
. . . this change proceeds fra the will of Christ . . . for
that thing is holie quhilh God calls holy, and that thing
is prophane quhilh God calls prophane." (Rev. Robert
Bruce, Sermons).

To whom is the Lord's Supper to be administered

The Lord's Supper is a feast for the Lord's people and
therefore those who have no interest in his covenant have
no right to partake of the symbols of the covenant. The
Lord's Supper is to be received only by those who, truly
repent of their sins, trust in the atonement of Christ for
their redemption, understand the meaning of the ordinance,
and have a holy desire to devote themselves to the service
of Christ. It is however a common opinion that all those
who communicate must be assured that they are in a saved
state, and that the officers of the church must satisfy themselves that the applicants are true believers. It is however

difficult if not impossible to discern who are the Lord's people; and besides, believers cannot always be sure of their interest in Christ even when they truly desire to be in Christ. The Larger Catechism, Q. 172, says that one who doubts of his being in Christ may have a true interest in him though not assured of it, and if such an one unfeignedly desires to be found in Christ and to depart from iniquity he is to labour to have his doubts removed, and he may and ought to come to the Lord's Table that he may be further strengthened. It should also be remembered that even the Lord's people may not always partake of this feast. If they are found to be ignorant or scandalous they are to be debarred from the Lord's Table until they receive instruction and make suitable acknowledgment of their repentance.

Open and Close Communion

Open communion broadly means that all persons who wish may be admitted to the Lord's Supper. Close communion means that only members of the denomination administering the sacrament or those of sister denominations are to be admitted. Rev. J. Vos maintains that the question has been greatly confused by the assumption that the only alternatives are "open" and "close" communion. Restricted communion — by which he means that members of other churches may be admitted after the officers of the congregation have satisfied themselves concerning their faith and life — is also a possibility and this same writer says that the argument that "it is the Lord's Supper and that all who are the Lord's should be invited to it" is based on an unconscious confusion of the visible with the invisible church, since it is not all who are born again but all who are living orderly, with a proper profession of faith and a corresponding life who are entitled to the privileges of the visible church, including the Lord's Supper. Even true believers according to the teaching of Scripture may be excluded from the Lord's Table if they are in a backsliding condition. The practice of allowing all and sundry who profess the name of the Lord to participate in this ordinance leaves no opportunity for the exclusion of the ignorant and scandalous and is therefore contrary to Scripture and calculated to introduce worldly professors, and to produce disorder in every church where this type of open communion is allowed. And indeed such a procedure would virtually put an end to the examination of candidates for church privilege and to the officers of the church whose office it is to observe order and discipline in the church of Christ.

ADDENDUM

1. The Ingredients of the Passover

Unleavened bread made of wheat, barley, oats, rye or spilt; a roasted egg; the shankbone of a roasted lamb; bitter herbs, made of lettuce, endive, beets, etc. These herbs were dipped once in salt water, once in vinegar, and in a mixture called charoseth, composed of dates, raisins, etc. There were also lettuce, barley and wine mixed with water. We take it that the wine was fermented and very mild.

2. The Ingredients of the Lord's Supper

Bread and wine.

3. The Order of the Passover

1. Drinking of the first cup of wine and giving thanks (Luke 22 : 17).
2. Washing of hands. Christ washed the disciples' feet (John 13 : 4, 5).
3. Bitter herbs dipped in salt water.
4. Singing of Psalms 113-114, giving thanks.
5. Second cup of wine, washing hands.
6. Bread broken, thanks given.
7. Pieces of bread with bitter herbs dipped in charoseth. This was the sop given to Judas at the beginning of the Passover.
8. Roasted lamb eaten last. The Jews sometimes conclude Passover with a piece of unleavened bread called the

after dish. According to Dr Eidersheim it was by taking the bread after the eating of the lamb that Christ began the Lord's Supper (The Temple, Dr Eidersheim, 1874, p. 208).

4. The Order of the Lord's Supper

1. Jesus took bread blest and brake. (Matt. 26 : 26; Mark 14 : 22; Luke 22 : 19).
2. Gave bread to disciples (Matt. 26 : 26; Mark 14 : 22; Luke 22 : 19).
3. Took cup, gave thanks, gave disciples (Matt. 26 : 27; Mark 14 : 23; Luke 22 : 20).
4. Supper Discourses (John 13-18).
5. Singing hymn (psalms) (Matt. 26 : 30; Mark 14 : 26).
6. Departure to Mount of Olives (Matt 26 : 30; Mark 14 : 26).

In the Gospel of John there is no record of the Lord's Supper but there is of the Passover (John 13 : 1, 2, 4, 26, 30).

Dr Eidersheim's view that Judas did not partake of the Passover or the Lord's Supper has been disputed on the basis of Luke 22 : 21. The question is not important for whether he did or not, it would have made no difference: his heart was not in it.

BIBLIOGRAPHY

1.	Dr Berkhof	Systematic Theology	Grand Rapids	1946
2.	Dr A. B. Bruce	Humiliation of Christ	Edinburgh	1881
3.	John Calvin	Institutes	Grand Rapids	1949
3a.	Prin. Cunningham	Historical Theology	Edinburgh	1864
4.	Dr A. Clarke	Commentary	New York	1840
5.	Dr Dabney	Systematic Theology	St. Louis	1878
6.	Dr Dick	Lectures on Theology	Edinburgh	1834
7.	Dr Wm. Fleming	Moral Philosophy	London	1874
8.	Rev. Fisher	Shorter Catechism	Edinburgh	1805
9.	Dr Gifford	The Incarnation	London	1897
10.	Dr A. A. Hodge	Outlines of Theology	New York	1891
11.	Dr Laidlaw	The Bible Doctrine of Man	Edinburgh	1879
12.	Prof. John Murray	Redemption	Grand Rapids	1955
13.	Dr John Owen	The Holy Spirit	London	1826
14.	Dr Ridgeley	Body of Divinty	New York	1855
15.	Dr Shedd	Dogmatic Theology	Edinburgh	1888
16.	Dr Strong	Systematic Theology	Philadelphia	1953
17.	Dr Treffrey	The Eternal Sonship	London	1849
18.	Dr G. Vos	Biblical Theology	Grand Rapids	1948
19.	Dr Warfield	Calvin and Calvinism	New York	1931
20.	Dr Shedd	History of Doctrine	Edinburgh	1888
21.	Principal Fairbairn	Typology	Edinburgh	1864
22.	Dr Eidersheim	The Temple	New York	1874
23.	The Westminster Confession of Faith			
24.	Dr Godet	Luke's Gospel	Edinburgh	1893
25.	Dr Owen	Vol 9. Sacramental Discourses	Edinburgh	1851

AUTHORS' INDEX

SUBJECT INDEX